# NAIS

Journal of the NATIVE AMERICAN and
INDIGENOUS STUDIES ASSOCIATION

## VOLUME 5.2

2018

*NAIS* (ISSN 2332-1261) is published two times a year in spring and fall (Northern hemisphere) by the University of Minnesota Press, 111 Third Avenue South, Suite 290, Minneapolis, MN 55401-2520. http://www.upress.umn.edu

Postmaster: Send address changes to *NAIS,* University of Minnesota Press, 111 Third Avenue South, Suite 290, Minneapolis, MN 55401-2520.

Information about manuscript submissions can be found at naisa.org, or inquiries can be sent to journal@naisa.org.

Books for review should be addressed to
*NAIS*, Department of American Studies, University of Kansas, Bailey Hall, Room 213, 1440 Jayhawk Boulevard, Lawrence, KS 66045-7594.

Address subscription orders, changes of address, and business correspondence (including requests for permission and advertising orders) to *NAIS,* University of Minnesota Press, 111 Third Avenue South, Suite 290, Minneapolis, MN 55401-2520.

## SUBSCRIPTIONS
- **Individual subscriptions to *NAIS*** are a benefit of membership in the Native American and Indigenous Studies Association. To become a member, visit http://naisa .org/. NAISA has four membership categories with annual dues that range from $25 to $100 and run on a calendar year.
- **Institutional subscriptions to *NAIS*** are $100 inside the U.S., $105 outside the U.S. Checks should be made payable to the University of Minnesota Press and sent to *NAIS,* University of Minnesota Press, 111 Third Avenue South, Suite 290, Minneapolis, MN 55401-2520.
- **Back issues of *NAIS*** are $25 for individuals (plus $6.00 shipping for the first copy, $1.25 for each additional copy inside the U.S.A.; $9.50 shipping for the first copy, $6 for each additional copy, outside the U.S.A.).
- **Digital subscriptions to *NAIS* for institutions** are available online through the JSTOR Current Scholarship Program at http://www.jstor.org/r/umnpress.

# NAIS

*Journal of the* NATIVE AMERICAN *and*
INDIGENOUS STUDIES ASSOCIATION

## CONTENTS
VOLUME 5 ● ISSUE 2

*Fall 2018*

## Articles

# Reviews

RANA BARAKAT

# Lifta, the Nakba, and the Museumification of Palestine's History

*A man builds a house and says,*
*"I am native now."*
. . . . . . . . . . . . . .
*"I don't like wars,*
*they end up with monuments."*
>     —FROM NAOMI SHIHAB NYE'S "JERUSALEM"

BEFORE APRIL 1948 and the start of the Nakba war, the "catastrophe" of Zionist settler expulsion of Palestinians to create the state of Israel, Lifta, like all the other urbanized villages in the Jerusalem area, was home to Palestinians. But after that and for nearly seventy years since, many have referred to Lifta as the "only abandoned Arab village in Israel not to have been destroyed or repopulated since 1948." However, while it may be popular to refer to it this way, this oft-repeated description is not entirely accurate.[1] Still, the village of Lifta, located in the western corridor of Jerusalem, just northwest of the main city center, is a rather unique site. In 1948 Zionist settlers violently destroyed and built over large parts of the village. However, there remain more than fifty standing structures in the lower section of the village that were spared the work of bulldozers in 1948 and 1949.[2] This essay argues that Lifta's history and fate as a Palestinian place with Palestinian people who continue to call it home is part of the larger Indigenous historical narrative of Palestine. However, the uniqueness of Lifta is often excised from the dominant narrative, creating a predicament that raises a series of epistemological, political, and ethical questions.[3] By examining the politics of Lifta on the local and international stages, I aim to understand how Lifta has been subject to a process of what I call "museumification." The main question posed here is how we can return Lifta to an Indigenous articulation of Palestinian history and how that restoration might in turn facilitate a different sort of return—one of Palestinians to Lifta as part of a collective right of return to a decolonized Palestine.

## History of the Present: The Israeli Court Case for Lifta

The complex story of *beginnings* is a part of a larger project on the Nakba in Palestine that I explore elsewhere for Lifta as well as the whole of historic Palestine.[4] By April 1948 Zionist forces had driven the entire Indigenous population of Lifta from their homes and village, leading the inhabitants who survived the Zionist attacks, like those from other surrounding villages, to begin their refugee journey. Today the descendants of the people of Lifta live in neighborhoods in eastern Jerusalem, Ramallah, and Amman and throughout the world. In the history of the "destroyed villages," this particular exodus story is actually only unique as far as the specificities of location within the larger Palestinian narrative of the war in 1947–49.[5] Various wings of the Zionist military forcibly emptied over five hundred villages, propelling nearly three-quarters of a million Palestinians into their refugee journeys during the Nakba war.[6] Lifta is part of this larger story, but it has also, through time as well as through various tactics of settler manipulation of the narrative and the space, become a story in itself.

In this settler narrative, the uniqueness of the story of Lifta begins with how this particular exodus is memorialized as a "beginning" to an "end" of the Palestinian history in Lifta. That is, as the "only remaining abandoned Arab village," the settler narrative of the place becomes one framed as a story of preservation. Lifta's story of preservation is a drama full of all kinds of actors—from settlers who want to be natives, settlers who want to make their own style of native chic, natives who were metamorphosed (and who in some ways and instances metamorphosed themselves) into folk stories, and, off this stage framed by the settler and imperial powers, Indigenous Palestinians who work to return.

To understand the unique part of Lifta's Nakba drama we must fast-forward to the twenty-first century. In 2003 the Israel Land Commission issued a public tender for construction in Lifta. Various arms of the settler state's motivation for this political move included the acceptance of proposals for urban building plans to transform this place, nestled on the edge of Jerusalem, into another site for Jerusalem's urban development. The goal, as stated by the Israeli developers at the time, was to "preserve the houses and meticulously restore them."[7] Part of the plan of this "meticulous restoration" was to make the old remaining structures into restaurants and galleries potentially alongside a public museum for Zionist collective memory, transforming Lifta into a settler colonial redevelopment plan par excellence.[8] According to one of the Israeli architects who helped design a Lifta redevelopment plan, "There is one approach that nothing should be done, which means the disappearance of the village. Our approach is one involving preservation and revival. The plan requires the most meticulous preservation rules and permits construction only after the historic buildings are preserved and everything is done under the supervision of the [Israeli] Antiquities Authority and a conservation architect."[9] In the privilege afforded him by his settler colonial position, this architect describes the act of preservation as one of revival—bringing back or preventing the final death of a location. Though he mentioned avoiding the death of a place in this context, this settler position does not come to terms with the continuous violence of settler colonialism and the Nakba. Perhaps understanding how death is a part of and not in opposition to preservation, Indigenous life can be understood and valued in actual opposition to this death.[10] Moreover, assertions of Palestinian vitality actively counter the operative logic of settler colonialism, what Patrick Wolfe theorized as the logic of elimination of the Native.[11] What was not mentioned, however, was whom this prevention of "death" serves? Never mind, of course, any mention of settler colonial structures or settler violence that lies at the heart of the process of death the architect quoted above referred to in the context of preservation. Nor, of course, did he mention the long decades of ongoing colonial violence or the policy of hard prevention of return for the original inhabitants of Lifta. Since settler narratives are often wrought with irony, this development plan for Lifta created a divide among Israelis regarding what they think Lifta represents, what and how that idea of place should be preserved, and for what purpose this preservation serves. Another Israeli architect, this time on the opposition side of the development plan, described his thoughts, envisioning Lifta as a World Heritage site and calling it "a 'Garden of Eden' of streams and fruit trees and beautiful landscapes and a site containing important Palestinian architecture."[12] The irony is that both views share a fundamental point: an assumption of no Palestinian agency and ongoing Palestinian disappearance is the common thread that links both divergent views of preservation.

After the Israel Lands Administration opened up the opportunity for building in Lifta, a nearly exclusively Israeli-centered discussion and opposition ensued. Since the original plan (urban building plan number 6036) called for 212 luxury apartments along with a commercial and tourist center, opposition (individual and organizational) called for various kinds of preservation mentioned earlier. Bimkom (an Israeli nonprofit), in its opposition to the planned luxury apartment complex, stated that issues of preservation "should be the basis of common cultural knowledge for every element of the population of Israel." Bimkom claimed that preservation of this place went hand in hand with Israeli reconciliation with its own past: "It is appropriate to find ways to strengthen Arab citizens' feeling of belonging to the nation without hurting their connection to their culture and community."[13] Even in opposition to the state's tender, the Israeli state remains the context by which to deal with the site. The symbolic value of the site is then read within its exclusive value for the settler state, even when this value is about how to deal with the memory of Indigenous dispossession and reconciliation with settler crimes. The story remains a settler-centered narrative where memory serves the settler state's collective consciousness.

Using this framework, this opposition actually had some nominal "success" within the Israeli court system. In February 2012 the Jerusalem District Court issued a decision based on a court case filed by a coalition of Israeli supporters and some former Palestinian residents of Lifta and their descendants living in eastern Jerusalem. The court decided to temporarily halt the real estate tender from going through, providing a minor reprieve for the "only abandoned Arab village in Israel not to have been destroyed or repopulated since 1948." The judge issued this decision based on a few factors, the most significant being that the Israel Antiquities Authority (an official state institution) was not satisfied with the terms of the original tender. It was decided that the Antiquities Authority should actually do a preservation survey before any development plans went forward.[14] Sami Ersheid, a Palestinian lawyer representing the appellants who brought forth the protest, praised the reasoning behind the court's reprieve: "Preservation isn't just preserving buildings, it's preserving heritage. . . . [T]his is a historic opportunity. . . . Lifta's history isn't just that of the Palestinians, it's the history of the State of Israel, for better or worse."[15] It was certainly not surprising within the structures of settler colonialism that the issue of the site of Lifta was put in the hands of the Antiquities Authority, for the questions of preservation are framed as questions of historical antiquity for the settler state, in other words, the work of museum makers.

By late 2016 the Antiquities Authority had completed its survey, which was lauded as unprecedented in that it was a massive undertaking that employed the latest techniques of archaeological investigation, applying them all the way from Lifta's most recent to its most distant past. The results were widely circulated in the Israeli press as a historic breakthrough: "Israel has never reconstructed any *former* village in this manner."[16] As the survey included a digital reconstruction of the village over historical periods, subterranean spaces of ancient history (dating back to the Hellenistic period) were "discovered." The vocabulary of settler discovery is common in settler colonial settings; similarly, Zionists have constructed their national myths by establishing a connection from their settler present to the ancient past.[17] The temporary reprieve actually served these same settler interests and further confirms that they were initiated and motivated by settler sensibilities. Even though researchers working on the survey consulted descendants of Lifta's families to reconstruct the more recent past of Palestinian Lifta, it was put within the context of the past tense: a *former* village as one part of centuries of history that can in some capacity serve the settler present.[18]

## The Dilemma of the "Preservation" of Lifta: Museumification

While the previous section covered the more recent Israeli court case of Lifta, this section addresses the dilemmas involved in confronting the obstacles put forward to thwart an Indigenous Palestinian historical narrative of Lifta, or, simply put, Lifta as caught in the matrix of impossibilities created by the settler present. In many ways, part of this story of Lifta has been stuck within the uniqueness of the settler categorization, referred to earlier as the "only abandoned Arab village in Israel not to have been destroyed or repopulated since 1948." As such, the question becomes, what does it mean to be destroyed yet to also remain for a people whose memory has been constructed by the destruction that remains and is ongoing? This destruction is ongoing, as is the Nakba, because more than seventy years after the violence that drove Palestinians from Lifta, Zionist settler colonial violence continues unabated in Palestine and upon Palestinians. In this sense, Lifta is not only a static symbol of the settler desire to come to terms with the past but also an active symbol for Palestinians who survived (or did not survive) this unending past—the ongoing Nakba. With this understanding, Lifta embodies the historical narrative of the Nakba (Lifta's Nakba), but it is also about how we treat the story of this Nakba in the present. The symbolic value of a "lost past" is not only a settler narrative, for it has framed Palestinian stories of exile since 1948. The tensions between the values of symbols from the past to the present and how loss frames this history are key to understanding an Indigenous historical interrogation of Nakba narratives, including Native voices adopting the "only village left" paradigm.[19]

Within the impossibilities of return produced by the preservation narrative, the question of the ruins of Lifta go through a process of *museumification*, where a not-so-distant past is preserved as a utopia (a Garden of Eden) that can only be preserved. As such, it is relegated to a static past that is, at best, about recognition within a settler reconciliation framework and, at worst, completely buried under the construction of a new modern building plan. All the plans and debates referred to earlier in the court case of Lifta were placed within settler state frameworks and were made to appease the low horizon of settler sensibilities. What was and remains at stake, nevertheless, is the final and complete destruction of what remains of the village, for within this framework the only change that can be made to the oft-repeated description of Lifta ("only abandoned Arab village in Israel not to have been destroyed" etc.) is that it can move into the category of over five hundred completely destroyed Palestinian villages. Nevertheless, even when facing this phase of imminent destruction, one should be circumspect about cultural heritage as savior.

In the 1970s the cultural argument around heritage, built heritage in particular, dominated urban development studies concerned with European cities as well as the discussions within UNESCO.[20] Like other aspects of historical preservation, built heritage is also a realm of contestation. According to G. J. Ashworth, the work of built heritage in European cities has overwhelmingly been a political exercise of power and a contest concerning the encoding of symbolic meaning to reinforce this power.[21] To explain the changes over time toward built heritage in European cities, Ashworth introduced the terms "eradification" and "museumification." Again, within the European context, Ashworth offered these concepts to explain the changing approaches toward built heritage. The concept of eradification means the destruction or disappearance of material culture (buildings, artifacts, etc.) due to political change. Museumification means change in the functional use of material cultural (artifacts, etc.), which Ashworth argues has also been brought about by political regimes in order to transform meanings that might better serve their political and economic purposes. Museumification in the European context in the post-1970s era is, according to Ashworth, mainly for economic concerns  specifically aimed at creating or increasing the tourist industry.[22] The culprit here is the state and its heavy hand of manipulation in the sense of both destroying and preserving.[23] The main objective, again, according to Ashworth, is the bold imprinting of national identities through a systemic decision-making process over urban forms, in sum, what to destroy and what to preserve to create a specific urban landscape as material support for the state's narrative.

The concept of museumification as a theorized notion has been used in a number of similar contexts. Jean Baudrillard played on the term "mummification" in his use of museumification: "The museum, instead of being circumscribed as a geometric, is everywhere now, like a dimension of life." Deconstructing this kind of science of knowledge, he says: "In order for ethnology to live, its object must die; by dying, the object takes its revenge for being 'discovered' and, with its death, defies the science that wants to grasp it." In regard to the goal of symbolic and cultural extermination, Baudrillard explains that only by forcing this kind of death on the past can the science of the present exist: "Because mummies don't rot from worms: they die from being transplanted from a slow order of the symbolic, master over putre-faction and death, to an order of history, science, and museums, our order, which no longer masters anything, which only knows how to condemn what preceded it to decay and death and subsequently to try to revive it with sci-ence. Irreparable violence toward all secrets, the violence of a civilization without secrets, hatred of a whole civilization for its own foundation."[24] The history of modernity is one of active destruction; as a result, the history of conquest and colonialism brought about by European modernity is a history of death.

As a commentary on modernity and devastation, which brought about postmodern epistemology, European cities were the most common back-drop for what has been called the "open air museum" as a studied physi-cal space that became the place of museumification. This order and order-ing of urban space as a museum was how the white world could represent itself for itself: "It is here, everywhere, in the metropolises, in the White community, in a world completely cataloged and analyzed, then artificially resurrected."[25] Museumification's emergence and sustaining popularity as a theorized concept have been in the general area of architecture, her-itage, tourism, and urban studies.[26] The intersections of the use of the con-cept seem to flow around a basic theme: representation. In fact, Michael A. Di Giovine defines the term as the "transition from a living city to that of an idealized re-presentation of itself, wherein everything is considered not for its use but for its value as a potential museum artifact."[27] Museums require material to exhibit, but when spaces become places for museumification, the heritage industry can overwhelm the space. Alexandra Mientjes referred to this process as making lived spaces dead through overcommodifica-tion.[28] In fact, Mientjes's questions were about representation and identity in a city like Amsterdam, where the tourist industry represents the place in a very narrow and particular way. She provides the example of the 2010 appointment by UNESCO of the canal ring of Amsterdam to the organiza-tion's World Heritage list. According to Mientjes, this triggered criticism and fears of "Disneyfication," where the museumification process becomes an uncontrollable phenomenon of commodification. Having a UNESCO stand-ing creates tourist value and capital, which can add to the museumification process. Even in a European city, World Heritage is the trigger (and result) of a museumification process.

## The Hegemonic Story of Lifta's "Ruins"

In official and popular discourse about Lifta, using the term "ruins" to describe the place has become quite common.[29] In her work on the imperial formations of ruins, Ann Laura Stoler emphasizes the ongoing process of imperialism, as she has been interested in investigating "dissociated and dislocated histories of the present." Though Stoler does not speak to the particular structures of settler colonialism and the unending violence of the settler state, her focus on the ongoing process of ruination might nevertheless illuminate some thoughts on the making of ruins and how that process is related to the museumification of Indigenous Palestinian history. Stoler states, "Ruins are also sites that condense an alternative sense of history. Ruination is a corrosive process that weighs on the future and shapes the present. . . . [T]he focus then is not on inert remains but on their vital refiguration." Treating Lifta as a site of ruins begs the question of whose history is being written through the various proposals of how to treat the site. More than focusing on memory formation, Stoler approaches the action of the verb "to ruin": "Attention here is on *to ruin* as an active process, and as a vibrantly violent verb." The focus on violence is key here; recognizing settler violence as *ongoing* can help illuminate the use of the word "ruins" in relation to Lifta rather than accepting the dominant narrative of "uniqueness," which implicitly poses it as an entity somehow independent or separate from Palestinian history. Nevertheless, the vitality referred to here needs a subject: For whom and for what purpose is this vitality, and can it be used to imagine the deruination of Lifta? Going from reading Franz Fanon's "tinge of decay" in reference to ruins, Stoler's focus on "'ruins of empire' provides not a melancholic gaze, but a critical vantage point. . . . Asking how people live with and in ruins redirects engagement."[30] But what of ruins that people are prevented from living in and have only been given the option of preserving for settler representation of indigenous absence? Stoler's concept of ruins, even in vitality, does not quite capture the making and maintaining of Lifta's ruins. The notion of a Palestinian Lifta thriving, present and alive, then, challenges the mere use of the word "ruins." The juxtaposition of how to approach the story of Lifta not as preservation but rather as vitality means a return to Lifta—not as a return to a vanished past of the ghosts of who Palestinians once were but as a return to the land for Palestinians to live not among the ruins but in the vitality of return as deruination.

The ruins of Lifta are only static ruins of history or decay when we accept the settler colonial prism. Following this logic, placing the ruins in a museum or, more appropriately in this sense, building a museum out of them promotes a certain historiography of the past that ignores ongoing settler colonial violence (from the past continuing in the present). As Gerald Vizenor rightly explained in terms akin to this kind of settler ruination, "The representations of the tribal past are more than mere human mimesis and more than the aesthetic remains of reason in the literature of dominance. . . . Simulations are new burdens in the absence of the real and the imposture of presence."[31] In other words, preseveration should be read as Indigenous presence *and* forced absence. Likewise, the vocabulary of preservation that pervades the actions (international and local) and campaigns of "saving Lifta" places a settler ethos of ruins to the forefront: settlers want to preserve something that is ruined.[32] With Lifta, like all of historic Palestine, the making of ruins is due to Israeli state destruction. The various manifestations of these nonindigenous campaigns' work to "save" Lifta are based on an implicit (or sometimes explicit) recognition of settler presence and focus on arresting the decay via preservation/museumification. Preservation, as I've argued here, is incommensurate with restoration (or deruination). If preservation serves settlers' interests, then restoration serves Indigenous interests. As such, restoration means Palestinians will return to their village—repatriated as a lived space, not as a symbolic museum space of a *former* past. What lies at the heart of this is the distinction between conceptualizing Lifta as a symbol of a dead past rather than as a living village thriving beyond museumification and preservation.[33]

Nadia Abu El-Haj has meticulously examined how the archaeology of Zionist settler colonialism served the interests of myth-making using the tools of ruins in the task of Zionist nation-building. She showed how, particularly in Jerusalem, the Zionist state used "ruins . . . to memorialize . . . histories of destruction."[34] In the context of settler myth making, then, why is destruction memorialized, and how does preservation serve these interests? This is made more complicated by the precarious position Palestinians are placed in by the reductive choice of "saving" (preservation) as the only choice available to them and their history. This is obviously motivated by the settler politics of recognition, where recognition only comes when the indigenous people accept their defeat as the price of entry into the settler historical narrative and settler present.[35] Here I want to borrow from Abdul Rahim Al-Shaikh's grammar concerning the Palestinian culture of defeat.[36] Using Al-Shaikh's description, preservation for Palestinians translates into preserving the moment of defeat when the ruined acknowledge ruination via being reduced to folkloric and aborted versions of their former selves (a form of museumification) as their only way of being, further reinforcing the settler colonial binary.[37] In other words, the "saving of Lifta" is bound by settler colonial confines, since in that limited framework it can only be saved without an active people who resist, a place without a people. This construction sounds all too familiar for those cognizant of Zionist tropes that described Palestine as a land without a people. This myth was a primary justification for the violence that wreaked the devastation of the Nakba upon Palestine and Palestinians. In this way, Lifta is merely a settler symbol if it means only recognition of past crimes rather than ongoing Indigenous dispossession. That kind of narrow recognition takes the ongoing part of the Nakba out and relegates it to a past historical event, from life to a lifeless, peopleless museum. Of course, preservation is one part of the settler colonial spectrum—the history of destruction, denial, and erasure of Palestine is a long and violent narrative. My argument here is that while preservation on the surface might appear different, it is actually part of that Zionist history of Palestinian erasure.

There are two levels (that are actually very connected) to this museumification of the ruins of Lifta: the international and the "national." One is centered in the United Nations via UNESCO, and the other (again via UNESCO) is centered on the nation-states Israel and, after 2011 and Palestine's inclusion in UNESCO, a Zionist and internationally recognized Palestine (not my Palestine). Part of the defense of retaining and appreciating what remains of Lifta, to prevent it from final physical destruction, is the claim that it must be preserved as cultural heritage. In fact, one line of the "saving" of Lifta has been to pursue UNESCO World Heritage site nomination, and it has recently been reported that UNESCO categorization might be the only path left to "save" Lifta.[38] Again, this is about saving what remains. I am all too aware of what opening up this argument might mean. The physical remains of this part of Lifta in the northwestern corridor of Jerusalem is all we materially have left from the Lifta that our Palestinian elders called home as a part of the history of Jerusalem and the history of Palestine. The significance and enormity of asking these kinds of questions regarding ruins and the museum as they pertain to what precious little material remains from this part of the Palestinian homeland are not lost on me.

## Conclusion: The Vengeance of Death

Understanding the intricacies of museumification speaks to the larger question of how the Palestinian narrative of the Nakba, of which ongoing settler colonial violence is a part, can be liberated from settler frameworks and how, through this process, Indigenous Palestinian historians can work to record the past outside this fruitless quest for recognition. Or maybe the question can be about not recording the narrative of the Nakba through a destroyed village history but about finding a language to see beyond the ruins and outside of the museum. Of course, these questions are fraught, because the answer might mean, in the immediate sense, the final physical destruction of what remains of Lifta. As it is, we have been *given an untenable quandary: work with settlers and save what remains, or let it all be destroyed.*

As a part of the larger project concerning the historiography of the Nakba referred to earlier, I conducted a series of interviews over the past several years with people who lived in Lifta until 1948 and their descendants. I found a common theme among all: they all spoke of the natural spring in the lower part of the village. While each person spoke of their personal stories and memories of place, they all recalled the spring in terms of daily life. Water for cooking, cleaning, living: water as life. In all the campaigns to "save Lifta," they use the spring as the Zionists have, mirroring its uses as a symbol for what once was. The Zionists use it as a religious metaphor, a place to perform rituals, and those who claim to want to save Lifta have also transformed it into a metaphor, a symbol of a former place. To arrest Lifta from the process of museumification is to steal the spring away from the world of symbols and metaphor of death and bring it back into the world of life and living.

RANA BARAKAT is assistant professor of history and contemporary Arab studies at Birzeit University in Palestine. Her research interests include the history and historiography of colonialism, nationalism, and the culture of resistance. She is currently working on a book project titled "Lifta and Resisting the Museumification of Palestine: Indigenous History of the Nakba."

## Notes

I want to thank J. Kēhaulani Kauanui and Rema Hammami for their invaluable help in listening and reading drafts of this article, as well as their incredible support in my intellectual journey toward understanding the Palestinian Nakba.

1. Lifta is not the only remaining Arab village in any sense of the term "remaining." The Palestinian landscape of land claimed by the state of Israel in 1948 is full of Arab villages where the politics of settler manipulation are at play: for just a few examples, see ʿAyn Houd, Jʼouna, Jaffa (the list goes on). Nonetheless, the politics of the use of this phrase is part of the argument in this article.

2. Why this part of Lifta was spared bulldozing remains a curious footnote to the narrative of the Zionist war. Noga Kadman suspects that the steep drop into the valley where these remaining structures are probably caused them to be spared, because the bulldozers at the time could not traverse the decline. See Noga Kadman, *Erased from Space and Consciousness: Israel and the Depopulated Villages of 1948* (Bloomington: Indiana University Press, 2015).

3. Rana Barakat, "Writing/Righting Palestine Studies: Settler Colonialism, Indigenous Sovereignty and Resisting the Ghost(s) of History," *Settler Colonial Studies* 8, no.3 (2017), DOI: 10.1080/2201473X.2017.1300048.

4. Rana Barakat, "Lifta and Resisting the Museumification of Palestine: Indigenous History of the Nakba" (monograph in-progress). The literature of the history of Palestine's Nakba is as vast as it is diverse. While that is the subject of my larger project and cannot be covered with any depth here, for a sense of this literature and the historiographical debates therein, see Ahmad H. Sa'di and Lila Abu-Lughod, *Nakba: Palestine, 1948, and the Claims of Memory* (New York: Columbia University Press, 2007).

5. For the Lifta story of dispossession and dislocation, see Walid Khalidi, ed., *All That Remains: The Palestinian Villages Occupied and Depopulated by Israel in 1948* (Washington, DC: Institute of Palestine Studies, 2006).

6. Walid Khalidi, "Plan Dalet: Master Plan for the Conquest of Palestine," special issue, "Palestine 1948," *Journal of Palestine Studies* 18, no. 1 (Autumn 1988): 4–33; Nur Masalha, *A Land without a People: Israel, Transfer and the Palestinians, 1949–1996* (London: Faber and Faber, 1997); Nur Masalha, *Expulsion of the Palestinians: The Concept of "Transfer" in Zionist Political Thought, 1882–1948* (Washington, DC: Institute for Palestine Studies, 1992).

7. "Israel Moves to Turn Deserted Palestinian Village into Luxury Housing Project," *Haaretz,* January 21, 2011, http://www.haaretz.com/israel-moves-to-turn-deserted-palestinian-village-into-luxury-housing-project-1.338280.

8. This kind of re-dressing of Palestinian villages by Zionist settler establishment is not unique, as it is well within the Zionist arsenal of settler colonial behavior. For example, see the story of 'Ayn Hawd in Susan Slyomovics, *The Object of Memory: Arab and Jew Narrate the Palestinian Village* (Philadelphia: University of Pennsylvania Press, 1998); Muhmmad Abu Al-Hayja' and Rachel Leah Jones, "'Ayn Hawd and the 'Unrecognized Villages,'" *Journal of Palestine Studies* 31, no. 1 (Autumn 2001): 39–49. Again, what is somewhat unique in Lifta is that this re-dressing had not been done to all of the abandoned homes and buildings, though, it *was* done to many of the actual structures of Lifta when homes were given to immigrant Jewish families by the Israeli state in the early 1950s.

9. *Haaretz,* January 21, 2011.

10. These questions have been informed by tensions of various projects about Indigenous revitalization. In particular, see Mark Allen Minch, "Return of the Indian: Bone Games, Transcription, and Other Gestures of Indigeneity" (PhD diss., University of California, Berkeley, 2014).

11. Patrick Wolfe, "Settler Colonialism and the Elimination of the Native," *Journal of Genocide Studies* 8, no. 4 (2006): 387–409; also see Wolfe, introduction to *The Settler Colonial Complex: Recuperating Binarism in Colonial Studies* (Los Angeles: American Indian Studies Center, UCLA, 2017).

12. *Haaretz,* January 21, 2011.

13. *Haaretz,* February 3, 2011.

14. *Haaretz,* February 7, 2012.

15. Ibid.

16. *Haaretz*, December 20, 2016, emphasis added.

17. Historical narratives based on these kinds of origin stories are a fundamental part of settler narratives not only in the Palestinian context but in settler colonial contexts in general. For more, see Mark Rifken, *Beyond Settler Time: Temporal Sovereignty and Indigenous Self-Determination* (Durham, NC: Duke University Press, 2017); and Jean O'Brien, *Firsting and Lasting: Writing Indians out of Existence in New England* (Minneapolis: University of Minnesota Press, 2010).

18. In the news coverage of the survey, it remained unclear what this meant regarding the tender process of construction in Lifta. Conservationists who worked on the survey were calling for a preservation process that would spare the historical content of the results of the survey, but it was also reported that the ILA (Israel Land Authority) still had no intention of reconsidering its initial plans to open the space up for building. This was further confirmed by the negotiations over compensation the ILA was conducting with the descendants of Jewish immigrant families who were placed in homes in upper Lifta (not considered as part of this Israeli discussion of Lifta, though many of the former residents of the village lived in the houses that were given to the immigrant families prior to 1948). As of late 2016 and early 2017, these families were being removed from their homes to make room for the construction process.

19. Working within this reductive paradigm, both the past and the present are tensions in Palestinian historiography and politics. This is obviously connected to the tensions involved in the politics of recognition in settler colonial settings, where Palestine is part of this larger story. For more on this, see Glen Sean Coulthard, *Red Skin, White Masks: Rejecting the Colonial Politics of Recognition* (Minneapolis: University of Minnesota Press, 2014).

20. 1972 World Heritage Convention, 1992 and 2003, "amendments" to it.

21. G. J. Ashworth, "The Conserved European City as Cultural Symbol: The Meaning of the Text," in *Modern Europe: Place, Culture and Identity,* ed. B. Grahm (London: Arnold, 1998). See also G. J. Ashworth, "Is There 'World Heritage'?," *Urban Age* 4, no. 4 (1997); Ashworth, *Dissonant Heritage: The Management of the Past as a Resource in Conflict* (London: Belhaven Press, 1996).

22. In addition to Ashworth, see Aspa Gospodini, "Urban Morphology and Place Identity in European Cities: Built Heritage and Innovative Design," *Journal of Urban Design* 9, no. 2 (2004): 225–48; Rose Aslan, "The Museumification of Rumi's Tomb: Deconstructing Sacred Space at the Mevlana Museum," *International Journal of Religious Tourism and Pilgrimage* 2, no. 2 (2014): 1–16; Nebojsa Camprag, "Museumification of Historical Centres: The Case of Frankfurt Altstadt Reconstruction," in *Tourism in the City*, ed. N. Bellini and C. Pasquinelli (Gewerbestrasse, Switzerland: Springer International, 2017); Paul H. Gobster, "Urban Park Restoration and the Museumification of Nature," *Nature and Culture* 2, no. 2 (Autumn 2007): 95–114.

23. In fact, during the post–World War II era, both forgetting and remembering were practiced by the state to control historical consciousness. This is never more clear than the post-Nazi era, when a state's power to manipulate "forgetting" has been as powerful (if not more) as the forced hand of

"remembering." See, among others, Sharon Macdonald, "Undesirable Heritage: Fascist Material Culture and Historical Consciousness in Nuremberg," *International Journal of Heritage Studies* 12, no. 1 (January 2006): 9–28; Simon Levis Sullam, "Reinventing Jewish Venice: The Scene of the Ghetto between Monument and Metaphor," *Cultural Representations of Jewishness at the Turn of the 21st Century,* European University Institute Working Papers (2010), 13–25.

24. Jean Baudrillard, *Simulacra and Simulation* (Ann Arbor: University of Michigan Press, 1994), 457, 460.

25. Ibid., 461.

26. Other fields have also picked up on the concept: literary critiques have provided some of the most interesting contributions to a general understanding of the term "museumification" in reference to a literary construct as a narrative tool. See John A. Stotesbury, "The Crime Scene as Museum: The (Re)construction in the Bresciano Series of a Historical Gibraltarian Past," *Coolabah* 20 (2016): 83–93.

27. Michael A. Di Giovine, *The Heritage-Scape: UNESCO, World Heritage, and Tourism* (Lanham, MD: Lexington Books, 2009), 261.

28. Alexandra Mientjes, "Is Amsterdam Turning into a Museum?," *Pop Up City,* August 8, 2013, http://popupcity.net/is-amsterdam-turning-into-a-museum/.

29. As popular as this discourse has become, it was incorporated to the big screen when a documentary film was released in 2016 under the title *The Ruins of Lifta: Where the Holocaust and the Nakba Meet* (directed by Menachem Daum and Oren Rudavsky).

30. Ann Laura Stoler, "Imperial Debris: Reflections on Ruins and Ruination," *Cultural Anthropology* 23, no. 2 (2008): 193, 194, 196.

31. Gerald Vizenor, "The Ruins of Representation: Shadow Survivance and the Literature of Dominance," *American Indian Quarterly* 17, no. 1 (Winter 1993): 7–30.

32. Daphna Golan, Zvika Orr, and Sami Ershied, "Lifta and the Regime of Forgetting: Memory Work and Conservation," *Jerusalem Quarterly* 54 (Summer 2013): 69–81.

33. A Tel Aviv–based anti-Zionist organization, Zochrot, moved on this point and had an open call for a project that was about imagining restoring Lifta for a return of Palestinians to Lifta. It asked the question, how can building be imagined not to preserve but to build for return?

34. Nadia Abu El-Haj, *Facts on the Ground: Archaeological Practice and Territorial Self-Fashioning in Israeli Society* (Chicago: University of Chicago Press, 2001), 164.

35. For an in-depth discussion of the politics of settler recognition, see Coulthard, *Red Skin White Masks*; and Audra Simpson, *Mohawk Interruptus: Political Life Across the Borders of Settler States* (Durham, NC: Duke University Press, 2014).

36. Abdul Rahim Al-Shaikh, "*Roshed al Hazima* (The Maturity of Defeat)," *Arab '48,* June 5, 2007, http://www.arabs48.com/?mod=articles&ID=45928. See also Abdul Rahim Al-Shaikh, "Al hawaya al-thaqafiyya al-filistinniyah: Al mithal', al-tamthil, wa al tamathol" [Palestinian cultural identity: The ideal,

the real, and the redemption], in *Palestinian Communities, Their Representations, and the Future of the Question of Palestine*, ed. Khalil Shahin (Ramallah: Masarat—The Palestinian Center for Policy Research and Strategic Studies, 2013), 69–143.

37. In addition to al-Shaikh, Faisal Darraj explores the many layers of employing symbols of a long-lost Palestinian past; see Faisal Darraj, *Bo's al thqafa fi muassa al Falastinyya* [The misery of culture in the Palestinian institution] (Beirut: Dar al-Adab, 1996).

38. This claim has been reported in the Israeli press, but it should be noted that for it to be nominated in order to be considered it would have had to have been submitted by Israel to UNESCO according to the rules of their nomination process. The last part of the article will discuss this as a de-Palestinized place.

DANIEL VOTH

# Order Up!
# The Decolonizing Politics
# of Howard Adams and Maria Campbell
# with a side of Imagining Otherwise

IT HAS BEEN MORE THAN FORTY YEARS since the publication of Maria Campbell's foundational text *Halfbreed* (1973) and Howard Adams's *Prison of Grass: Canada from the Native Point of View* (1975). Both authors emerged out of Indigenous organizing movements and established themselves as articulate and persuasive Métis writers, activists, and leaders. Campbell and Adams provided pointed and powerful criticisms of the Canadian colonial milieu grounded in their respective local contexts and experiences. Both Adams and Campbell were featured on Indigenous media programs such as the Canadian Broadcasting Corporation's (CBC) radio show *Our Native Land.* Adams also gave comments to major daily newspapers; magazines such as *New Breed;* and films, including the National Film Board's *Pow Wow at Duck Lake* and *The Other Side of the Ledger: An Indian View of the Hudson's Bay Company.* Campbell went on to write acclaimed children's books and translated Cree and Michif stories in *Stories of the Road Allowance People.* Through their activism, Campbell and Adams came to be leaders in both formal and protest Métis political movements, and they built bridges between the leaders of the previous generation and a new generation of Métis agitators.

While many in Indigenous communities will reflect fondly on both Adams's and Campbell's teaching, mentorship, and public appearances, both scholars ought to also be noted for their important intellectual contributions to understanding Canadian colonialism and theorizing Indigenous resistance.[1] With the exciting rise in Métis scholarship and Métis studies, the time seems right for a reexamination of both Adams and Campbell as intellectual leaders on whose shoulders many of us stand tall. Importantly, though, these works have a great deal to say to each other. In what follows, I start by arguing that, more than forty years after its publication, *Prison of Grass* continues to have the power to inform scholars and activists engaged in the study and practice of Indigenous resurgence as well as the politics of decolonization, colonialism, and settler colonialism in Canada. This appreciative critique, however, cannot abide one of the central theoretical failings of Adams's intellectual work: his colossal failure to adequately and appropriately address Indigenous gender and Indigenous gendered power dynamics within his explication of colonial domination. While Adams's thought remains useful as a tool both for Indigenous activists in community and for scholars in the academy, there is a pressing need to name, deconstruct, and then imagine and act otherwise about the sexism and the reproduction of heterosexual norms of life he advances in his thought. To this end, I contrast Adams's interventions with Maria Campbell's insightful engagement with gendered colonial violence in *Halfbreed* to demonstrate that Campbell understood better than Adams the gendered and intersecting dimensions of colonial power and violence.

The article is divided into three sections. In the first, I argue that Adams's interventions continue to have explanatory strength for Indigenous political struggles and the study of those conflicts. In the second, I work through Adams's failure on gender and contrast his theory with Campbell's. The problem created by this critical engagement is that it leaves much of the fight against gendered colonial oppression unfinished. Phrased differently, the critique that I offer here does not in itself substantially contribute to the building of a decolonizing politics attuned to gendered colonial violence. To address this, the final section takes up James Tully's call to act otherwise in struggles *of* freedom along with the calls of literary scholars to imagine otherwise. The aim of the final section is to offer a framework that at once harnesses a rich appreciation of Indigenous gender diversity toward creating an anticolonial politic, thereby combining the strengths of both Campbell and Adams. The way I approach this is to engage in an alternative imagining of the formulation of Adams's orientation to both gendered colonial domination and the way gender is animated in a decolonizing political movement.

## Howard Adams as Foundational in Decolonizing Politics in Canada

This section outlines the continued relevance of Adams's contributions to Indigenous thought, politics, and the Indigenous experience in Canada. Adams's thought provides important elucidation of the underpinnings of colonial domination for Indigenous peoples in general and Métis people in particular. He accomplishes this by examining the psychological, economic, and political modes of domination that manifest in the historical and daily lived experiences of Indigenous peoples. Adams's work forces non-Indigenous readers to confront the icy reality that the just society they thought they lived in is in fact fundamentally unjust. For Indigenous readers, the work provides theory and empirics that relate to their daily lives. The result is that Adams's work makes several foundational interventions that have the power to continue informing Indigenous activists and scholars today. I will discuss two particularly key elements of Adams's contribution to the politics of decolonization: his elaboration of the deceitful and racism-laced mechanisms of Indigenous land dispossession in Canada, and his views on the colonizer's divide-and-rule tactics.

Adams's thought is deeply indebted to the anticolonial scholarship of Frantz Fanon and other anticolonial thinkers from the African context.[2] Like Fanon, Adams situates within the program of colonizing Indigenous people in Canada a need to dehumanize Indigenous peoples using profoundly racist logics. He identifies the roots of this dynamic in fur-trade history.[3] Adams argues that "white supremacy, which had been propagated since the beginning of European imperialism, became woven into Canadian institutions such as the church, the schools, and the courts, and it has remained the working ideology of these institutions" (8). Adams articulates a critique of the process of building Canada that laid down a fundamental and shocking (to non-Natives) element of Canadian life: deep-seated institutionalized racism. Adams traces the way this racism seeps into the minds of Indigenous people in Canada such that they come to see themselves as their colonizers do: lazy, dishonest, freeloading, and morally bankrupt (4–11). Adams sums up the power of racist oppression in writing published after his death. In his reflection on the range of tools at an oppressor's discretion, he argues, "As my absolute commander, oppressor and mythmaker, you screwed into my head all these distortions and myths. You used all your weapons so effectively: your schools, church, court, and parliament."[4]

For Adams, racist attitudes and history came to be institutionalized through Canadian efforts to subjugate Indigenous peoples. Following the destruction of the buffalo herds, Adams argues, the Riel Resistance in 1870 and the subsequent treaty process served as methods of Indigenous land theft in service of Canadian expansionist policy (64–67). Adams points to the steep power imbalance between Indigenous peoples and the Canadian state in the nineteenth-century treaty processes and problematizes the ability for parties to come to equitable terms. He argues that conducting negotiations under conditions where Indigenous peoples faced starvation meant the resulting treaties were a means to first "legitim[ize] the imprisonment of native people under white agents backed by police and soldiers" (68) while making "Indian subjugation look honourable, or at least legal" (71). This effort to justify unjust relationships was key to the removal of Indigenous peoples from their lands in order to facilitate the transfer of land from Indigenous hands into non-Indigenous hands. Adams argues that the core of this process was predicated on the belief that non-Native peoples are racially superior to Indigenous peoples (73).

This remains a helpful contribution to the political history of Canadian Indigenous relations. By first using the language of Fanon to expose the racist underpinnings of Canadian society on which Métis and other Indigenous peoples' subjugation is justified and then illustrating the manifestation of those perverse relationships of power in the lives of both Indigenous and non-Indigenous peoples, Adams makes both theoretical and empirical interventions into the structure and operation of Canadian projects of Indigenous land dispossession. These interventions are key to students and scholars tracing the intellectual development of Indigenous resistance and Indigenous critiques of the settler state. Where scholars like Patrick Wolfe, Lorenzo Veracini, Audra Simpson, Glen Coulthard, and others have made recent and important contributions to understanding settler colonialism as a structure rather than an event, Adams was engaged in elucidating a similar process in the early 1970s.[5] Like those who came after him, Adams saw this process as possessing a number of intersecting relations of power, with access to Native land as the centerpiece of building the settler state.

This is not to say that Adams should be seen as a proto—settler colonial theorist. Rather, my point in drawing out this element of Adams's work is to say that Adams's intellectual contribution to understanding Indigenous oppression continues to have the power to inform scholars in their engagement with the ongoing processes of Indigenous land dispossession with kernel contributions that predate settler colonial theory. Further, Adams's deployment of himself and his people's history within these examinations of power provides a helpful glimpse into some of the implications of the devastation he is illustrating north of the 49th parallel. Finally, his blunt rejection of the fairness and honesty within Indigenous-Canadian institutional relations also is a helpful educational tool in light of the desire by some to sanitize and then glorify Canadian expansion to the Northern Plains as a grand and just Indigenous/Canadian achievement.[6]

Adams also makes important contributions to understanding the Indigenous political landscape that remain instructive today. Adams might be most well known for his biting critique of "middleclass native élites [who] provide support for . . . [imperial] administration" (180). Adams shows deep disdain for collaborator Indigenous leaders. He argues that their purchased acquiescence to the plight of their people contributes to the continuing conditions of oppression and poverty in Indigenous communities. Adams contrasts the wealth possessed by leaders of recognized organizations to the poverty faced by the general Indigenous population to emphasize both the relative unrepresentativeness of Indigenous political organizations and the inflated importance of formal leaders. For example, in the mid-1970s the Métis Society of Saskatchewan, which Adams led in 1969–70, represented approximately 2 percent of the Métis population in Saskatchewan. However, this organization inflated its relative importance and representativeness to protect the "personal position, prestige, and salary" (183) of its leaders. Despite the lack of broad representation, "governments continue to give recognition to these national and provincial organizations as the official voice of native people and grant them millions of dollars annually" (183).

Adams's examination of these entities provides a still salient critique of Indigenous political organizing in Canada. Indeed, key components of this orientation can be seen in the #IdleNoMore movement's effort to recenter power away from formal, recognized Indigenous political organizations in favor of broad Indigenous decolonizing political movements.[7] There remains an ongoing tension within Indigenous political organizing about whether formal, government-recognized political organizations are the best vehicles for agitating against the settler colonial state. Adams warns us that Native leaders who backstop their power and authority with government-subsidized salaries and recognition rather than their communities serve to forestall change within Indigenous nations. Not only do these organizations impart false hope to Indigenous youth clamoring for change, they alter none of the conditions of Indigenous oppression and thereby perpetuate the lived experiences of "poverty and wretchedness" (183) in Native communities.

As Indigenous youth continue to organize and challenge the conditions of their political surroundings, Adams's insights provide a still-useful lens to think through *how* one ought to engage colonial oppression. Adams's analysis cuts through the din of self-congratulating Indigenous political organizations to provide reasons for looking at government money and recognition suspiciously. This is healthy and, from the perspective of cultivating critically informed decolonizing action, desirable.

While Adams is probably best known for these critiques, he also set out a key explication of the challenges to broad Indigenous political unity:

> "Divide and rule" is a basic method of oppressive action that is as old as imperialism itself. Since the colonizer subordinates and dominates the rank-and-file natives, it is necessary to keep them divided in order to remain in power. The oppressor cannot permit himself the luxury of tolerating the unification of indigenous people, which would undoubtedly cause a serious threat to the status-quo rule. Accordingly, oppressors prevent any method and any action by which the oppressed could be awakened to the need for unity. . . . It is in the interest of the colonizer to continuously weaken the oppressed, to isolate them, to create and deepen rifts among them. This is done by various means,

from repressive methods of police action to forms of cultural imperialism and community action programs. The colonizer manipulates the people by giving them the impression that they are being helped, e.g., community development programs, free education, etc. (178)[8]

Adams argues that successfully dividing the Indigenous political landscape hinges on Indigenous peoples not seeing themselves as part of a larger colonized and oppressed Indigenous world. In the 1960s and 1970s a great deal of emphasis was placed on the need for government-funded community development projects to "help" Native communities. Adams views these projects as government strategies to focus Indigenous people inward on their specific and contained problems, thus serving the program of dividing Indigenous peoples. This inward focus discourages Indigenous people from critically examining their plight within the framework of colonial oppression more broadly. Today, one would likely add to this intervention that it also shifts one's gaze away from the related struggles of one's kin in other Indigenous nations.[9]

The upshot of this tactic of divide and rule is that it can be used to fracture both intra-Indigenous politics and inter-Indigenous relations. When Adams returned to Saskatchewan in 1966 after completing his PhD at UC Berkeley, he arrived at a time when the Métis political movement was divided over the acceptance of government funding. In the south, the Métis Society of Saskatchewan wanted to accept government money, while the Métis Association of Saskatchewan in the north believed it should be shunned. This battle was said to have been highly divisive.[10] The two organizations ultimately united under the Métis Society of Saskatchewan's banner, with Adams as the president. However, the point here is that with only the threat of providing funding, the government of Saskatchewan fractured the Métis political landscape. Further, the government recognition provided to one group as the official voice of the Métis is used to first divide and then shut out other voices within Métis politics.[11]

Nor is this issue unique to Saskatchewan Métis politics. In the 1990s Sheila Jones Morrison argued that the question of acquisition, control, and disbursement of government funds had divided the Manitoba Métis Federation (MMF).[12] Indeed, more recently, similar fights have raged in British Columbia over which Métis organization is fit to receive government funding, the Métis Nation British Columbia or the BC Métis Federation. While Adams helps frame these conflicts over securing and disbursing government funds, it is his analysis of the emergence of a divided Métis political world perpetuating Métis oppression that continues to prove instructive to activists and scholars. Just as this dynamic is not localized to one place in the Métis homeland, neither is it exclusive to relationships between the Métis. Fights over government money also divide Métis and First Nations peoples. The point in all of this is to say that his interventions in 1975 continue to have purchasing power beyond the time they were written, because Métis and other Indigenous peoples *continue* to live with the violence of racism, land dispossession, and numerous forms of intersecting oppression. Adams's work contains contemporary lessons for those who walk in and between the worlds of scholarship and decolonizing community-based activism.

## The Thought of Maria Campbell Teaches Howard a Thing or Two, or Three, or Four

Adams's articulation of colonial power operates in an overtly gendered and hypersexualized fashion. In *Prison of Grass* Adams gleans an insight into the way colonial power constructs Native people generally and Métis women in particular during an interaction with the Royal Canadian Mounted Police (RCMP) in the fall of 1939 (37). Two Mounties drove him to work and ridiculed Métis women as depraved sexual beings. Adams recounts the conversation he had with the Mounties: "Although they seemed to have an obsessive interest in native girls, they were also implying that Métis girls were little more than sluts and too dirty for Mounties. One asked, 'Is it true that they'll go to bed with anyone for a beer?'" (37–38). When Adams threatens to jump out of the moving squad car to escape his tormentors, the Mounties turn up their racist and sexist hate speech:

> "Jump off, so that's it." They roared on about "jump on, jump off, breed games, up and down, in and out, and halfbreed fun." Finally they let me out and drove away in a thunder of laughter. I turned and ran down the road with their mockery ringing in my ears. Shame was burning in my mind like a hot iron. I ran as if I was trying to outrun the Mounties' image of the Métis. I ran till I was exhausted, swearing, spitting, and half crying. That is how the famous red-coats of law and order respect the native people and their society. (38)

As one can see from his reaction to this exchange, Adams is deeply hurt by the Mounties' portrayal of Métis women.[13]

This experience shows both the gendered element of racist colonial violence and the way Adams constructs his own gendered colonized mentality. Colonial power for Adams contains a troubling desire for whiteness that manifests in a decidedly gendered way. This desire is more than wanting to become white; it is a sexualized desire for white women alongside the spurning of Indigenous women. Adams enunciates this dynamic when reflecting on his relationship with his family. He states that his family was an unwelcome reminder that he was Indigenous. He states that his family "reminded me of everything that was halfbreed. I was making it in the white world and

I didn't want anything holding me down. *All my friends were white, especially girlfriends*" (165, emphasis added). Adams expands on this "especially girlfriends" comment and explains that the desire for white women as lovers is itself an expression of colonial domination.

He describes his overwhelming attraction to white, blonde-haired, blue-eyed women and situates this within a desire for a white ideal that is imposed by white power structures. In the operationalization of this ideal, Native women symbolize oppression, and white women symbolize freedom (165). Adams said the white ideal made him hate those things and people that reminded him of being Native. He explains, "Every time I put my arms around a native girl I embraced oppression, but when I hugged a white girl I hugged freedom. I always felt that I would never have complete freedom until I had a white woman in my arms, in my life, in my bed. Until that day came my entire existence would be plagued with oppression" (165). Adams explicitly grounds this view in Eldridge Cleaver's *Soul on Ice*.[14] Adams believed he and Cleaver experienced colonial oppression in the same way, where domination makes one's people or, more precisely, Native women ugly and undesirable.

This expression does not only stem from Adams's personal experience. Rather, this is an experience that Adams argues is generalizable to other Indigenous people and peoples. When bringing Bonnie, his non-Indigenous girlfriend, to his home community, he says he was convinced that all the other Native men in his life envied him for being with a white woman and that they all secretly lusted after white women (166). Putting a sharper point on it, Adams argues that "every native person has this inclination towards acceptance and success in white society. . . . The supposed splendour of whiteness and the ugliness of things non-white deeply affects native people in their thought and behaviour" (167). Adams sees sexual desire of whiteness as a feature of colonial power experienced by *all* Native people.

This formulation becomes even more problematic as Adams constructs Native male desire for Native women as a type of gauge for one's engagement with one's colonial mind-set. While at UC Berkeley in the 1960s, Adams became steeped in the resistance movements of colonized people around the world. This education formed an important catalyst in his Indigenous anticolonial political awakening. Adams explicitly connects this consciousness to his new appreciation for the beauty of Métis women. He argues that "now that I was able to understand the white-deal and the profound effect it had on my life, I was able to appreciate the beauty of my own people. The women were indeed beautiful and they possessed a warmth and charm of which I had previously been unaware" (177). The operationalization of this framework means that the more Adams sees Métis women as beautiful (and this includes as objects to be desired), the more he engages with resisting the white ideal and, relatedly, successfully resists colonialism.

Adams and his thought are gripped by a particular brand of sexual power. On its face it is exclusively heterosexual; it is sexualized power that constructs women without political agency and with no heed paid to Native women as political leaders. Indeed, his relationship with Maria Campbell, an accomplished Métis political leader in her own right as well as an accomplished writer and committed activist, shows that Adams struggled to see her as a political figure in the resistance movement in which they both were engaged. Campbell talked about her interactions with Adams at the end of Hartmut Lutz's edited book *Howard Adams: Our Thoughts and Prayers Are with You.* She describes how Adams never saw her as a political person with ideas and unique contributions of her own.[15]

Campbell first met Adams in 1969 when they both were presenting to a Canadian Senate committee on poverty. Campbell was there on behalf of the Métis Association of Alberta. This context is key to their future interactions. Even though they were meeting in an explicitly political context, Adams did not see Campbell as a political person. Campbell recalls that some years later Adams invited her to speak to his class about the early Métis political movement, a topic Campbell is eminently qualified to speak about. However, in his introduction, Adams was exclusively focused on how pretty he thought she was. He recounted to the class that when he met Campbell in Ottawa years earlier she looked like she had just stepped out of a *Vogue* magazine.[16]

In contrast to Adams, Campbell works through the way colonial power manifests in a form that is horrendously violent and predatory in the lives of Métis women. In *Halfbreed* Campbell describes how gendered colonial violence is perpetrated through domestic violence, racism, and the exploitative sex trade. She captures the complex way this violence intersects along racial, gendered, and psychological lines in the lived experiences of Indigenous women. This includes a close engagement with what Adams would later call the desire for the white ideal among the colonized. This important intersection came together in vivid terms during a trip home to Spring River. Campbell had developed relationships of support and friendship while writing to inmates in Prince Albert Penitentiary's Alcoholics Anonymous (AA) program.[17] As an act of appreciation for the relationships she cultivated, Campbell was invited to attend a conference at the prison, where she met the people she had been corresponding with.[18] This conference also afforded Campbell the chance to go home to Spring River and visit her family. While at home, she made a trip to the town of St. Michel, where she ran into her friend Smokey and was confronted by his relationship with two white, blonde-haired women. After visiting friends around the town with Smokey,

Campbell "drove him home, his blonde-haired wives came out and listened to him say to me, 'Hell, some of us are lucky enough to have a white woman to make us feel we've moved up.' I went home, feeling like I wanted to get Daddy's rifle and go out and shoot everything" (149).

Campbell is identifying the way falling in love with a white partner comes to be thought of, in some people's lives, as a marker of social mobility and status. Key to this is the rage the experience elicits in Campbell. When placed in the context of her life in Vancouver and her treatment at the hands of Canadian hospitals, social services, and law enforcement, all of which are shown to be violently opposed to the presence and experiences of Indigenous women, this rage against the white ideal seems to also be rage against the marginalization of her people. This is not to say that the ideal does not have heterosexualized power attached to it—it does. Rather, the point is that Campbell illuminates the sexualized elements of the white ideal without needing to then sexualize the path to decolonization in the way Adams does.

Indeed, she is also able to explain the complex set of relationships this gendered violence creates between Indigenous women, on the one hand, and Indigenous and non-Indigenous men, on the other. Campbell takes her reader through the happy and difficult times in her life. She confronts violence at the hands of Indigenous men, non-Indigenous men, and drug addiction. After a lengthy period away from Native community, Campbell is helped by a community of Indigenous people in Arizona on her way back from being abandoned in Mexico. These Indigenous people shared what they had with her, and when Campbell left, the family's grandmother gave her a few dollars to make sure Campbell could get something to eat on the long journey home (123). This was the first occasion since leaving her community that Campbell had been back among Indigenous people, and she remarked that the expectation to help others within Native community made it hard for her to survive. Deepening and nuancing this thought, Campbell remarks: "There was a part of me that hated them as well. The drunken Indian men I saw would fill me with a blinding hatred; I blamed them for what had happened to me, to the little girl who had died from an overdose of drugs, and for all the girls who were on the city streets. If they had only fought back, instead of giving up, these things would never have happened. It's hard to explain how I felt. I hated our men, and yet I loved them" (123). This comment, which seems to have roots in her father's disillusionment with the early Métis political movement after its co-optation by government salaries and recognition (67), shows a great deal more complexity about the way domination impacts Indigenous women. Where Adams saw Native female attractiveness as a marker on the road to male decolonization, Campbell is pointing out that Indigenous men are both sources of violence *and* wells of potential strength for Indigenous resistance. Campbell's work is helpfully alerting us to how relationships of gender, Indigeneity, and colonial power intersect in complex and nuanced ways for Indigenous women.

In this same vein, during her return visit to St. Michel, Campbell deepens this relational intersection by working through the normalized and cavalier nature of gendered violence for Indigenous women.

> Later on I went in to St. Michel, and because it was Saturday night it seemed as if the pages had been turned back. Only now it was worse, like a nightmare too horrible to forget. The streets were full of Native people in all stages of intoxication. There were children running everywhere; babies crying with nobody to care for them. A man was beating his wife behind a building, while little children looked on as though it was all quite normal. . . . There were drunken women with faces badly scarred and bruised from numerous beatings. The old angry bitter feeling came back to my stomach—the feeling of hate—as I saw people whom I had known as a child, now with such empty, despairing faces. (148)

Campbell captures the intense impact that gendered violence has on Indigenous women and children and its capacity to undermine Métis political resistance movements by creating states of despair in the lives of individuals. One of the consequences of Campbell's recounting is that the powerlessness and despair not only keep women in conditions of atrocious violence but also undermine the ability of the community to organize and fight back against these conditions of oppression. In this formulation, despair is disempowering. This proves to be a far more nuanced and robust explication of gendered colonial violence in the lives and politics of Indigenous women than anything outlined by Howard Adams.

These interventions lay bare one of the key distinctions between Adams's formulation of colonial domination and Campbell's. They are engaging women's experiences very differently. Adams's lustful heterosexual desire, along with its predatory overtones, renders the importance of women down to being objects of male desire along the road to decolonization. His framing not only normalizes a fundamentally unsafe state of predation and disempowerment on/of Indigenous women but also makes that state virtuous and decolonial. The position in which Adams places women also undermines the important role that women play in the political movements that Campbell and others are trying to build.[19] Campbell, on the other hand, forces us to confront the predatory and violent behavior endemic in St. Michel—she *insists* that it be seen. Recall that Campbell points out that "little children looked on as though it was all quite normal." This statement makes us see the normalization of violence while also alerting us to its potential to become intergenerational.

In all this, Campbell provides an account of colonial power that brings together complex struggles of resistance, psychology, gender, and indigeneity. Her work locates a bona fide rage against colonial oppression alongside the complex relationship that Indigenous women navigate in and between the spaces they move through. This complexity is marked by its resistance to colonial structures of power and by a powerful and insightful critique of Indigenous men. Taken together, she helpfully illuminates the contours of gendered colonial violence in the lives of Indigenous women. As Indigenous activists and scholars continue to grapple with violence against Indigenous women, these insights remain a grounded, salient, and helpful framework to understand and resist gendered colonial violence.

While Adams may very well experience colonialism in the terms he describes, the generalization of his consciousness to the whole of Métis people is neither compelling nor redeemable. For these reasons I do not believe Adams's views on the gendered dynamics of colonial power are recoverable. However, the critique offered above creates a new problem. In light of the contrast between Adams's and Campbell's works and the rejection of Adams's lustful decolonial consciousness, it is not clear where this leaves the potential for building decolonizing political action informed by the types of gendered considerations discussed by Campbell. In essence, the criticisms provided above do not in themselves contribute to a world where gender is treated seriously in decolonizing struggles.

The criticisms offered in this article need to be paired with imagining how one might envision alternative, gender-robust modes of decolonizing politics. Doing so requires drawing on both Campbell's and Adams's method of grounding their intellectual interventions in community experiences and activism. The strength of this approach lies in providing guidance to subsequent generations of Indigenous people about the ways in which research can be combined with action to inform the choices Indigenous nations are confronting in our complex world. My suggestion for achieving this is to practice imagining a political engagement in which the strengths of both authors are combined toward cultivating a politics attuned to the types of intersections that Campbell works through. To inform such an act of political imagining, I argue that combining two key decolonizing theoretical approaches, acting otherwise and imagining otherwise, takes the action-deficient state of the above critique and turns it into a springboard from which to launch decolonizing political action grounded in a deeply robust relationship with Indigenous gender diversity. In the next section, I work through the intellectual traditions of acting otherwise and imagining otherwise with the aim of using these interventions to inform a reimagining of a fictional Howard Adams confronted by the political complexity of gender politics in his fight against the Trudeau/Chrétien 1969 *White Paper on Indian Policy.*

## Imagine Howard Adams Walks into a Diner

James Tully offers a framework to think through Indigenous struggles *for* freedom and *of* freedom in the first volume of *Public Philosophy in a New Key.* For Tully, struggles *for* freedom encompass Indigenous peoples as peoples "resisting the colonial systems as a whole, in each country and throughout the world of 250 million Indigenous people." Despite these struggles being marked by vast power imbalances, Indigenous peoples have engaged in a range of activities *for* their freedom. From "appeals to the Privy Council in the seventeenth century to statements to the Working Group on Indigenous Populations of the Sub-Commission on Prevention of Discrimination and Protection of Minorities of the United Nations today, their 'word warriors' have never ceased to declaim the illegitimate system of internal colonisation and proclaim their sovereignty and freedom." Indigenous peoples also engage in struggles *of* freedom in which "they struggle within the structure of domination vis-à-vis techniques of government, by exercising their freedom of thought and action with the aim of modifying the system in the short term and transforming it from within in the long term." As is characteristic of Tully's thought, each of these interventions operates through a series of logically constructed supporting lists and sublists of characteristics and properties. Common to these struggles is disrupting what Tully calls the dual colonial hinge propositions, which assert that, first, settler rule over Indigenous peoples' territories is argued to be effective and legitimate, and second, even if it is not legitimate, it is argued that there is no viable alternative. Tully offers that these two propositions can be efficaciously disrupted by Indigenous struggles and practices *of* freedom: "The multiplicity of immanent activities of challenging specific strategies and techniques by the available democratic means of dissent, insubordination and *acting otherwise* may not only modify this or that rule of the system, which is important in itself, but may also in the long run bring about the self-overcoming of the system itself." Tully believes that such activities done in struggles *of* freedom come to intersect with struggles *for* freedom.[20]

Within this framework, Tully's notion of "acting otherwise" possesses some important characteristics that might helpfully reimagine Adams in light of Campbell's work. By acting otherwise, Indigenous activists deploy their own contextually grounded norms of political engagement as a means to change the domination they experience. While I am open to this potential of acting otherwise, it seems that to productively intersect with struggles *for* freedom, there also needs to be work done to disrupt the cemented power relationships between Indigenous peoples and colonizers *and* between Indigenous peoples and nations. Tully's second hinge proposition is important because it circumscribes and truncates the universe of decolonizing possibilities. As such, imagining and dreaming about different modes and norms of relationality are key prior conditions to one acting otherwise and unhinging the proposition.

Several literary scholars have offered the potential to "imagine otherwise" as a robust theoretical intervention and scholarly engagement. Kandice Chuh argues in her critique of Asian American literatures that "to imagine otherwise is not simply a matter of seeing a common object from different perspectives. Rather, it is about undoing the very notion of common objectivity itself and about recognizing the ethicopolitical implications of multiple epistemologies—theories about knowledge formation and the status of objects of knowledge—that underwrite alternative perspectives."[21] Thus, for Chuh, imagining otherwise is also about interrogating what appear to be cemented power relations. Joseph Bauerkemper also pulls at this intellectual thread when he reflects on the theory-building work of Robert Warrior and writes, "The task of theory, then, is to illuminate the worlds in which we live, to enable us to imagine otherwise, and to encourage us to work toward the realization of alternatives."[22]

To this end, what I offer next is a preliminary, imagined otherwise experience for Howard Adams. Though Adams captures important elements of the lived colonial struggle for Métis people, one can learn a good deal more by imagining him, within his context, fully alive to the colonial gender relations that Campbell captures in her work. This turns my above action-deficient critique into a reimagining that is explicitly oriented toward unhinging colonial propositions at the intersection of struggles *for* and *of* freedom.

*Howard walked into his favorite diner in Prince Albert. The place was exactly as he had seen it last, packed full of Métis talking both emphatically and intensely, with conversations interspersed with uproarious outbursts. All the usual suspects were there: his cousins Keith and Henry, his ex-lover Mert, her new beau, and a rash of other relations, friends, and enemies. But he wasn't here to see any of them.*

*"Howard! How the hell are ya!" bellowed Keith through his brother. "We didn't know you were in town. We'd a picked you up!"*

*"I'm in drumming up support to fight this goddamned Canadian White Paper," replied Howard. He hated uttering the name of that genocidal abomination in this place. "We gotta shut this thing down before it shuts us down. Is Billy here?"*

No sooner had the words fallen out of his mouth than a voice cut through the din. It was a voice that sounded as though it had endured years of twice-daily gargling with rusty nails. "Well if it isn't the King of the Breeds, returned from the Tyndall Palace."

Out from behind the small order pick-up window, there she stood. Howard had seen her a hundred times, but every time there seemed to be something different about her that made the experience feel new. Her purple metallic hair sheened to pink as the angle of the light changed. Howard could never fully comprehend her bright blue eyeshadow and lashes that curved up from her eyelids to touch her bushy eyebrows. All of this set upon a weathered face with rail lines radiating out from the ends of her eyes and running truncated down her cheeks. It didn't matter how many times it happened, when Billy's gaze fell on Howard he could feel himself being pierced by those yellow eyes and hypnotized by the methodical movement of her Adam's apple.

"What the hell is wrong with you? Aren't you gonna give your aunty a hug!?" Billy stepped out from behind the kitchen order window, snapping something unintelligible to one of the servers, and made a beeline for Howard. She wrapped him in a hug so crushing that Howard's spine cracked from ass to head.

When they released each other from their embrace Howard was able to fill his lungs enough to get out "got time to talk?"

"Anything for you, Howard" Billy barked.

Billy marched back into the kitchen with her grease-stained apron brushing gently against her knees. She flipped two burgers and reappeared in the kitchen order pick-up window.

"Order up! Buffalo burger, extra fried onions on a bannock bun!" A young man dutifully scurried over, grabbed the plate, and rushed away, never making eye contact with Billy. Howard recognized this particular dance. Making eye contact with Billy might invite some biting remark about the young server's haircut or what he got caught doing after work last week.

Billy said something to one of the other cooks and reappeared outside the kitchen. Motioning for Howard to follow, Billy marched into a small, dimly lit office at the back of the diner with a No Smoking sign (complete with the Prince Albert bylaw number) hanging on the wall behind the table. A low-hanging ceiling light gave off a soft glow that didn't seem to reach any of the four corners of the wood-paneled room. They both sat down, and Billy lit up a smoke. She took a long drag, and just before she exhaled Billy used the ember end of her smoke to point to the No Smoking sign. "We don't take orders from them," she said and let out a long stream of exhaust.

And here they talked. Howard explained his struggle to fight the 1969

*White Paper and expressed his concern that the government's policy was dividing Native peoples. Billy wasn't surprised at all by this. It had happened before. Billy told Howard about the deep need colonizers have to ensure Natives are divided. "Divided politically, but also divided internally. Keep the Indians fighting each other, and they won't be able to fight the real enemy." Billy then told Howard a story about missionaries laying the groundwork for Métis men to distrust anything but the most simple understandings of the world. "Hate women who speak, hate people who aren't men or women, hate following women. Our men had to learn that bullshit."*

*Here Billy trailed off and stared intensely into the dark corner of the room. Her yellow eyes glimmered as they made sense and shape out of the darkness. After a moment Billy snapped her head back toward Howard. "They've been doing it for a long time, and it starts with making us hate ourselves and then each other."*

*Howard and Billy continued to talk for some time. Their intense talk of strategy was interrupted by a knock on the door. The knock wasn't so much a sound as it was a request for permission to be a sound. Billy got up and whipped open the door.*

*"Umm, we're getting swamped out here, Billy," said the young server. Billy growled, and the young man bolted back to his duties. Howard could see Billy's perma-scowl slowly morph into a crooked, playful smirk. "We'll pick this up another time, Howard."*

*Howard's visit was over, and he knew it. He could either order something or get the hell out. Howard thanked Billy, and she cracked his spine back to the shape it was in when Howard had walked into the diner. Billy had given him a great deal to think about, and as he crossed over the threshold a cool, dry wind ran its fingers through his inkwell-black hair. He figured he had a plan.*

In this account, the Indigenous world in which Adams engages with Billy offers a gendered complexity to Indigenous politics that is far more likely to lead to different understandings about the pathways and forms of Métis struggles *for* and *of* freedom. Though Adams, a heterosexual man, remains the central figure in this political agitation, there is a complex and normalized gender diversity to his world that is absent from Adams's 1975 work. This imagined Adams is uncomplicatedly engaged in complex kin relationships with a queer Indigenous relation. There is also added complexity to Billy's gender identity in the community as a Rougarou. Billy, a queer Rougarou, is situated simultaneously in and alongside Métis community as restoried by Campbell in *Stories of the Road Allowance People*.[23] This character is also imbued with an explicitly political orientation to her surroundings. The result is that this experience expands the gendered horizons of imagined Adams while providing an imagined alternative to retheorize Indigenous resistance to settler colonial oppression.

At the same time, the story continues to orient Adams to the devastation wreaked by divide-and-rule tactics among Indigenous peoples and suggests that he has the strength, called for by Campbell, to address it. However, here the method of division is neither self-evident nor divorced from gendered power dynamics. Billy explains that the divisions are built on a foundation of focused oppression of nonconforming gender identities. Further, in the diner, gender diversity is imagined and normalized into the present, thereby challenging the lived gender oppression of the real world. The result is that the diner and Adams's movement through it form a complex space that is deeply relational with an orientation to gender grounded in Métis community. All the while, this moment leads to a strategy that could inform acting otherwise in a struggle *of* or *for* freedom.

Returning for a moment to the contrast between Adams's and Campbell's lived experiences and the reimagined experience outlined here, one of the advantages of this act of imagining otherwise is that it empowers those who may have been disempowered in the authors' actual lives while also challenging the seemingly cemented power relationships they both moved through. For example, an aunty or relative may actually have sat Adams down to have a very similar conversation with him during his life. But gendered colonial power dynamics may have disempowered both that voice and that experience's relative importance in Adams's life. That is what Campbell is pointing out to us. These voices of Indigenous women and other relatives are not respected. Imagining otherwise takes Campbell's interventions and empowers those relations and those experiences, making them central to decolonizing action. Conversely, the experience of a normalized gender diversity, as imagined here, is difficult to contemplate in the real world in light of the role played by the Catholic and Protestant Churches in Métis communities. These religions contribute to Tully's second hinge proposition by circumscribing the ability of Métis to imagine an alternative to the cemented power relationship between Métis people/communities, churches, and church leaders. However, this imagined alternative also undermines that power dynamic by opening up new ways of relating that are not policed by priests and parishioners.

It is important to note that this is not a utopic exercise. Adams, a heterosexual male, continues to be the lead character in organized agitation confronting a manifestation of settler-colonial domination. This suggests that the work of challenging the power of gendered colonial oppression is not yet done. Importantly, though, fictional Adams answers Campbell's call to think more about the strength that Indigenous men possess in our political struggles. As Indigenous peoples grapple with the devastation wreaked by a multipronged system of oppression, this moment of imagination brings into existence an alternative emphasis of being grounded by close relationships with one's people, and that moment comes to inform creative political action.

Nor is this type of exercise without complications. It is not my desire in this reimagining to fully divorce Adams from his contradictions. One must be equally careful not to sanitize Adams's failings to try and save him from himself. The risk in imagining otherwise is that Adams's sexualized and gendered construction of colonial power comes to be made innocent of its transgressions. However, by placing Adams and Campbell in conversation with each other concerning the context and operation of gendered violence, my hope is to unlock and then animate the strengths of both authors' interventions. Doing so leads to very different understandings of the gendered dimensions of decolonizing politics and provides pathways for gender-informed and gender-diverse decolonizing action.

## Conclusion

Howard Adams and Maria Campbell made important and lasting contributions to understanding being Métis in Canada. This work has argued that, forty years after publication, *Halfbreed* and *Prison of Grass* continue to have the power to inform scholars and activists engaged in the study and practice of Indigenous resurgence as well as the politics of decolonization in Canada. Adams's blunt yet robust enunciation of racism in Canada and its incorporation into the institutional mechanisms of land dispossession still proves useful for both Indigenous and non-Indigenous readers. Campbell provides thoughtful insight into the way colonial power intersects with gender and Indigeneity. Both works were published at a time marked by constitutional nation building in Canada and a desire to reinforce a supposedly just and unified Canadian community. Together, both works paint a portrait of Canada that captures the racist colonial project's effects on Métis families' psychologies, economies, and politics. Their works challenge Canada's image as a bright light of tolerance and inclusiveness in the global community advanced by successive Canadian governments. Their discussions of the white ideal, Indigenous political organizing and mobilization, and the risks of divide-and-rule tactics continue to have purchasing power more than forty years after publication.

Adams was personally and professionally gripped by the sexual power of colonial domination. His understanding of this power troublingly frames Indigenous women as objects of lustful desire rather than as empowered political people in our communities. My work here endeavors to show that one can find a significantly more robust understanding of the gendered nature of colonial violence in the thought and life of Maria Campbell. Campbell understands that there is a complex interplay between gender, psychology, and Indigeneity within colonial power that makes Indigenous men sources of violence and, potentially, wells of strength. Adams's work never appreciates this complexity. Instead, his thought contributes to an environment that is, at its core, unsafe and predatory toward Indigenous women, while Campbell's work demands that we see the violence and predation and address it head-on.

Indigenous peoples have suffered greatly at the hands of the intersecting power dynamics of settler colonial oppression. If we are to engage in struggles *of* and *for* freedom and imagine, act, think, and love otherwise, it might be helpful to spend some moments with our relations reimagining other ways of acting, thinking, and loving. As Avery Gordon reminds us, power manifests in obvious and invisible ways in our lives, and "it causes dreams to live and dreams to die." But "we need to know where we live in order to imagine living elsewhere. We need to imagine living elsewhere before we can live there."[24] Adams and Campbell help us know more about where we live. The work of imagining and acting otherwise puts us on the road to living elsewhere.

DANIEL VOTH (Métis) is an assistant professor of political science and an instructor in the International Indigenous Studies program at the University of Calgary in the territory of Treaty #7 Peoples. In addition to this work in *NAIS*, his research has been published in the *Canadian Journal of Political Science* and the *University of Toronto Law Journal*.

## Notes

I would like to thank all my blind peer reviewers for their thoughtful and generous engagements with this work. I feel deeply grateful to be part of an intellectual community that responds so generously when reading the work of others.

1. I use the terms "Indigenous" and "Native" interchangeably throughout this work.

2. Adams drew heavily from Fanon's work yet cited him sparingly. Many who have worked with Adams will recall his deep engagement with African anticolonial thought. Indeed, added to this should be Adams's close engagement with Marx. There is a pressing need for further research on these intellectual connections. However, teasing out these connections is beyond this article's scope and requires a different methodology than is being deployed here.

3. Howard Adams, *Prison of Grass: Canada from the Native Point of View* (Toronto: New Press, 1975), 8. Hereafter cited parenthetically in the text.

4. Howard Adams, *Howard Adams: Otapawy! The Life of a Métis Leader in His Own Words and in Those of His Contemporaries*, ed. Hartmut Lutz, Murray Hamilton, and Donna Heimbecker (Saskatoon: Gabriel Dumont Institute, 2005), 36.

5. Please see Audra Simpson, *Mohawk Interruptus: Political Life across the Borders of Settler States* (Durham, NC: Duke University Press, 2014); Patrick Wolfe, "Settler Colonialism and the Elimination of the Native," *Journal of Genocide Research* 8, no. 4 (2006): 387–409; Lorenzo Veracini, "Introducing Settler Colonial Studies," *Settler Colonial Studies* 1, no. 1 (2011): 1–12; Lorenzo Veracini, *Settler Colonialism: A Theoretical Overview* (New York : Palgrave Macmillan, 2010), 182; Glen S. Coulthard, *Red Skin, White Masks* (Minneapolis: University of Minnesota Press, 2014).

6. In his October 20, 2014, Killam Lecture at the University of British Columbia, J. R. Miller portrays the numbered treaty process as one rooted in kinship and laudable nation building between Canada and the Indigenous nations of the Northwest. His analysis inexplicably divorces Canada's betrayal and deceit, which has now been well cataloged in many of the numbered treaties. See Daniel Morley Johnson's PhD dissertation, "'This Is Our Land!': Indigenous Rhetoric and Resistance on the Northern Plains" (University of Alberta, 2014). For an insightful and critical view of contemporary treaty making in British Columbia, see Andrew Woolford, *Between Justice and Certainty: Treaty Making in British Columbia* (Vancouver: UBC Press, 2005).

7. Interestingly, one of the things that made #IdleNoMore so successful among Indigenous peoples and their settler allies was its emphasis on nonviolent action. Adams, on the other hand, remarked in an interview with Hartmut Lutz that growing up with a life of violence made him never one to shy away from violent agitation. For the full interview, see "Interview with Howard Adams," in *Contemporary Challenges: Conversations with Canadian Native Authors*, ed. Hartmut Lutz (Saskatoon: Fifth House Publishers, 1991), 135–54.

8. See also Howard Adams, *Prison of Grass: Canada from a Native Point of View*, 2nd ed. (Saskatoon: Fifth House Publishers, 1989), 154.

9. For excellent examinations of these dynamics and robust theoretical approaches for their study, see Robert Alexander Innes, *Elder Brother and the Law of the People: Contemporary Kinship and Cowessess First Nation* (Winnipeg: University of Manitoba Press, 2013); Brenda Macdougall, *One of the Family: Métis Culture in Nineteenth-Century Northwestern Saskatchewan* (Vancouver: UBC Press, 2010).

10. James M. Pitsula, "The Thatcher Government in Saskatchewan and the Revival of Metis Nationalism, 1964–1971," *Great Plains Quarterly* 17 (Summer/Fall 1997).

11. Ibid., 222.

12. Sheila Jones Morrison, *Rotten to the Core: The Politics of the Manitoba Métis Federation* (Victoria: J. Gordon Shillingford Publishing, 1995).

13. One year after this interaction Adams joined the Mounties and served with them for four years (1940–44).

14. Eldridge Cleaver, *Soul on Ice*, 1st ed. (New York: McGraw-Hill, 1967).

15. Adams, *Howard Adams: Otapawy!*, 242.

16. Ibid., 237, 242.

17. Maria Campbell, *Halfbreed* (Toronto: McClelland and Stewart, 1973), 146. Hereafter cited parenthetically in the text.

18. It was at the conference that Maria received a gift of a painting depicting "a burnt-out forest, all black, bleak and dismal. In the centre was a burnt-out tree stump, and at the roots were little green shoots sprouting up" (ibid., 146–47).

19. Sam McKegney, "Remembering the Sacredness of Men: A Conversation with Kim Anderson," in *Masculindians: Conversations about Indigenous Manhood* (Winnipeg: University of Manitoba Press, 2014), 89–90; Kim Anderson and Maria Campbell, *Life Stages and Native Women* (Winnipeg: University of Manitoba Press, 2011).

20. James Tully, *Public Philosophy in a New Key* (Cambridge: Cambridge University Press, 2008), 265, 276, 287, emphasis added.

21. Kandice Chuh, *Imagine Otherwise: On Asian Americanist Critique* (Durham, NC: Duke University Press, 2003), x.

22. Joseph Bauerkemper, "Indigenous Trans/Nationalism and the Ethics of Theory in Native Literary Studies," in *The Oxford Handbook of Indigenous American Literature*, ed. James H. Cox and Daniel Heath Justice (Oxford: Oxford University Press, 2014), 405.

23. Maria Campbell, *Stories of the Road Allowance People* (Penticton, BC: Theytus Books, 1995), 28–49; see also Warren Cariou, "Dances with Rigoureau," in *Troubling Tricksters: Revisioning Critical Conversations*, ed. Deanna Reder and Linda M. Morra (Waterloo: Wilfrid Laurier University Press, 2010), 157.

24. Avery Gordon, *Ghostly Matters: Haunting and the Sociological Imagination* (Minnesota: University of Minnesota Press, 1997), 3, 5.

KHALIL ANTHONY JOHNSON JR.

## Problem Solver or "Evil Genius": Thomas Jesse Jones and *The Problem of Indian Administration*

WHEN LEWIS MERIAM VISITED FORT WINGATE on March 29, 1927, construction crews were busy converting the old military post into an off-reservation boarding school for Navajo youth.[1] The pupils attending the Charles H. Burke Indian School, located in a valley just east of Gallup, New Mexico, played on a field where US soldiers once paraded.[2] Their grandparents and great-grandparents had endured forced relocation and four years of internment on a meager scrap of eastern New Mexico desert before negotiating the Treaty of Bosque Redondo in 1868. The treaty secured their release and created the reservation. It also stipulated compulsory education for every child age six to sixteen, but the US government would take decades to fulfill that promise. Fort Wingate, once the final sojourn for Navajo exiles returning to ancestral homes on the new reservation, had now entered a new era of US rule in which education increasingly shouldered colonial policy.[3] The school already housed 200 students, some clearly too young to enroll, all visibly diminished next to the imposing stone facilities.[4] After the construction crews completed their work later that year the boarding school would become home to as many as 750 students.[5]

Meriam, a white Harvard Law graduate with a mind geared toward administrative efficiency, had been in the field for 137 days investigating reservation schools, hospitals, and Indian agencies across the United States on behalf of the nonpartisan Institute for Government Research (now the Brookings Institution). A Navajo girl had died from tuberculosis in the hospital on school grounds the morning of his visit, he learned. And upon touring Fort Wingate's dim and dismal dormitories, he confessed, "I was rather depressed at seeing the development of another large boarding school, especially by the attempt to utilize a lot of the old army post buildings which were poorly adapted for school use." On day 138 Meriam wrote that the boarding school at Fort Wingate "was as distressing as any place I have visited."[6]

Meriam submitted his findings to Secretary of the Interior Hubert Work nearly a year later, on February 21, 1928. Although the report singled out the Charles H. Burke Indian School, observing that "the army barracks and other structures there will never make satisfactory school buildings," the report avoided direct criticism of its namesake, the current commissioner of Indian affairs. Still, Meriam and the nine members of his survey team felt obliged to state "frankly and unequivocally that the provisions for the care of the Indian children in boarding schools are grossly inadequate." They pilloried the Office of Indian Affairs for working students to a degree that made a mockery of child labor laws, for neglectful Indian health services that threatened public welfare, and for a highly centralized administrative structure that dictated orders from afar yet staffed local offices with underpaid and often ill-qualified personnel.[7]

Published as *The Problem of Indian Administration*, Meriam's report proved to be a masterpiece of political publicity. Its recommendations set a new benchmark for reforms. Better yet, the thrust of its 847 pages could be distilled into a single sentence: "He who wants to remain an Indian and live according to his old culture should be aided in doing so."[8] More than money or congressional oversight or improved facilities, what US Indian policy needed most was "a change in point of view." The report urged the United States to recognize that American Indian policy had always been "primarily educational" because the overarching objective had been to "adjust" primitive Native people to meet the economic, social, and vocational realities of the dominant society. If the old view insisted that Indian children should be detribalized in distant boarding schools and remade as individual allottees, the new vision maintained that education must be gradual, "locally relevant," and "adapted to individual abilities, interests, and needs."[9]

Historians have justifiably presented *The Problem of Indian Administration,* better known as the Meriam Report, as the culmination of a progressive movement in US Indian policy that catapulted radical reformist John Collier into the office of commissioner of Indian affairs in 1933 and served as a blueprint for the 1934 Indian Reorganization Act, reversing a half century of federal policies directed toward assimilating Native Americans and bringing the federal boarding school era to a close. In recommending that Indian culture should be incorporated into the school curriculum and that education should be adapted to the local needs of Native communities, moreover, the Meriam Report remains a defining moment in the struggle for self-determination in Native America.[10] But like so much of boarding school history, the story of how Lewis Meriam, a statistician with no prior experience in US Indian policy, became the technical director of "the most significant inquiry into Indian conditions and administration during the twentieth century," to quote historian Donald Parman, has been oversimplified.[11]

Retracing the genesis of the Meriam Report takes us on a world tour—from the US South, to British colonial Africa and Oceania, and back to the Charles H. Burke Indian School—during a moment in which new ideas in sociology, anthropology, philanthropy, and politics combined to institute a sea change in policies directed toward Indigenous people. As Commissioner of Indian Affairs John Collier observed in 1937, "The thinking of educated people about the needs and the potentialities of so-called backward peoples has been revolutionized."[12] The revolution Collier described involved a twenty-five-year period in which colonial governance shifted away from aggressive assimilation of Indigenous populations in favor of a more gradual, pluralist approach of incorporating and recognizing Indigenous people as *Indigenous people*. This policy reorientation resulted not from an idea caught high in the winds of progress and dispersed across the globe; instead, a small cadre of people worked behind the scenes to reverse decades of assimilation. "A great many personalities and influences have entered into the change," noted Commissioner Collier, "but surely one of them, consistently and to an important extent, has been the personal contacts and the writings of Thomas Jesse Jones."[13]

From 1917 until his retirement in 1944, Dr. Thomas Jesse Jones served as the educational director of the Phelps-Stokes Fund, a New York–based philanthropy established in 1911 for the purpose of promoting "the education of negroes, both in Africa and the United States, North American Indians and needy and deserving white students."[14] Best known for its endeavors in African and African American education, the Phelps-Stokes Fund has garnered relatively little attention among scholars of American Indian history, perhaps because scholars have generally neglected the influence of industrial philanthropy on US Indian policy, instead emphasizing the prominence of the federal government, Christian missionaries, and Indian rights organizations.[15] Likewise, scholars of African and African American history, often attentive to Jones's frequent sparring with W. E. B. Du Bois, have largely overlooked his historic contributions to US Indian policy. As Philip J. Deloria has observed of Gilded Age and Progressive Era history, the "naturalization of Indian disappearance and American settlement" has fostered narratives that "leave us knowing W. E. B. DuBois and Booker T. Washington,"[16] while virtually erasing from US history Native American contemporaries such as Henry Roe Cloud and Ella Deloria, both of whom collaborated with Jones during and after the Meriam survey.[17] Yet W. Carson Ryan, the progressive reformer who authored the Meriam Report's education section and subsequently served as the BIA's director of Indian education, not only believed that the Meriam survey "could hardly have been made were it not for Dr. Jones's skills in negotiation" but also maintained that significant reforms that occurred during the Collier administration "would not have been possible without [Jones's] marvelous skill in bringing divergent groups together and smoothing out difficulties."[18] Indeed, between 1917 and 1939 Jones and the people he knew would reshape a world connected through histories of colonialism, transatlantic slavery, and Indigenous dispossession.

Jones's biography and career unlock a hidden history of *The Problem of Indian Administration.* At the turn of the twentieth century, he became the steward of an idea that was born in the aftermath of the US Civil War and that attempted to resolve the quandary of black citizenship and territorial expansion through a racially qualified approach to education. As an arbiter of power within international philanthropic circles, he translated this idea into educational policies that affected millions of Indigenous peoples in Anglophone colonies across the globe. Indeed, Jones and his network of associates enabled two New York—based nongovernmental institutions—the Phelps-Stokes Fund and the Rockefeller Foundation—to directly influence government policymakers in both the United States and the United Kingdom. The following pages map colonial influences on the imperial frontier between the United States and the British Empire during the interwar period, connecting three boarding schools across time and space: Hampton Institute in Virginia, Achimota College in the British Gold Coast, and the Charles H. Burke Indian School. In linking progressive social reformers across these seemingly disparate regimes, from Jim Crow segregation to British indirect rule to American Indian reservations, this essay argues that each can be understood within a common colonial matrix.

## Who Was Thomas Jesse Jones?

Thomas Jesse Jones was born on the Isle of Anglesey, off the northern coast of Wales, in 1873 to Benjamin and Sarah Williams Jones. His father was the village saddler in Llanfachraeth, and his mother was keeper of the Mona Inn, the epicenter of local politics and gossip.[19] By the 1870s, native Welsh communities were experiencing profound economic and cultural pressures under British rule. Industrialization in the south and northeast had brought increasing numbers of English immigrants. Not unlike their peers in the United States, the British had imposed a universal English curriculum in Welsh schools. Meanwhile, rural farmers from northwestern villages such as Llanfachraeth were immigrating to the United States, including Sarah's sister, Margaret William Davis.[20] Sarah put her literacy and associations with English travelers to use defending the rural peasantry against exploitative public servants and absentee landlords, but her husband's unexpected death in the spring of 1880 left her a widow with mounting difficulties of her own.

Sarah immigrated to the United States with her mother, younger sister, and four children in 1884, where the family joined Margaret alongside the Ohio River in Meigs County, Ohio.[21]

Eleven years old and speaking little English, young Thomas adjusted to the United States while working in a butcher shop owned by his uncle, who evidently paid Thomas and his brother Robert John in raspberries and lemonade. Outside the shop, Thomas would find much richer reward for his work. He became active in the local Presbyterian church and excelled in his public school studies. Seven years after immigrating, he graduated from Pomeroy High School and headed to college on a ministerial scholarship. On August 4, 1894, he became a naturalized US citizen. Education and religion worked a kind of alchemy upon him. In pursuing his own transformation from Welsh foreigner to US citizen, Jones would move far beyond his working-class origins to the upper echelons of society. In 1900 he received a bachelor's of divinity from Union Theological Seminary and earned a doctorate in sociology from Columbia University in 1904.[22]

Though assimilated, Jones thought of himself as both a Welshman and an American. "I believe in Wales and love the Welsh," Jones pledged in a 1917 interview. "Cymru fo am byth" (Long live Wales).[23] He spoke Welsh fluently, delighted in its culture and history, and was known to lift his voice in a lilting Welsh folksong when the mood compelled him. Yet he loved the United States above all nations.[24] He wielded this insider-outsider status to his advantage, positioning himself as the consummate mediator in the fractious field of US race relations. As his friend and Meriam Report coauthor Fayette Avery McKenzie put it, "In Dr. Thomas Jesse Jones we have a man in whom great diversities meet. He is a white man but possessed of a 'black heart'—a heart that beats in sympathy with the black man as well as with the white. An immigrant, he represents America to the rest of the world. Born to poverty he associates with those who are wealthy and advises with those who sit in seats of authority and power."[25] Short, swarthy, and foppish, Jones projected what someone once described as a "purring manner." But he was no housecat. His friends considered him to be "absolutely fearless, both physically and morally," possessing "a keen sense of humor, and a fine sense of justice."[26] His enemies, the African American intellectual and activist Du Bois among them, considered him an "evil genius."[27]

Prior to joining the Phelps-Stokes Fund, Jones served as the director of research and sociology at Hampton Institute from 1902 through 1909. Originally founded in 1868 as a teacher training and industrial school for emancipated African Americans, Hampton famously educated American Indian students from 1877 through 1923, acting as a foil and rival to Carlisle Indian Industrial School. Although both institutions stressed vocational education,

Hampton practiced a gradualist, evolutionary approach to Indian and black advancement. Known as "the Hampton Idea," this philosophy emphasized self-reliance, community uplift, and racial pride over the Carlisle brand of total assimilation.[28] But Hampton also possessed deeper, colonial roots. Its founder, Samuel Chapman Armstrong, had been born in the Kingdom of Hawai'i in 1839 to US missionaries Clarissa Chapman and Rev. Richard Armstrong, the so-called father of American education in Hawaii. Under the elder Armstrong, missionaries created a two-tiered system of Christian education. One system, which the Kamehameha School and Lahainaluna Seminary exemplified, provided leadership and academic training for the royal family and ruling ali'i class. The other school system targeted the Kanaka Maoli masses while serving American interests in the growing plantation economy. To that end, missionaries developed a pedagogy at Hilo Boarding and Vocational School that sought to produce a disciplined Indigenous laboring class through surveillance, routinization, and, above all, manual training.[29] Hilo provided both inspiration and precedent for the Hampton Idea.[30]

Following in the footsteps of his more famous contemporary Booker T. Washington, the Hampton acolyte who rose up from slavery to found Tuskegee Institute, Jones inherited the Hampton Idea and refined it for the twentieth century, developing a new curriculum that he dubbed "social studies." Eschewing traditional academics, social studies emphasized the development of "good citizenship" and encouraged teachers to attend to the social, moral, and material conditions affecting students and the local community.[31] Jones's social studies curriculum aspired to teach minority students to understand their subordinate social standing in terms of social Darwinist theories and to prepare students to adjust to a segregated world in which they would slowly achieve greater economic and social power within the dominant society. He believed that African Americans and American Indians could attain the same level of intellectual, social, political, and economic achievement as their white peers. But until both groups moved beyond their respective disadvantages, he insisted that their education must be adapted to "the vocational outlook of the pupils, their homes, their recreations, their health, their morals, their disposition."[32]

If the last sentence sounds familiar, it is because Jones published a series of highly influential reports elaborating upon his philosophy that education, rather than being a liberating intellectual force, should promote social change by addressing specific deficits in targeted minority populations.[33] The first report, *Negro Education,* was the springboard for those that followed. Published in 1917 under the auspices of the US Bureau of Education and the Phelps-Stokes Fund, *Negro Education* endorsed the concept that education should be adapted to fit the current mental capacities of African

Americans and the needs of local communities. Du Bois, an outspoken critic of the Hampton Idea, excoriated the study. Because African Americans in the Jim Crow South faced complete political exclusion, local control could only mean white control. "There is not a single protest against a public school system in which the public which it serves has absolutely no voice, vote, or influence," Du Bois wrote. "There is no defense of those colored people of vision who see the public schools being used as training schools for cheap labor and menial servants."[34] The report, in Du Bois's view, promoted a narrowly defined education that would train a black underclass to fit the needs and desires of the white community. But in constructing a set of concepts justifying "different futures for differently endowed individuals," Jones won acclaim from policymakers and philanthropic organizations alike.[35]

## The American Prophet

The first Phelps-Stokes study produced and disseminated a worldview that worked to contain an alternative set of ideologies about the relationship of African Americans to the state, and as it turned out, that idea had legs. An April 1918 review in the *International Review of Missions* offered the first widespread indication of Jones's potential contributions to education in British Africa. Journal editor and International Missionary Council secretary Joseph H. Oldham placed Jones's *Negro Education* in dialogue with Charles T. Loram's *The Education of the South African Native*, published concurrently in 1917. Hampton-Tuskegee-style education had already gaining renewed currency among British educationists, and world missionary agencies alternately sought to pacify, civilize, and evangelize "the world in this generation." Both studies, Oldham concluded, insisted that the most appropriate method toward these ends would eschew the traditional literary model and instead focus "on training in such necessities of actual life, as health, hygiene, the making and keeping of a home, the earning of a livelihood and civic knowledge and spirit." Moreover, it was "inevitable," Oldham insisted, "that missionary efforts to educate the negro [sic] race should be supplemented and outdistanced by the larger resources of the state."[36] By January 1919 the American Baptist Foreign Missionary Society had requested that the Phelps-Stokes Fund undertake a survey of West Africa in cooperation with the British government. The trustees recognized Jones's "birth in Wales as a British subject, his thorough training in sociology at Columbia University," and "his long experience as director of the research department of Hampton Institute" among his many qualifications for leading the commission.[37] And when Jones and Oldham met in England later that summer, the encounter would mark Jones's entrée into an elite circle of academics, civil servants, missionaries, and industrial philanthropists who would systematically translate their collective enthusiasm for educational adaptations into official British policy.

One member of that elite circle was Oldham's brother-in-law, Alexander G. Fraser. As principal of Trinity College in Kandy, Ceylon (now Sri Lanka), Fraser had steered his ecumenical prep school away from the traditional British grammar school model toward a more Hampton-inspired curriculum.[38] Replacing Latin and Greek with Sinhala and Tamil, Fraser argued that teaching in vernacular languages made "it simpler also to interest boys in the social and economic welfare of their people. The exclusion of the vernaculars favours the tendency to think all local knowledge and local problems are unworthy of respect."[39] A few English-educated locals were familiar enough with the British civil service examination to brand the white principal as a heretic more interested in turning out "hewers of wood and drawers of water" than developing a self-governing Ceylon.[40] Unorthodoxy secured Fraser admirers within British imperial circles, however. In preparation to chair a British survey on village education in India in late 1919, Fraser toured the southern and midwestern United States over three months, studying US education under Jones's guidance. Unsurprisingly, his report recommended that village missionaries in India select trainees to teach for a year at Hampton or its sister school, Tuskegee Institute. Jones and Fraser became friends and frequent collaborators.[41]

"In his work for Africa and in the British Empire," Fraser later wrote, "Dr. Jones did a prophet's work."[42] Hyperbole aside, Fraser struck a fundamental truth. Jones's first survey of British West Africa, published in 1922 as *Education in Africa*, had received such acclaim that the British government immediately offered Jones a second commission. Sheltered away at the Phelps-Stokes Fund's London headquarters, five blocks south of the Buckingham Palace Gardens, and chain-smoking over drafts of his second report, *Education in East Africa*, Jones wrote: "The winning of the great rural West and the successes and failures of racial adjustments in America are rich in valuable lessons" for British endeavors in Africa.[43] Following its independence, the United States had generated a corpus of technologies, court presidents, legislation, public discourse, and pedagogical techniques used to conquer a continent once wholly populated by American Indians, exploit ten million African-descended people, and alternately subordinate or assimilate millions more foreign-born immigrants into the body politic.[44] Jones drew upon this corpus of knowledge to devise adaptable solutions to pressing issues of the moment. Cultivating a kind of settler-colonial futurity, he superimposed the United States upon British Africa, an insight that proved particularly enticing in Kenya, Rhodesia, and South Africa, all colonies seemingly destined to become permanent homes for white settlers. "Who is ultimately to occupy East Africa?" he asked. "Will it be the story of the American Indians dwindling and withdrawing into the difficult places? Or will it be an adjustment of white and black for the mutual benefit of each?"[45] If the American Old West was the colonial African present, then his frontier vision promised to usher East Africa toward a future that evoked the American vision of a New South.

Such a transition would require a concerted government effort. Like the decentralized public and parochial education system in the United States, education in the British colonies had heretofore been left to missionaries such as Alexander Fraser in Ceylon or devised on the ground via local administrators such as Charles Loram in South Africa. That all changed in 1925, when His Britannic Majesty's government published a white paper, "Education Policy in British Tropical Africa." This formal statement of government policy owed as much to the Phelps-Stokes Fund's two surveys of colonial education as it did to the singular efforts of Oldham, the Indian-born Scottish missionary who lobbied for the creation of the Advisory Committee on Native Education in British Tropical Africa, which penned the report.[46] The white paper thus called for a realignment more akin to the strong federal role that the United States played in American Indian education and in colonial territories such as Puerto Rico and the Philippines. The committee's membership, meanwhile, included Lord Frederick Dealt Lugard, former British governor of Nigeria, and Michael Sadler, master of University College at Oxford. As the primary architect of British "indirect rule," Lugard believed that Britain had failed to comprehend that in British India the classical model of education had produced "Indian unrest" and that "the time must come when this purely intellectual type of education and emancipation of thought would produce its inevitable results, undermining respect for authority, whether of the State or the parent."[47] The pedagogy of adaptive education forged at Hampton and Tuskegee thus fit British indirect rule like a glove. Quoting the Phelps-Stokes surveys almost verbatim, the white paper consequently recommended that colonial education be "adapted to the mentality, aptitudes, occupations and traditions of the various peoples, conserving as far as possible all sound and healthy elements in the fabric of their social life."[48] According to Lugard, a newly conceived government-run boarding school at Achimota in Gold Coast Colony had been "equipped to put the policy to a practical test."[49]

Prince of Wales College, known colloquially as Achimota, was the first educational institution in British Africa to fully implement Jones's recommendations. In 1924 his friend Fraser ended a twenty-year career at Trinity College in Ceylon to accept the principalship of the new Gold Coast boarding school.[50] Officially inaugurated in January 1927, the school accepted pupils as young as six years old and trained young adults to become government teachers in the normal school. "Those children who come to Achimota at the kindergarten stage," reported Fraser, "may well stay fourteen years before leaving." Like its US counterparts, the school stressed the character-building value of manual labor. Its boarding houses, gardens, classrooms, and dining halls were "looked after and cleaned by the students, great and small. They wash and iron their own clothes. They do all eagerly and with zest," he claimed. Primary education was conducted in Twi, Fanti, Ga, and Ewe, with English taught as a second language until secondary school. Faculty offered courses in West African history, and in consultation with paramount chiefs from neighboring ethnic polities, the curriculum incorporated aspects of Gold Coast history and tribal traditions. Native goldsmiths and ivory workers trained students in tribal handcrafts. Students practiced tribal drumming and dancing, while a Tamil games master from Ceylon taught English football, hockey, and cricket.[51] As the British governor of the Gold Coast explained at Tuskegee Institute on October 27, 1927, "What we are trying to do in the Gold Coast is to give the natives sufficient opportunity for education [so] that gradually they may be able to bring their tribal customs in line with the practices of modern civilization. We are trying to develop them from within rather than from without by exterior force."[52] As it turned out, that idea had legs too.

The 1925 white paper scattered the seeds of educational adaptations beyond the Gold Coast and across the British Empire. After fifty years of assimilationist policy in Oceania, the inspector of Native schools in New Zealand began incorporating Maori history and culture into the curriculum to insure "all instruction be practical and related to the actual needs of the Maori."[53] Across the Java Sea, the British Advisory Committee on Colonial Education elaborated upon Principal Fraser's early emphasis on the vernacular. "It is for the African or the Malay," the committee wrote, "to decide for himself as he advances educationally to what extent he will drop indigenous traits and develop external ones."[54] This paradigm shift in education policies of Indigenous peoples would also ripple back to the United States— not at Hampton, Tuskegee, or Fisk University, where student activists were already revolting against almost sixty years of industrial education, but two thousand miles west at the Charles H. Burke Indian School in Fort Wingate, New Mexico.[55]

## Thomas Jesse Jones and
## The Problem of Indian Administration

It was late November 1925 when Jones began a conversation with Kenneth Chorley at the Town Hall Theater in Manhattan that ended half a mile away at Grand Central Terminal and subsequently became a catalyst that quickened an incipient shift in American Indian policy.[56] For months Jones's thoughts and schedule had revolved around colonial Africa, but as the conversation with Chorley unfolded, he pivoted toward a new matter.[57] How would he organize a study of the present conditions of American Indians in the United States? What ideological perspective and methodology might such a survey adopt? Who should undertake the inquiry? These were hardly rhetorical questions.

Kenneth Chorley represented the Laura Spelman Rockefeller Memorial Foundation. Through its General Education Board, the Rockefeller Foundation had exerted control over African American educational and social policies since 1902.[58] With the incorporation of the International Education Board, the Rockefellers had extended that reach abroad, providing funding for Jones's recent East African survey, among other ventures.[59] And now John D. Rockefeller Jr. had emerged from a camping expedition in Montana with an interest in conserving the American West, including its American Indians.[60] Of his New York staff, Chorley possessed the most experience in Indian Country. Born in Bournemouth, England, to an Episcopal clergyman in 1893 and reared in suburban New York, Chorley made a name for himself in the US Southwest as an indefatigable rail yard superintendent. When he returned east he made the acquaintance of Col. Arthur Woods, the former New York City police commissioner who directed the Spelman Rockefeller Memorial Foundation. Woods hired Chorley in 1923.[61] With little knowledge of Indian affairs, Chorley wisely turned to the Phelps-Stokes Fund and Jones, its renowned education director, for advice.

Jones turned the conversation over in his mind, puzzling over the politics, pitfalls, and potentialities of a survey of US Indian affairs.[62] The topic had been on the Phelps-Stokes Fund's back burner since Fayette McKenzie, the white sociologist who cofounded the Society of American Indians in 1911, and Henry Roe Cloud, a member of the Ho-Chunk Nation and Yale-educated anthropologist, conducted a preliminary investigation of American Indian schools that ended prematurely in 1915, when McKenzie became president of Fisk University, which also happened to be Du Bois's alma mater.[63] A full decade later, with three monumental reports on African and African American education behind him, Jones began to envision a reprise for the Phelps-Stokes Fund venture. As he dictated his observations over the telephone on

December 2, the project emerged in broad sketches. He could all but guarantee cooperation with the Bureau of Indian Affairs because as recently as 1919 the chairman of the Board of Indian Commissioners, George Vaux Jr., had asked him if "that Indian survey" was still in the works.[64] Indeed, it was.

Jones suggested that the study should carve out an ideological middle ground between primitivists, who "would likely condemn most of the process of adjustment to modern conditions," and assimilationists, who "would disregard the tribal past of the Indians and throw him ruthlessly into a maelstrom of modern life." It would be best to avoid the rivalry between Catholic and Protestant missionaries altogether by selecting an independent organization to undertake the study. Ranked highest among three suitable contenders was Lewis Meriam at the Institute of Government Research, whom Jones had known professionally since 1917.[65] Following the template of the Phelps-Stokes African commissions, the survey membership should include an American Indian person. "I have in mind such a trustworthy and sane student as Mr. Henry Roe Cloud, the Principal and Founder of the Indian Institute, at Wichita, Kansas," he said. Jones mentioned McKenzie's sterling record on American Indian advocacy as well.[66] Chorley agreed to arrange a meeting with the secretary of the interior a month later to propose Rockefeller support for a nonpartisan study conducted by the US Indian Service.[67]

At six feet five inches Chorley stood a full foot taller than Jones, but evidently they saw eye to eye on how to gain influence in US Indian affairs.[68] On January 29, 1926, he wrote to Jones, "It seems to me that you and I have done all the promoting that we can do now. We have started the ball rolling, and it is now up to other people to keep it going."[69] After months of negotiations, Meriam and W. F. Willoughby, the director of the Institute of Government Research, won the secretary of the interior's approval that June. The Rockefeller Foundation wrote a $125,000 check, with the Phelps-Stokes Fund providing a modest grant of $5,000 but lending the substantial experience of its education director, Thomas Jesse Jones.[70]

"I wonder if you realize what a whirlpool you have set in motion and how swiftly many important world affairs are circling around you," marveled the correspondent who informed Jones in October 1926 that Meriam's survey was under way.[71] Quick to downplay publicity and fearing "an avalanche of requests and suggestions from various propaganda organizations desiring to be allied with the study," Jones contented himself with the role Oldham had played in the 1925 British white paper: a hidden hand orchestrating diverse elements into harmony with a narrow sociopolitical agenda while maintaining an illusion of nonpartisan disinterest.[72] Privately, Jones confessed to Chorley his belief that "the study will be regarded by some as quite unimportant because it deals with only a quarter of a million people who are being merged into American life with considerable rapidity, in many instances by unfortunate means." "Others," however, "will regard the survey as a study of American self-respect in dealing with the original inhabitants of this great country. In this sense, I feel that the undertaking is exceedingly important."[73]

The Problem of Indian Administration carried Meriam's name, but it bore Jones's imprimatur. In hindsight, it was almost as if its primary components sprang fully formed from his initial memorandum.[74] In addition to Meriam, Cloud and McKenzie also joined the nine-member survey staff, as did the author of the education section of the report, W. Carson Ryan, a respected progressive educationist who had given editorial assistance on Negro Education and the two Phelps-Stokes African commissions.[75] On Jones's recommendation, the survey team included "a woman to study the home and child welfare," Mary Louise Mark, a professor of sociology at Ohio State University. During fieldwork, Jones guided the survey team from afar, and he was actively involved in the manuscript right down to final revisions in December 1927.[76] So when the authors observed that the "first and foremost need in Indian education is a change in point of view," not surprisingly, the viewpoint suggested in the report aligned squarely with the pedagogical model Jones had promoted for twenty years.[77]

"It is commonly understood that the young Indian hates school. The real marvel is that he endures it at all, considering what school life often means," Jones had written in "Social Studies at Hampton" in 1906. He promoted day schools over boarding schools, citing the children at Day School No. 27 on Pine Ridge, who "are daily taking from the school and from the teachers' home bits of the leaven of civilization and carrying it into their own homes and lives." He insisted that an "Indian teacher, even if his [sic] literary attainments are not great, must be a far more stimulating example to his young pupils than a foreigner can possibly be, for what the Indian teacher has done the Indian pupil may do."[78] The Meriam Report's major recommendation—that Indian schools "must be adapted to individual abilities, interests, and needs"—could be found almost word for word in each of Jones's Phelps-Stokes commissions since Negro Education.[79]

As he had with the 1925 white paper on Africa, Jones would hail The Problem of Indian Administration as "the beginning of a new era in Indian Affairs," and like his British counterpart, Oldham, Jones understood that publication of the report was useless unless its recommendations were translated into public policy.[80] Jones subsequently collaborated with Chorley and Meriam on what he called "follow up" work to implement the recommendations.[81] Jones had proven himself a master at maximizing the influence of his previous studies. For example, within the decentralized landscape of education at the state and local levels, *Negro Education* provided the General Education Board, the Julius Rosenwald Fund, and the Carnegie Foundation with a playbook for molding southern education into shape through selective philanthropic giving. The Phelps-Stokes African commissions aided the transition from missionary-led to government-operated education in the Anglophone colonies, which the 1925 white paper then codified into colonial policy. Now, however, because American Indian education fell under the purview of the US federal government, the Rockefeller-backed triumvirate of Jones, Chorley, and Meriam faced a different task: they had to influence federal policy. This meant navigating a fraught political machine to produce results. They approached their task from the top down.

In January 1929 the trio wrote a memorandum concerning recommendations for the commissioner of Indian affairs and worked through back channels to deliver the report to President-elect Herbert Hoover and his pick for interior secretary, former Stanford president Ray Lyman Wilbur.[82] As Chorley wrote to Jones, "I have a very good direct contact through one of our people with Dr. Wilbur and I am going to get in some dirty work."[83] Meanwhile, Jones elicited help from a prominent Phelps-Stokes Fund associate to deliver the memo directly to the president. The lobbying and "dirty work" proved successful. Hoover selected their top candidate, Charles J. Rhoads, for the position. As Chorley wrote to his boss, Col. Arthur Woods, "It seems to me that the cost of the Survey has been paid for many times over by these increased appropriations and by the appointment of Mr. Charles J. Rhoads as Indian Commissioner."[84]

With their man now in office, the Rockefeller group set about implementing the report. Chorley secured an additional $100,000 in grants from the Spelman Rockefeller Memorial Foundation so that the incoming commissioner could retain Meriam and other staff members at the Institute for Government Research as technical experts. Then, in 1929, Commissioner Rhoads appointed a special committee of advisors to the Indian education program, consisting of Thomas Jesse Jones, Carson Ryan, and Mabel Carney of Columbia Teachers College, the latter a noted authority on rural education in the US South and British Africa.[85] When the director of Indian education later resigned, Ryan claimed the position upon the advisory committee's recommendation and shortly after taking office replaced traditional academics with vocational programs adapted to fit the perceived needs of American Indian pupils.[86] The Hampton Idea had come home to roost.

### Achimota, USA

The Great Depression doomed the Hoover administration, but Jones and his associates had shifted the politics and policies in their favor, thanks in part to a symbiotic relationship with John Collier, whose left-wing political muck-raking through the American Indian Defense Association (AIDA) not only contributed to the reformist mood but also made the Meriam recommendations appear moderate and actionable in comparison. Ever wary of radicals, Jones initially fretted that "Collier's hectic activities threaten to involve us in his campaign," but Collier quickly developed a productive partnership with the group. From 1929 to 1931, when the BIA retained Meriam's team of consultants, Collier worked especially well with Nathan R. Margold, the brilliant Harvard attorney the IRG brought in to draft reform legislation to end the 1887 Dawes General Allotment Act and restore tribal land claims.[87]

Like Jones, Collier thought globally in reference to US Indian policy. Shortly after founding the AIDA in 1923, he observed: "In these United States there is an equivalent of the Belgian and the French Congo. The denial of land rights of the Congo—it is here. The decimation of victims—it is here. . . . The insolence of denial and of whitewash of the Congo—it is here."[88] He so easily identified parallels between the worst abuses in colonial Africa and the contemporary administration of Indian affairs because he understood the relationship between the United States and American Indians to be fundamentally colonial.

In contrast to the destructive policies of the United States and Belgian Congo, Collier praised an alternative model: Lord Frederick Lugard's ideas of indirect rule in British Africa, which integrated aspects of Indigenous government into the mechanics of the colonial system rather than imposing a foreign system of governance from the top down. British Africa, he argued, offered the United States both the administrative techniques and the legislative models necessary to avert a full-blown "American Congo." Embracing the Meriam Report, Collier believed its recommendations would pave the way for future legislation that would eventually produce radical changes in government policies along British colonial lines.[89] But he was not inclined to wait for that eventuality.

"There is one great field of Indian work not dependent on changes of law for the swift realization of the philosophy of 'indirect rule.' That is the Indian school," Collier declared in 1931.[90] A mere three years had passed since the Meriam Report debuted, and Collier observed that the boarding school at Fort Wingate remained "handicapped by a monstrous lay-out of inherited buildings and by staff deficiencies and misfits." Yet he also discerned "epoch-making possibilities" afoot.[91] In October 1930 the former supervisor of vocational education for Los Angeles public schools, Edward B. Dale, had been appointed superintendent of the Charles H. Burke Indian School. Dale was redesigning the curriculum to equip Navajo graduates for employment in the Indian Service and leadership positions on the reservation. Vocational tracts now included agriculture, "native arts and crafts," and stock raising, each with parallel academic programs. These programmatic changes made the Navajo secondary school a national model for implementing the new point of view in Indian policy.[92] And for Collier, this first step was a giant leap toward setting the world aright.

When Collier observed the efforts under way at Fort Wingate, he did not view the educational reforms as a fresh branch off the old Hampton-Tuskegee method. Instead, he overlooked the idea's genealogy and embraced its most recent incarnation: Fort Wingate was Achimota, USA. "Here was a new concept," he wrote, "a new and efficient social technique, an embodiment in the flesh of a new and great idea, and a way into the future for more than one hundred million of the 'backward races.'"[93]

When President Roosevelt took office two years later, in 1933, John Collier became the next commissioner of Indian affairs, and Nathan Margold was appointed solicitor in the Department of the Interior. By then the Rockefeller team knew that it could work with both men. "The new appointments," Meriam observed the day Collier was sworn in, "seem to me to go as far as is humanly possible to guarantee not only a continuation of the Indian program for which we have been working but accelerated progress toward our goals."[94] Indeed, the model legislation Collier and Margold began with Meriam served as a basis of the 1934 Indian Reorganization Act, which included many elements of the administrative reforms proposed in *The Problem of Indian Administration* and rolled back the worst excesses of US assimilatory policies.[95]

## Swan Song in Dinétah

On the one hand, Jones's philosophy of educational adaptation and cultural adjustment was far preferable to the alternative of total assimilation. The notion that education should be adapted to suit the outlook of American Indian pupils and the needs of the local community empowered American Indian activists such as Henry Roe Cloud with leverage against the assimilatory pressures of a paternalistic state. To be sure, Cloud's assessment of Jones stood in stark contrast to that of Du Bois. "I am not competent to say how much Dr. Jones has accomplished for the Africans overseas or the Negroes in our great Southland, but I do know that he has profoundly influenced educational procedure with respect to our Native American Indians," Cloud remarked in 1937. "He has brought about normal relationships between the Indian child and the home and has led the way in directing our educational enterprise to community needs."[96]

Privately, Cloud may have harbored some bitterness against the Rockefeller group. While Jones, Meriam, and Chorley were vetting potential candidates for the commissioner of Indian affairs, Cloud decided to throw his hat into the ring as well. On January 28, 1929, he wrote to Meriam seeking his support for the commissionership. Cloud realized his potential shortcomings but asked nonetheless, "What are young men born into this world for if not to attempt and do things?"[97] Meriam forwarded the letter to Jones, whose response is not extant. But Meriam wrote in reply: "As an individual I should derive the greatest pleasure from the appointment of my good friend Henry Roe Cloud as Indian Commissioner. I believe he would make a good one, and if given the necessary support by the President and the Congress he could bring about the desired reforms." He continued, "So much for the individual point of view. The institutional point of view is that at most we could recommend to the President not a particular man but a particular type of man."[98] Cloud was not that type of man.

Meriam believed that Cloud would have been capable of the job, yet he feared that Cloud's Indianness posed a political liability. Simply put, Commissioner Cloud would have made an easy target for political enemies of the Indian reform movement because he could be attacked as racially biased, racially incompetent, or both. Meriam felt, therefore, that supporting Cloud for the commissionership would not only ruin any chance at enacting reforms but also ruin Cloud.[99] Therein lies a darker side of the Meriam Report and the laudable move in favor of gradualism and cultural pluralism over rapid and total assimilation. From the 1925 white paper to the 1934 Indian Reorganization Act, a small group of white men dictated international policies for their own purposes and consistently constrained the possibilities and personalities suitable for African American, African native, and Native American leadership.

Jones, meanwhile, minimized his influence on the Hoover administration and the Meriam Report. "As you know," he informed Collier in 1932, "I have been very much on the 'side-lines' of Indian Affairs. My only participation has been cooperation with Lewis Meriam in his wise services. Behind the lines I have tried to exert any possible influence to advance the Indian cause."[100] The Collier administration, while more independent, had enlisted Jones during the summer of 1934 to visit BIA schools from Lawrence, Kansas, to Riverside, California, where he inspected the pedagogical reforms under way. He had shared the stage with Collier and Carson Ryan at a bureauwide conference for Indian Service teachers held at the Charles H. Burke Indian School in Fort Wingate, where the commissioner touted a new program to introduce soil conservation efforts into the day school curriculum.[101] Jones came to see Collier as a reasonable commissioner who could both reform Native education and steer clear of resurgent young Native American activism. He wrote to Chorley, "Your influence still continues through the new Commissioner [and] is bordering close to revolutionary in some directions. We are now doing our best to keep close to the surging streams of new policies, so that the Administration may not fall into destructive whirlpools."[102]

Thus at the twilight of his career, Jones employed the US Indian Service to stage his final act.[103] By the late 1930s, the Collier administration's heavy-handed implementation of indirect rule on the Navajo Nation had engendered fierce opposition from Jacob C. Morgan, a Diné graduate of Hampton Institute who had ridden a wave of discontent into the tribal council chairman's office. As an associate known to both Commissioner Collier and Chairman Morgan, Jones volunteered to mediate the feud away from any "destructive whirlpools" by conducting a two-month-long survey of the Navajo Nation in January 1939.[104] As he had in the four previous Phelps-Stokes Fund surveys, Jones served as chairman of the Navajo inquiry. Rounding out the team were Harold B. Allen, former education director at the Near East Foundation; Ella Deloria, a Columbia University—trained Yankton Dakota anthropologist and educator; and Yale professor Charles Loram, an early architect of apartheid education in South Africa and Sterling Professor of Education at Yale University.[105]

Published as *The Navajo Indian Problem* in 1939, gradualism and cooperation rang as keynotes throughout the report, and its recommendations on education echoed the Phelps-Stokes African commissions, which had emphasized the importance of classroom instruction in vernacular languages and cultivating an Indigenous teaching corps. Yet Ella Deloria also found strong opposition against the new day school program, focused on instruction adapted to local conditions. Some Navajo parents insisted that schooling should equip their children to escape reservation life, while others favored boarding schools not only because they provided clothing, food, and shelter but also because students' families could integrate the boarding school calendar into age-old seasonal migration practices.[106] One petition to build a boarding school in Greasewood, Arizona, read, "We are not village Indian. We move from place to place depending upon the conditions for our sheep. At times we are two or three miles from the school house and at some times we are ten or more miles from the school house."[107] Boarding schools like the one at Fort Wingate, in contrast to the assessment of men such as Meriam, Jones, and Collier, provided at least some Navajo families with a means to educate their children for a new future while protecting Diné lifeways.

In attempting to tell this new and more complicated story about the Meriam Report and American Indian boarding schools, this essay has drawn together substantial evidence of direct influence between the United States and the United Kingdom in fashioning Indigenous education policy across the globe.[108] Like the colonial policies that historian Margaret Jacobs chronicled between the United States and Australia, the equally important and understudied connections between African, African American, and American Indian education in the twentieth century suggest that the lens with which historians examine the boarding school era can offer new insights into a more elaborate mapping of colonial relations and genealogies operating within the United States. Indeed, in September 1939 the links between generations of American Indian activists and BIA administrations to African and African American education crystallized at the University of Toronto, where Yale educationist Charles Loram had organized the two-week Conference on the North American Indian. The participants included not only former and current directors of Indian education, Carson Ryan and Willard Beatty, but also John Collier, who delivered a paper in absentia, and two future commissioners of Indian affairs, Philleo Nash and Louis R. Bruce Jr. The General Education Board sent Jackson Davis, an international figure in African and African American education. Although Fayette McKenzie was absent, one attendee, Arthur C. Parker, had been a founding member of the then-defunct Society of American Indians. Several more active attendees, D'Arcy McNickle, Archie Phinney, and Ruth Muskrat Bronson, would usher in a new generation of Native activism, founding the National Congress of American Indians in 1944.[109] In the group photograph from the conference, Thomas Jesse Jones stands smiling at the very center.

In the end, Jones was neither an educational prophet, as Alexander Fraser and others dubbed him, nor an "evil genius," as W. E. B. Du Bois once claimed.[110] Perhaps the most accurate assessment of his long career with the Phelps-Stokes Fund came from fellow white educationist Emory Ross: "He waited not for government to formulate and fund and function. He roused himself, drew in others, examined and weighed, and a plan was drawn. Men were gotten. Money came. Governments followed."[111]

KHALIL ANTHONY JOHNSON JR. is an assistant professor of African American studies at Wesleyan University. He is currently at work on a book manuscript about the role of education in shaping the intertwined histories of black and Indigenous people in the United States and other Anglophone colonies.

## Notes

1. Donald L. Parman, "Lewis Meriam's Letters during the Survey of Indian Affairs 1926–1927 (Part II)," *Arizona and the West* 24, no. 4 (1982): 359–60.

2. Since time immemorial the Navajo have called the site Shash Bitooh, Bear Springs. In 1861 the United States hoisted Old Glory over the newly erected fort during Kit Carson's war against the Navajo in the heart of Dinétah. Ruth Murray Underhill, *Here Come the Navaho! A History of the Largest Indian Tribe in the United States* (Washington, DC: United States Indian Service, 1953), 108, 182–85.

3. Ibid. On the Long Walk and treaty negotiations, see Peter Iverson, *Diné: A History of the Navajos* (Albuquerque: University of New Mexico Press, 2002), 35–66. See also Jennifer Nez Denetdale, *Reclaiming Diné History: The Legacies of Navajo Chief Manuelito and Juanita* (Tucson: University of Arizona Press, 2007). By 1925 nine boarding schools had been erected in Arizona at Chinle, Leupp, and Tuba City and in New Mexico at Crownpoint, Tohatchi, Shiprock, and Toadlena. For Navajo education prior to 1930, see Hildegard Thompson, *The Navajos' Long Walk for Education: A History of Navajo Education* (Tsaile, Navajo Nation: Navajo Community College Press, 1975), 25–34.

4. Photos of the Charles H. Burke Indian School, Fort Wingate, New Mexico, G. E. E. Lindquist Native American Photographs, the Burke Library Archives, Columbia University, http://lindquist.cul.columbia.edu/.

5. Board of Indian Commissioners, *Annual Report of the Board of Indian Commissioners to the Secretary of the Interior* (Washington, DC: US Government Printing Office, 1929), 9.

6. Parman, "Meriam Letters (Part II)," 359, 360. The survey began on November 22, 1926, in Norman, Oklahoma. See Donald L. Parman, "Lewis Meriam's Letters during the Survey of Indian Affairs 1926–1927 (Part I)," *Arizona and the West* 24, no. 3 (1982): 253.

7. Lewis Meriam et al., *The Problem of Indian Administration: Report of a Survey Made at the Request of Honorable Hubert Work, Secretary of the Interior, and Submitted to Him, February 21, 1928* (Baltimore, MD: Johns Hopkins Press, 1928), 423, 8.

8. The authors, however, subsequently argued that certain "adjustments" were necessary in the areas of economics, education, health, and sanitation. Failure to implement such changes, particularly in health and sanitation, would mean "not only that they [the Indians] may become a menace to the whites but also that they themselves will go through a long drawn out painful process of vanishing. They must be aided for the preservation of themselves" (Meriam et al., *The Problem of Indian Administration*, 88).

9. Ibid., 32. For a critical historical account of the reforms and their effectiveness, see K. Tsianina Lomawaima and Teresa L. McCarty, *To Remain an Indian: Lessons in Democracy from a Century of Native American Education* (New York: Teachers College Press, 2006), 64–90.

10. Margaret Connell Szasz, *Education and the American Indian: The Road to Self-Determination since 1928* (Albuquerque: University of New Mexico Press, 1999), 2–4.

11. Donald Parman, *Indians and the American West in the Twentieth Century* (Bloomington: Indiana University Press, 1994), 83. Contrary to the conventional wisdom established in Parman's scholarship, Vine Deloria and Clifford M. Lytle have argued, "Although almost every commentator on Indian matters credits the Meriam Report with providing the motivation and framework for the subsequent reforms initiated by the New Deal, there is not much evidence to support such an idea conceptually or in execution." Drawing upon overlooked records from the Phelps-Stokes Foundation and Rockefeller Foundation Archives, this essay presents a wealth of evidence in favor of the Meriam Report's substantial influence in shaping US Indian policy during the 1930s. See Deloria and Lytle, *The Nations Within: The Past and Future of American Indian Sovereignty* (Austin: University of Texas Press, 1984), 43–45.

12. John Collier to Anson Phelps-Stokes, September 22, 1937, in *Education for Life: Phelps-Stokes Fund and Thomas Jesse Jones, a Twenty-Fifth Anniversary, 1913–1937* (New York: Phelps-Stokes Fund, 1937), 154.

13. Ibid.

14. The quote is from the seventeenth clause of the will of Caroline Phelps-Stokes, which directed a group of trustees to establish the Phelps-Stokes Fund on April 28, 1910. See Thomas Jesse Jones, *Educational Adaptations: Report of Ten Years' Work of the Phelps-Stokes Fund, 1910–1920* (New York: Phelps-Stokes Fund, 1920), 15.

15. Indeed, while Donald T. Critchlow offers a partial account of the report's origins, he erroneously credits the impetus for the study to Secretary of the Interior Hubert Work and underestimates the role the Rockefeller Foundation and Phelps-Stokes Fund played in planning and initiating the study. See "Lewis Meriam, Expertise, and Indian Reform," *Historian* 43 (1981): 325–26. Parman correctly notes that the "inquiry resulted from conversations between Thomas Jesse Jones of the Phelps-Stokes Fund and Lewis Meriam and W. F. Willoughby of the Institute of Government Research of Washington, DC." Yet because of Parman's reliance on the Brooking Institution archives, his account overlooks the greater role that Jones and Kenneth Chorley of the Rockefeller Foundation played in both initiating the report and implementing its recommendations. See Parman, *Indians and the American West,* 83. Meanwhile, others frequently credit John Collier and the American Indian Defense Association for creating the climate responsible for the report. See Kenneth R. Phillip, *John Collier's Crusade for Indian Reform* (Tucson: University of Arizona Press, 1977), 90–93; Szasz, *Education,* 16–25; Deloria and Lytle, *The Nations Within,* 43–45; Lomawaima and McCarty, *To Remain an Indian,* 64–68; Elmer Rusco, *A Fateful Time: The Background and Legislative History of the Indian Reorganization Act* (Reno: University of Nevada Press, 2000).

16. This quote is selectively adapted from the original, which reads, "Nonetheless, if one is ranking the relative strength of these master narratives, 'conquest' is surely among the weakest—a reflection of the power of other narratives in centering other issues, the incredibly thorough ideological naturalization of Indian disappearance and American settlement, the physical separations of the reservation regime, and the demographic realities of Indian country, all of which leave us knowing W. E. B. Du Bois and Booker T. Washington

well, but leaving behind a less-visible imprint of Arthur C. Parker, Laura Cornelius, and Zitkála-Šá—and an even fainter trace of the 4,000 Indians they hoped
would join them as colleagues in the SAI [Society of American Indians]." See
Deloria, "American Master Narratives and the Problem of Indian Citizenship in
the Gilded Age and Progressive Era," *Journal of the Gilded Age and Progressive
Era* 14, no. 1 (January 2015): 11.

17. For a sample of oversights on Jones's influence in American Indian his-
tory, particularly the Meriam Report, see Paullette Dilworth, "Competing Conceptions of Citizenship Education: Thomas Jesse Jones and Carter G. Woodson,"
*International Journal of Social Education* 18, no. 2 (2003–4): 1–10; Donald
Johnson, "W. E. B. DuBois, Thomas Jesse Jones, and the Struggle for Social Education, 1900–1930," *Journal of Negro History* 85, no. 3 (2010): 71–95; Eric S.
Yellin, "The (White) Search for (Black) Order: The Phelps-Stokes Fund's First
Twenty Years, 1911–1931," *Historian* 65, no. 2 (2001): 319–52. For monographs
that incorporate American Indians into Gilded Age and Progressive Era his-
tory, see, for example, Cathleen Cahill, *Federal Fathers and Mothers: A Social
History of the United States Indians Service, 1869–1933* (Chapel Hill: University
of North Carolina Press, 2011); Frederick E. Hoxie, *A Final Promise: The Cam-
paign to Assimilate the Indians, 1880–1920* (Lincoln: University of Nebraska
Press, 1984); Michelle Wick Patterson, *Natalie Curtis Burlin: A Life in Native and
African American Music* (Lincoln: University of Nebraska Press, 2010), 222; Kim
Carey Warren, *The Quest for Citizenship: African American and Native American Education in Kansas, 1880–1935* (Chapel Hill: University of North Carolina
Press, 2010). See also Boyd Cothran and C. Joseph Genetin-Pilawa's coedited
forum, "Indigenous Histories of the Gilded Age and Progressive Era," in *Journal
of the Gilded Age and Progressive Era* 14, no. 4 (October 2015): 503–79.

18. W. Carson Ryan Jr. to Thomas Jesse Jones, October 6, 1937, in *Education
for Life*, 38.

19. Dr. Emory Ross, President, Phelps-Stokes Fund, "In Memoriam Thomas
Jesse Jones, 1873–1950," 7, Thomas Jesse Jones, Reports and Pamphlets, folder
2713, box 262, subseries 2, series 1, General Education Board Archives (1901–
64), Rockefeller Archives Center, Sleepy Hollow, NY; Stephen Taylor Correia,
"For Their Own Good: An Historical Analysis of the Educational Thought of
Thomas Jesse Jones" (PhD diss., Pennsylvania State University, 2003), 56–57.

20. Gerald Morgan, "The Place of School in the Maintenance of the Welsh
Language," *Comparative Education* 24 (1988): 248; Kenneth O. Morgan, "Welsh
Nationalism: The Historical Background," *Journal of Contemporary History* 6
(1971): 153–59, 161–72; Correia, "For Their Own Good," 57.

21. During the War of 1812 the region had been a battleground between
Tecumseh's Indigenous confederacy, their British allies, and the fledgling
United States. By 1843 the Shawnee, Wyandott, and other Indigenous nations
had been removed from the state, clearing the way for Welsh immigrants, who
fueled the burgeoning coal- and salt-mining industries along the Ohio River
during the 1850s, when Margaret and her husband settled there. Ross, "In
Memoriam Thomas Jesse Jones," 7; Correia, "For Their Own Good," 57. For European American settlement in Ohio, see Francis Paul Prucha, *The Great Father:*

*The United States Government and the American Indians* (Lincoln, University of Nebraska Press, 1984) 76–79.

22. It is possible that Jones spoke some English, since his mother certainly did. But his lack of English at the time he immigrated became central to his personal biography. See Correia, "For Their Own Good," 57–85; *Education for Life*, iv–v; Ross, "In Memoriam Thomas Jesse Jones," 7–8.

23. William Anthony Aery, "Dr. Thomas Jesse Jones," *Cambrian* 37, no. 19 (1917): 6.

24. Ibid. Jones's correspondence is replete with references to his Welsh identity. For instance, Jones wrote to John Collier, "I have never before had the honor of being called a mystic. If I deserve the title the quality is probably rooted in my Celtic nature. Welshmen are inclined to be mystics, even to a dangerous degree" (November 26, 1934, file 127, Jones, Thomas Jesse, educational director of the Phelps-Stokes Fund, box 7, series I, Correspondence of John Collier, part 1, 1922–23, John Collier Papers [MS 146], Manuscripts and Archives, Yale University Library, New Haven, CT).

25. McKenzie, "A Man His Own Philosophy," 40. In its review of Jones's 1916 report, *Negro Education, the Sewanee Review* noted that Jones was "perhaps better equipped than any other man in this country to plan and give temper to such an investigation." Indeed, as Anson Phelps Stokes informed Jones, the trustees of the Phelps-Stokes Fund appointed him educational director because he "knew, from personal experience, the point of view of the North, of the Southern white man, of the Negro, and [his] Welsh background gave [him] a certain detachment which we thought would prove valuable." See Broadus Mitchell, review of *United States Department of the Interior, Bureau of Education: Bulletin, 1916, No. 39: Negro Education, a Study of the Private and Higher Schools for Colored People in the United States*, by Thomas Jesse Jones, *Sewanee Review* 26 (1918): 246; Phelps-Stokes to Jones, in *Education for Life*, i.

26. Jones's "purring manner" was described in a letter published anonymously in *Crisis* 31, no. 5 (1926): 217. Director of Indian Education Willard Beatty wrote, "Jones is short and dark and rather effeminate looking. Don't allow these outward characteristics to mislead you with regard to the man. He is experienced in the study of native peoples, both in this country and in Africa, where he did a thoroughly fine piece of work, evaluating the program of native education. He is absolutely fearless, both physically and morally. He has a keen sense of humor, and a fine sense of justice" (Beatty to E. R. Fryer, December 15, 1938, 100 Phelps-Stokes Report, Dr. Thomas J. Jones, 1938–41, box 55, Central Classified Files, Navajo Area Office, Records of the Bureau of Indian Affairs, Record Group 75, National Archives and Records Administration—Pacific Region, Riverside, CA; hereafter BIA Records).

27. Du Bois commented on Jones's association with Robert Moton, president of Tuskegee University, while on a tour for black US soldiers stationed in World War I France: "He [Moton] took with him and had at his elbow every moment that evil genius of the Negro race, Thomas Jesse Jones, a white man" (*Crisis* 18, no. 1 [1919]: 9). Jones also famously sparred with Carter G. Woodson over the direction of black education policy and avenues for African American

leadership. Upon Jones's death in 1950, Woodson wrote, "To say that Jones did not accomplish some good in the various positions which he filled would be far from the truth. He would have achieved greater success, however, if he had not been so narrow-minded, short-sighted, vindictive and undermining" ("Thomas Jesse Jones," *Journal of Negro History* 35 [1950]: 109). For more on the conflict between Jones and Woodson, see Jacqueline Goggin, *Carter G. Woodson: A Life in Black History* (Baton Rouge: Louisiana State University Press, 1993), 59–63, 81–83; and Paulette Patterson Dilworth, "Competing Conceptions of Citizenship Education: Thomas Jesse Jones and Carter G. Woodson," *International Journal of Social Education* 18 (2004): 1–10. For Du Bois and Jones, see Kenneth James King, *Pan-Africanism and Education: A Study of Race Philanthropy and Education in the Southern States of America and East Africa* (Oxford: Clarendon Press, 1971), 25–35, 41–42; Donald Johnson, "W. E. B. Du Bois, Thomas Jesse Jones, and the Struggle for Social Education, 1900–1930," *Journal of Negro History* 85 (2000): 71–95; and Correia, "For Their Own Good," 225–44.

28. See James D. Anderson, *The Education of Blacks in the South, 1860–1935* (Chapel Hill: University of North Carolina Press, 1988), chap. 2; Donal F. Lindsey, *Indians at Hampton Institute, 1877–1923* (Chicago: University of Illinois Press, 1994); and David Adams, "Education in Hues: Red and Black at Hampton Institute, 1878–1893," *South Atlantic Quarterly* 76 (Spring 1977). For contrasts between Hampton and Carlisle, see Jacqueline Fear-Segal, "Nineteenth-Century Indian Education: Universalism versus Evolutionism," *Journal of American Studies* 33 (1999): 323–41.

29. On Samuel Chapman Armstrong's biography, see Robert Francis Engs, *Educating the Disfranchised and Disinherited: Samuel Chapman Armstrong and Hampton Institute, 1839–1983* (Nashville: University of Tennessee Press, 1999). For pedagogy at Hilo, see C. Kalani Beyer, "The Connection of Samuel Chapman Armstrong as Both Borrower and Architect of Education in Hawai'i," *History of Education Quarterly* 47 (2007): 29. For history of education in Hawai'i, see Benjamin O. Wist, *A Century of Public Education in Hawaii* (Honolulu: Hawaiian Educational Review, 1940); and Noenoe K. Silva, *Aloha Betrayed: Native Hawaiian Resistance to American Colonialism* (Durham, NC: Duke University Press, 2004), 32, 46.

30. The emphasis on manual labor as "the correct means of training" ideal subjects within "disciplinary regimes," to quote theorist Michel Foucault, was not limited to Hawai'i. Citing Foucault and historian James D. Anderson, K. Tsianina Lomawaima observed in her study on Chilocco Indian School that the assumption that manual labor instilled discipline and respect for authority "also underlay practices in French prisons and schools for American blacks." The critical issue here is that the ethos of manual training for both African Americans and American Indians resulted in large part because of Samuel Chapman Armstrong's work at Hampton and its sister schools, Carlisle Indian Industrial School and Tuskegee Institute. See Foucault, *Discipline and Punish: The Birth of the Prison* (New York: Vintage Books, 1991), 170–94; and Lomawaima, *They Called it Prairie Light: The Story of Chilocco Indian School* (Lincoln: University of Nebraska Press, 1994), 82–83.

31. Thomas Jesse Jones, *Social Studies in the Hampton Curriculum* (Hampton, VA: Hampton Institute Press, 1906), books.google.com. See also Diane Ravitch, "A Brief History of Social Studies," in *Where Did Social Studies Go Wrong?*, ed. James S. Leming et al. (Washington, DC: Thomas B. Fordham Foundation, 2003), 1–5; Kliebard, "That Evil Genius of the Negro Race," *Journal of Curriculum and Supervision* 10, no. 1 (Fall 1994): 5-20; and Correia, "For Their Own Good."

32. The above quotation is gleaned from Jones's *Educational Adaptations: Report of Ten Years' Work of the Phelps-Stokes Fund, 1910–1920* (New York: Phelps-Stokes Fund, 1920), 37. However, regarding the Hampton curriculum specifically, Jones wrote, "The study of civics in Hampton Institute is not limited to the subjects ordinarily included in that course. Its scope and character are determined as much by the needs of the student as by the logical analysis of the study." Anson Phelps-Stokes wrote of Jones in 1948, "For educational fads and trimmings he cares little. He has wanted to emphasize that education, whether for the Negro or the white man, should be related to what he likes to call the four essentials—health, capacity for earning a living, re-creation, and meeting community needs. It was these convictions that led him to have such a profound reverence for the ideals that have dominated Hampton Institute, especially under General Armstrong and Dr. Frissell" (*Negro Status and Race Relations in the United States, 1911–1946: The Thirty Five Year Report of the Phelps-Stokes Fund* [New York: Phelps-Stokes Fund, 1948], 28). See also Yellin, "The (White) Search."

33. Kliebard, "That Evil Genius," 19.

34. W. E. B. Du Bois, "Negro Education, a Review," *Crisis* 15, no. 4 (1918): 175. Eric Anderson and Alfred A. Moss have argued that historians have largely mischaracterized *Negro Education* and Jones more broadly. "Though Du Bois—and the scholars who have followed his lead—described Jones as a man with a distinctive program of caste education, in fact, he repeatedly based his arguments on general theories of 'modern' or 'progressive' education." Anderson and Moss also note that Jones not only advocated for similar reforms forms in all schools, including urban and rural white people, but also protested certain aspects of the Jim Crow racial order. See Anderson and Moss, *Dangerous Donations: Northern Philanthropy and Southern Black Education, 1902–1930* (Columbia: University of Missouri Press, 1999), 202–11.

35. Robert F. Arnove had argued that this was the predominant aim of US industrial philanthropy during the first half of the twentieth century. See the introduction to *Philanthropy and Cultural Imperialism: The Foundations at Home and Abroad*, ed. Robert F. Arnove (Bloomington: Indiana University Press, 1982), 9.

36. Joseph Houldsworth Oldham, "Christian Missions and the Education of the Negro," *International Review of Mission* 7 (1918): 244.

37. Thomas Jesse Jones, *Education in Africa: A Study of West, South and Equatorial Africa by the African Education Commission* (New York: Phelps-Stokes Fund, 1922), xii–xiii.

38. Richard Symonds, "Alexander Garden Fraser (1873–1962)," in *Oxford*

*Dictionary of National Biography* (Oxford: Oxford University Press, March 2016).

39. Quoted in J. C. A. Corea, "One Hundred Years of Education in Ceylon," *Modern Asian Studies* 3, no. 2 (1969): 161.

40. Ibid., 160.

41. According to Kenneth J. King, J. H. Oldham first suggested Jones to lead the Indian survey ("Africa and the Southern States of the U.S.A.," *Journal of African History* 10, no. 4 [1969]: 663). See also A. G. Fraser, *Village Education in India* (Oxford: Oxford University Press, 1920).

42. A. G. Fraser, August 1937, "Chapter I: Quality of Services," in *Education for Life*, 6.

43. Thomas Jesse Jones, *Education in East Africa: A Study of East, Central and South Africa by the Second African Education Commission under the Auspices of the Phelps-Stokes Fund, in Cooperation with the International Education Board* (New York: Phelps-Stokes Fund, 1925), xxv, 6. The International Missionary Council, of which J. H. Oldham served as secretary, loaned the office space to the Phelps-Stokes Fund.

44. As contemporary Cornelius W. de Kieweit observed, "South African schoolboys play at Cowboys and Indians, not at Boers and Zulus; for Zulus, Basuto and Bechuana are too manifestly an unheroic and desperate social problem" (*The Imperial Factor in South Africa: A Study in Politics and Economics* [Cambridge: Cambridge University Press, 1937], 2). For a broader comparison between the US and South African frontier, see Howard Lamar and Leonard Thompson, eds., *The Frontier in History: North America and Southern Africa Compared* (New Haven, CT: Yale University Press, 1981).

45. Jones, *Education in East Africa*, 6.

46. W. G. A. Ormsby-Gore et al., "Education Policy in British Tropical Africa: Memorandum Submitted to the Secretary of State for the Colonies by the Advisory Committee on Native Education in the British Tropical Dependencies," Cmd. 2374 (London: His Majesty's Stationery Office, 1925); T. Walter Wallbank, "The Educational Renaissance in British Tropical Africa," *Journal of Negro Education* 3 (January 1934): 105–22; Frederick James Clathworthy, "The Formulation of British Colonial Education Policy, 1923–1948" (PhD diss., University of Michigan, 1970); Clive Whitehead, "Education Policy in British Tropical Africa: The 1925 White Paper in Retrospect," *History of Education* 10 (1981): 195–203; and "The Advisory Committee on Education in the [British] Colonies 1924–1961," *Paedagogica Historica* 27 (1991): 384–421.

47. F. D. Lugard, "Education in Tropical Africa," *Edinburgh Review* 242 (July 1925): 2.

48. Ormsby-Gore et al., "Education Policy," 4.

49. Lugard, "Education in Tropical Africa," 17.

50. Gita Steiner Khamsi and Hubert O. Quist, "The Politics of Educational Borrowing: Reopening the Case of Achimota in British Ghana," *Comparative Education Review* 44 (2000): 272–99; Jones, *Education in Africa*.

51. Alexander Garden Fraser, "Native Education in Africa," *Journal of the Royal Society of Arts* 81 (July 1933): 812–31, quotes on 816. See also Ransford

Slater, "The Gold Coast of To-Day," *Journal of the Royal African Society* 27 (1928): 325–26.

52. "Tuskegee Idea Works in Africa," *Pittsburgh Courier*, October 29, 1927, 13.

53. Quoted in Judith Simon et al., "The End of Assimilation?," in *A Civilising Mission? Perceptions and Representations of the Native School System* (Auckland: Auckland University Press, 2001), 190. See also John M. Barrington, "Cultural Adaptation and Maori Educational Policy: The Africa Connection," *Comparative Education Review* 20 (1976): 1–10.

54. Quoted in Kessing, *Education in Pacific Countries: Interpreting a Seminar-Conference of Educators and Social Scientists Conducted by the University of Hawaii and Yale University, Honolulu, Hawaii, 1936* (Shanghai: Kelly and Walsh, 1937), 72.

55. For African American student unrest against industrial education, see Raymond Wolters, *The New Negro on Campus: Black College Rebellions of the 1920s* (Princeton, NJ: Princeton University Press, 1975).

56. Chorley wrote to Jones regarding "a memorandum about our conversation the other day at the Town Hall." Some fourteen years later, Jones wrote to Carson Ryan, "You will recall that I was at the very beginning of the Meriam et al survey. My first conference with Chorley in front of the Grand Central Station is dramatically vivid in my memory." And to Chorley, "I regard this study as a continuation of all the fine efforts that began in our conversation on 42nd Street so long ago." Kenneth Chorley to Thomas Jesse Jones, December 1, 1925, Navajo Indian Study, folder 7: Correspondence, 1919-1938, box 47, Subjects, Thomas Jesse Jones Files, 1912–46, Office Files, Phelps-Stokes Fund Records, Schomburg Center; Thomas Jesse Jones to Carson Ryan, January 17, 1939, file 100, Phelps-Stokes Report, Dr. Thomas J. Jones, 1938–41, box 55, Central Classified Files, Navajo Area Office, BIA Records; Jones to Chorley, December 23, 1938, Navajo Indian Study, folder 7: Correspondence, 1919-1938, box 47, Subjects, Jones Files.

57. Three weeks earlier, Jones had represented the Phelps-Stokes Fund at the second International Conference on Africa. Organized through J. H. Oldham's International Missionary Council, the three-day conference had met in Hartford to discuss education in East Africa. Meanwhile, throughout November, the Phelps-Stokes Fund had sponsored African missionaries from Uganda, Rhodesia, and Gold Coast to tour southern industrial schools. The cohort included Dr. James Emman Kwegyir Aggrey of Achimota and members of both Phelps-Stokes commissions. See "Quarterly Notes: Being the Bulletin of the International Missionary Council," *International Review of Mission*, October 1925, viii; Anson Phelps Stokes to Du Bois RE invitation to International Missionary Council, November 17, 1925, file 277, box 18, series I, Phelps-Stokes Papers (MS 299), Yale University Library, New Haven, CT; "Prof. of African Languages in Berlin Addresses Student Body at Hampton," *New York Age*, November 14, 1925, 9; "African Missionaries Visit Hampton Institute," *New York Age*, November 7, 1925, 9.

58. The Rockefellers and other industrial philanthropists also supported education and research concerning white Americans. As historian Natalie

Ring has argued, the northern industrialists and social reformers conceptualized the South alongside US territories such as Puerto Rico and the Philippines as a so-called problem region. Therefore, studies for possible solutions to the "southern problem" mirrored approaches to other colonial economies. One result, as Tiffany Willoughby-Herard has recently uncovered, was that research into white poverty in the Jim Crow South set the stage for the American Carnegie Corporation's 1932 inquiry on race in South Africa, *The Poor White Problem in South Africa*, which, like Jones's *Negro Education*, provided an intellectual and purportedly scientific rational for apartheid. In the United States, the foundations also increased access to higher education by endowing institutions such as the University of Chicago and colleges for African Americans but distributed resources unevenly and in ways that often reinforced the segregationist status quo. As Anderson and Moss have argued, "The foundations did little to attack directly segregation, poverty, or disfranchisement. Believing 'our work is education not agitation,' they did, however, greatly strengthen selected black colleges and universities, and advocate, with some success, increased public support for black education." See Ring, *The Problem South: Region, Empire, and the New Liberal State, 1880–1930* (Athens: University of Georgia Press, 2012); Willoughby-Herard, *Waste of a White Skin: The Carnegie Corporation and the Racial Logic of White Vulnerability* (Berkeley: University of California Press, 2015); Saul DuBow, "The Elaboration of Segregationist Ideology," in *Segregation and Apartheid in Twentieth-Century South Africa*, ed. William Beinart and Saul DuBow (New York: Routledge, 1995), 151–52; R. Hunt Davis Jr., "Charles T. Loram and an American Model for African Education in South Africa," *African Studies Review* 19 (September 1976): 87–99; and Anderson and Moss, *Dangerous Donations*, 11.

59. See James D. Anderson, "Philanthropic Control over Private Black Higher Education," in Arnove, *Philanthropy and Cultural Imperialism*, 147–78; Anderson, "Training the Apostles of Liberal Culture: Black Higher Education, 1900–1935," in *The Education of Blacks in the South*, 238–79; C. Vann Woodward, "Philanthropy and the Forgotten Man," in *Origins of the New South, 1877–1913* (Baton Rouge: Louisiana State University Press, 1971), 396–428; and Anderson and Moss, *Dangerous Donations*.

60. This is Lewis Meriam's account, which also emphasizes that when Secretary of the Interior Hubert Work "learned that the Rockefeller people were also interested in a survey he immediately took action" ("Assignments since Coming with the Institute for Government Research," October 4, 1932, 5, Lewis Meriam File, Brookings Institution Files, Washington, DC). Rockefeller's trip to Montana would also lead to the Snake River Land Company, a front company established to purchase private lands near Yellowstone in a conservation scheme that ultimately created Grand Teton National Park. His office tasked Kenneth Chorley with the operation in 1926. See Marian Albright Schenck, "One Day on Timbered Island: How the Rockefellers' Visits to Yellowstone Led to Grand Teton National Park," *Montana: The Magazine of Western History* 57 (2007): 22–49, 93–94; J. W. Ernst, ed., *Worthwhile Places: Correspondence of John D. Rockefeller, Jr. and Horace Albright* (New York: Fordham University Press, 1991); "Biographical/

Historical Note," Finding Aid, Kenneth Chorley Papers (FA067), Rockefeller Archive Center, http://dimes.rockarch.org/FA067/biohist.

61. Philip Kopper, *Colonial Williamsburg* (New York: Harry N. Abrams, 2001), 165–69; Richard Massock, "Arthur Woods Is Old Hand: Career Has Been One of Giving Aid in Difficult Situations," *Gettysburg Times*, November 4, 1930, 3.

62. Jones to Chorley, December 2, 1925.

63. For McKenzie's involvement, see Christopher L. Nicholson, "To Advance a Race: A Historical Analysis of the Intercession of Personal Belief, Industrial Philanthropy and Black Liberal Arts Higher Education in Fayette McKenzie's Presidency at Fisk University, 1915–1925" (PhD diss., Loyola University, 2011), 24–25. On Cloud, see Henry Roe Cloud, "From Wigwam to Pulpit," *Southern Workman* 45 (July 1916): 400–406; and for biographical treatments, see Joel Pfister, *The Yale Indian: The Education of Henry Roe Cloud* (Durham, NC: Duke University Press, 2009); David W. Messer, *Henry Roe Cloud: A Biography* (Lanham, MD: Hamilton Books, 2010); and Renya K. Ramirez, "Henry Roe Cloud to Henry Cloud: Ho-Chunk Strategies and Colonialism," *Settler Colonial Studies* 2 (January 2012): 117–37. For a scuttled survey, see Anson Phelps-Stokes to Cato Sells, December 5, 1914, file 7: January–February 1915, box 15, Chronological Files, Anson Phelps Stokes Files, 1912–46, Office Files, Phelps-Stokes Fund Records, Schomburg Center. For McKenzie's tenure at Fisk, see Lester C. Laymon, "The Black Community in Nashville and the Fisk University Student Strike of 1924–1925," *Journal of Southern History* 40 (May 1974): 225–44; Wolters, *The New Negro*, 230–74.

64. George Vaux Jr. to Thomas Jesse Jones, January 21, 1919, Navajo Indian Study, folder 7: Correspondence, 1919-1938, box 47, Subjects, Jones Files.

65. Jones to Chorley, December 2, 1925. Jones also suggested two other potential directors for the planned survey: Columbia University sociologist Frank Ross and Dr. T. J. Woofter of the Commission for Interracial Cooperation. In the same memo, Jones later recommended that the Institute of Government Research should carry out the study: "As I think of the various qualifications to which I am referring it occurs to me now that the Institute of Government Research in Washington is probably even better fitted for this undertaking than the Russell Sage Foundation. The Director of this Institute is Dr. W. W. Willoughby. You will note on the first page that Mr. Meriam is an officer of this Institution" (ibid.).

66. Ibid.

67. In the back-and-forth between Jones and Chorley hashing out a memorandum for the Phelps-Stokes Fund trustees' approval, it became evident that Jones did not want to be on record approaching the secretary of the interior and that the matter should be kept confidential. See Jones to Chorley, RE Phelps-Stokes Trustees Proposal, January 27, 1926, Navajo Indian Study, folder 7: Correspondence, 1919-1938, box 47, Subjects, Jones Files; "Memorandum for Dr. Stokes on the Survey of the American Indians," undated, Jones Files; Jones to Chorley, RE Phelps-Stokes Trustees Vote, January 28, 1926, Jones Files.

68. Kopper, *Colonial Williamsburg*, 165; Thomas Jesse Jones, US Passport Application, March 24, 1920, roll 1117, 1795–1925, certificates: 376–749, March

24, 1920—March 25, 1920, Passport Applications, January 2, 1906-March 31, 1925, NARA, Washington, DC, Ancestry.com.

69. Chorley to Jones, January 29, 1926, Navajo Indian Study, folder 7: Correspondence, 1919-1938, box 47, Subjects, Jones Files.

70. W. F. Willoughby to the Board of Trustees of the Institute for Government Research, RE: "The Survey of Economic and Social Conditions among American Indians," 1, Meriam File. Donald T. Critchlow offers a partial account of the report's origins; however, he erroneously credits the impetus for the study to Secretary of the Interior Hubert Work and underestimates the role Chorley and Jones played in planning and initiating the study because his sources largely rely upon Brookings Institution and Rockefeller Foundation records, missing the Phelps-Stokes records entirely. See "Lewis Meriam, Expertise, and Indian Reform," *Historian* 43 (1981): 325—26. For the official accounting of the report's origins, see also W. F. Willoughby, "Letter of Transmittal," February 21, 1928, in Meriam et al., *The Problem of Indian Administration*, vii—x.

71. See Roy to Jones, October 19, 1926, folder 7: Correspondence with L. A. Roy, 1924—1927, box 44, Correspondence, Jones Files. The same letter details a dinner honoring Charles T. Loram at the Astor Hotel, Tuskegee president Robert R. Moton's world tour, and a compliment from Mr. Rockefeller Jr. about Jones's latest book, *Four Essentials of Education*.

72. Jones to Chorley, December 2, 1925.

73. Jones to Chorley, April 13, 1926, Navajo Indian Study, folder 7, box 47, Subjects, Jones Files. Here, too, Jones raised the question "whether the study shall be instituted through a quiet approach to the whole problem with only enough publicity to assure the friends of Indians that a thoroughgoing consideration is to be given to the whole field, as against a study that may be heralded abroad as of national significance thus awakening a degree of expectation that may result in states of mind inimical to the field work" (ibid.).

74. In a letter from the field, Meriam informed Jones that he had been able to earn an extraordinary level of cooperation from staff members of the Indian Field Service, "securing cooperation such as I received from you, [Carson] Ryan, and Capon at the time I made the survey of the Bureau of Education" (Meriam to Jones, April 5, 1927, Meriam File). Indeed, the philanthropic support for the study was contingent upon Meriam's being selected as its director. Even before Chorley solicited support from Secretary Work, the Phelps-Stokes Fund board of trustees had voted "to authorize the Educational Director to inform the Laura Spelman Rockefeller Foundation that the Phelps-Stokes fund will be glad to cooperate with it to a modest extent in making possible an Indian Survey by the Institute of Government Research . . . provided the Institute is able to set apart Mr. Lewis Meriam as proposed for the direction of the Survey" (Jones to Chorley, January 26, 1926).

75. W. Carson Ryan to Stokes, in *Education for Life,* 38; and Jones, "Ryan, W. Carson," in ibid., 182.

76. On including a woman, see Jones to Lewis Meriam, April 16, 1926, Navajo Indian Study, folder 7: Correspondence, 1919-1938, box 47, Subjects, Jones Files. Jones quotes a letter from Meriam: "'I had a conference with Thomas Jesse in

New York on Sunday Night and Monday and a brief interview with Secretary Work yesterday. Jones is of the opinion that the report can be materially improved by further revision" (Jones to Chorley, December 7, 1927, Jones Files). For involvement in fieldwork, see Parman, "Lewis Meriam's Letters," Parts 1 and 2.

77. Meriam, *The Problem of Indian Administration*, 32.

78. Jones, "Social Studies at Hampton," 61, 62.

79. Meriam, *The Problem of Indian Administration*, 32.

80. Thomas Jesse Jones, *The Navajo Indian Problem* (New York: Phelps-Stokes Fund, 1939), 118.

81. Thomas Jesse Jones to Kenneth Chorley, RE "Memorandum—the Reorganization of Indian Administration and the Indian Commissionership," January 8, 1929, folder 195, Brookings Institution—Indian Affairs 1929, box 2, series 4, Spelman Fund of New York, Rockefeller Foundation Archives.

82. Ibid.

83. Chorley to Jones, February 27, 1929, Spelman Fund.

84. Chorley to Arthur Woods, April 18, 1929, Spelman Fund.

85. Commissioner Charles J. Rhoads to Spelman Fund of New York, "How the Special Fund Was Used," March 30, 1931, Spelman Fund; and Critchlow, "Meriam and Indian Reform," 335–40.

86. See Szasz, *Education*, chap. 3, "W. Carson Ryan: From the Meriam Report to the Indian New Deal." As Lomawaima and McCarty argue, "A new idea—schools should serve the needs and interests of Native students—was wedded to an old idea—federal policymakers were best qualified to define those needs and interests." That old idea also included the Hampton idea. See Lomawaima and McCarty, *To Remain an Indian*, 69.

87. Jones to Meriam, March 21, 1929, folder 195, Brookings Institution—Indian Affairs 1929, box 2, series 4, Spelman Fund. Regarding Margold, see Meriam to Guy Moffett, folder 196, Spelman Fund; Rhoads to Spelman Fund of New York, "How the Special Fund Was Used," Spelman Fund.

88. John Collier, "The American Congo," *Survey* 50 (August 1923): 476.

89. Ibid., 467–76; Laurence M. Hauptman, "Africa View: John Collier, the British Colonial Service and American Indian Policy, 1933–1945," *Historian* 48 (1986): 359–74; Rusco, *A Fateful Time*, 156–59, 160–65.

90. Collier's comments appeared in his review of the famed British biologist Julian Huxley's *Africa View,* a sprawling travelogue elaborating upon observations Huxley gleaned during a sixteen-week survey of East Africa. Huxley himself acknowledged in his original 1929 report, "I am attempting to build upon the general ideas and recommendations of the Phelps-Stokes Commission, and to extend them a stage further." See John Collier, "Africa View—and Indian," *American Indian Life* 17 (January 1931): 35; Julian S. Huxley, *Africa View* (New York: Harper and Brothers, 1931), 1; Huxley, "Report by Professor Julian Huxley, M.A., on Biology and the Biological Approach to Native Education in East Africa," in *War and Colonial Department and Colonial Office: Africa, Confidential Print: Nos. 1124 to 1141 and 1144* (1930), 1.

91. Collier, "Africa View," 35.

92. Board of Indian Commissioners, *Annual Report*, 29; "The Progress of Indian Legislation and Administration: Extension of Remarks of Hon. Scott Leavitt of Montana, in the House of Representatives, Tuesday, March 3, 1931" (Washington, DC: US Government Printing Office, 1931), 16–17. For a list of school superintendents at the Burke School, see Robert W. Young, *The Navajo Yearbook: 1951–1961, a Decade of Progress* (Window Rock, AZ: Navajo Agency, 1961), 601.

93. Collier, "Africa View," 32.

94. Meriam to Guy Moffett, April 21, 1933, folder 196, Brookings Institution—Indian Affairs 1929, box 2, series 4, Spelman Fund.

95. Rusco, *A Fateful Time*, 179, 184–87.

96. Cloud to Phelps-Stokes, September 28, 1937, in *Education for Life*, 157.

97. Cloud to Meriam, January 28, 1929, file 195, Brookings Institution—Indian Affairs 1929, box 2, series 4, Spelman Fund.

98. Meriam to Cloud, February 5, 1929, file 195, Brookings Institution—Indian Affairs 1929, box 2, series 4, Spelman Fund.

99. Ibid.

100. Jones to John Collier, March 30, 1932, box 7, folder 127 (reel 3), series I, Correspondence of John Collier, part 1, 1922–23, Collier Papers.

101. "Collier Will Open Indian Conference at Fort Wingate," *Gallup Independent,* August 25, 1934, 1, 4; "Dr. Thomas Jesse Jones Visits Indian Schools," *New York Age,* September 29, 1934, 2; Jones to Collier, October 30, 1934, box 8, folder 168 (reel 14), series I, Correspondence of John Collier, part 1, 1922–23, Collier Papers.

102. Jones to Chorley, December 31, 1934, Navajo Indian Study, folder 7: Correspondence, 1919-1938, box 47, Subjects, Jones Files.

103. The sixty-five-year-old educationist remained involved in Africa through Phelps-Stokes Fund ventures such as the Booker T. Washington Institute, an industrial training school in Liberia geared toward workers on Firestone rubber plantations, and he expanded his colonial purview through his collaborations with the Near East Foundation. Though active in African American social policy via the Commission on Interracial Cooperation and seats on the board of trustees at Howard, Fisk, and Hampton, his influence among black people in the United States had waned since McKenzie had been ousted. He admitted that his ideas were unpopular among African Americans in a 1936 essay. Regarding the trend in African American education away from "pioneers" such as Samuel Chapman Armstrong and Booker T. Washington, "It is unfortunate but probably certain that Negro education must for a time, and possibly for a long time, give up the objectives and methods of the pioneers who served the Negro people better than current opinion can possibly understand" (Jones, "Universality of Educational Objectives," *Journal of Negro Education* 5 [1936]: 411). For the arc of his career, see Anson Phelps-Stokes, Channing H. Tobias, and Thomas Jesse Jones, *Negro Status and Race Relations in the United States: The Thirty-Five Year Report of the Phelps-Stokes Fund* (New York: Phelps-Stokes Fund, 1948), 17–22, 28–30.

104. Donald Parman, *The Navajos and the New Deal* (New Haven, CT: Yale University Press, 1976), 234–36.

105. Jones, *The Navajo Indian Problem.*

106. "Impressions from Talks of Loram, Jones, Allen, Deloria," file 100, Phelps-Stokes Report, Dr. Thomas J. Jones, 1938–41, box 55, Central Classified Files, Navajo Area Office, BIA Records. For Navajo settlement patterns, see Stephen Jett, "The Origins of Navajo Settlement Patterns," *Annals of the Association of American Geographers* 68, no. 4 (1978): 351–62. For Navajo opinions on the day school program, see Parman, *The Navajos*, 198–99.

107. Members of Greasewood, AZ, Community to Commissioner of Indian Affairs, April 14, 1932, in *"For Our Navajo People": Diné Letters, Speeches & Petitions, 1900–1960, ed.* Peter Iverson (Albuquerque: University of New Mexico Press, 2002), 53.

108. In her seminal study of Indigenous education in the United States and Australia, *White Mother to a Dark Race*, historian Margaret Jacobs observed that despite the striking similarities between government policies in both nations, she had "found no evidence . . . that officials in the two countries were aware of each other's policies. American officials did not discuss or refer to Australian policy, and Australian officials seem to have known only the vague outlines of federal Indian policy in the United States" (*White Mother to a Dark Race: Settler Colonialism, Maternalism, and the Removal of Indigenous Children in the American West and Australia, 1880–1940* [Lincoln: University of Nebraska Press, 2009], 51).

109. C. T. Loram and T. F. McIlwraith, eds., *The North American Indian Today: University of Toronto–Yale University Seminar Conference, Toronto, September 4–16, 1939* (Toronto: University of Toronto Press, 1943).

110. W. E. B. Du Bois, *Crisis* 18, no. 1 (1919): 9.

111. Ross, "In Memoriam Thomas Jesse Jones," 29.

JENNIFER CAROLINA GÓMEZ MENJÍVAR AND WILLIAM SALMON

# Mopan in Context: Mayan Identity, Belizean Citizenship, and the Future of a Language

MAYAN COMMUNITIES IN BELIZE have been largely excluded from the linguistic inquiry into Mayan languages that began in the late nineteenth century, as well as from the grassroots movements that have promoted the revitalization of Mayan languages in Guatemala more recently.[1] In the absence of academic interest, limited attention to grassroots activism, and a lack of publishing opportunities for authors, the issues affecting Mayan languages in Belize have been relegated to the periphery of larger discussions about Mayan languages in Mesoamerica.[2] Even as attention turns to speakers of Mayan languages living in the United States, Mayan migrants from Belize continue to be absent from research on the Mayan diaspora.[3] As such, the study reported on in this article is the first to look in depth at the ecology in which the Mopan language resides.[4] Significantly, it is also the first study to consider the implications of a young generation of ethnic Mayans growing up as native speakers of Kriol. Our findings in this article suggest that a language shift from Mopan to Kriol is underway among the younger generations of Mopan speakers and that if its use among this demographic is not revitalized, it could lead to Mopan's endangerment in the near future. The larger discussion focuses on geopolitical and socioeconomic factors that influence language attitudes toward Spanish, English, and Kriol in Belize, contributing to an ongoing body of work on Belizean languages in general.[5]

## The Mopan Language Family and History

Mopan belongs to the Yucatecan branch of the Mayan language family, which also includes Yucatec, Itza', and Lacandón. Yucatec and Lacandón are primarily spoken in Mexico, with the former having an estimated eight hundred thousand speakers and the latter seriously endangered, with approximately one thousand speakers. Itza' is spoken in the Petén region of northern Guatemala and is also severely endangered. Mopan is one of two Yucatecan languages spoken in Belize, and it is believed to have approximately ten thousand speakers.[6] There are an additional five thousand speakers of Mopan in

Guatemala; they are concentrated in in San Luis and in the Lake Petén Itzá road area (an enclave between Dolores and Poptun) within the department of Petén.[7] Both of the Mayan languages spoken in this area of Guatemala, Mopan and Itzá, have been identified by the Academia de Lenguas Mayas de Guatemala (ALMG) as endangered languages and have been targeted for revitalization efforts.[8]

Over the last few centuries, speakers of Mayan languages in Guatemala, including Mopan, have been subjected to a process of *castellanización*, or Hispanicization, that parallels the experiences of speakers of indigenous languages in other former Spanish colonies.[9] Unlike Guatemala and the rest of Central America, however, the official language of colonial British Honduras (now Belize) was standard British English. Speakers of Mayan languages were subjected to a process of Anglicization. This process has continued since Belize gained its independence in 1981 and become increasingly complex: the American English standard variety has overtaken British English in terms of overt prestige, and Kriol now holds both covert and overt prestige as a lingua franca qua national language.[10]

## Political Setting

While most former English colonies obtained their independence from the British Empire in the 1960s, Belize had to assess three interrelated factors before claiming its independence. It had to consider first the threat of a Guatemalan invasion of Belize during the former's civil war (1960–96); second, the brutal genocide against Mayan populations across the border in the Petén region; third, the ongoing territorial dispute between the countries over the existence and precise location of the Belizean-Guatemalan border.[11] The factors remain salient, as their potential threat has not attenuated in the years since the end of the Guatemalan civil war. The territorial dispute is still very much alive, with the territory involved including the southern section of Belize District, most of Cayo District, and the entirety of Stann Creek and Toledo Districts, which are home to the Kekchi and Mopan Maya linguistic communities.[12] Importantly, this disputed territory also includes the entirety of the Maya Mountains, which are shown in Figure 1.

San Antonio, San José, Na Luum Caj, Santa Elena, and Pueblo Viejo are important Mopan villages in Toledo and, as seen in Figure 1, are located on the foothills of the Maya Mountains.[13] In addition to the mountain range, the disputed territory easily includes half the land of Belize, as shown in Figure 2. This includes valuable forestlands, coastland, and approximately one hundred islands; a large percentage of the country's agricultural sites; archaeological sites; and conservation zones, all of which are on ancient

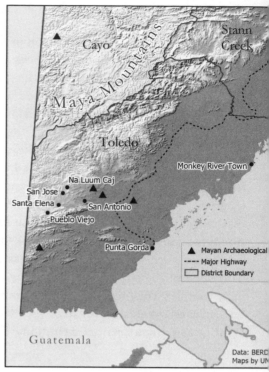

**FIGURE 1.** Map of Belize showing all districts and close-up map of Toledo. Courtesy of University of Minnesota Duluth Geospatial Analysis Center.

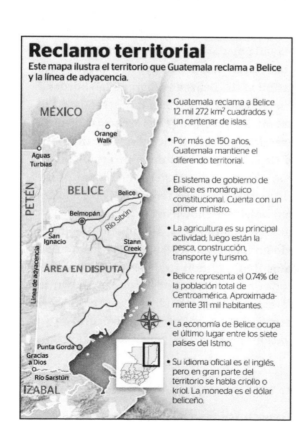

**FIGURE 2.** Area of Belize claimed by Guatemala. Map by Nelson Xuya for *La Prensa Libre*, Guatemala City, 2013.

Mayan homelands.[14] Annexation would provide Guatemala with access to the Caribbean Sea and control over the highways transporting raw materials out of this lush landscape.

The red lines in Figure 2 that define the 12,272 kilometers (4,738.25 square miles) of disputed territory correspond to three of the four major highways in operation in Belize today.[15] The territory is roughly bordered in the north by the George Price Highway (formerly known as the Western Highway), which originates in Belize City; goes through the capital, Belmopan; and terminates at Benque Viejo del Carmen at the border/adjacency line with Guatemala. The area also includes the Hummingbird Highway, which originates in Belmopan and cuts through the Maya Mountains to end in Dangriga. The Southern Highway originates in Dangriga and runs south to conclude at Punta Gorda, the largest town in Toledo.

Even after thirty-seven years of Belizean independence, the threat of annexation continues to be a matter of great importance to Belizean citizens of all ethnic groups, particularly those who reside in the districts within the disputed territory, such as Toledo. Evidently, annexation by Guatemala is far from an attractive option to the Mayan communities, given the Spanish-speaking country's role in the genocide and disenfranchisement of its own Mayan communities in the recent past.[16] Thus, the territorial dispute with Guatemala continues to play a role in the expression of a national Belizean identity, holding Kriol as the lingua franca that binds the newer nation's inhabitants together within the same borders.

## Economic Setting

Toledo, where Mopan is mainly spoken, lies in the southernmost district of Belize, which is often referred to as "the forgotten district of Belize." Census data illustrate how this district compares with Belize District, the largest city in Belize and former capital of the country. Belize District has the largest urban population (72 percent), while Toledo has the smallest urban population (17 percent). Furthermore, 88 percent of the working-age population in Belize District had completed at least a primary school education, compared to 58 percent in Toledo. Belize District has the highest rate of Internet usage (38 percent), while Toledo has the lowest rate of Internet usage (16 percent). Homeownership was higher in Toledo, but the homes in the two districts were very different: 24 percent of the homes in Toledo had earth/sand as the main flooring material (compared to 0.2 percent of the homes in Belize District), and 48 percent of the inhabitants in Toledo used wood/coal as their primary cooking fuel (compared to 2 percent of the homes in Belize).[17] While the tourist industry has historically created a wider array of professional opportunities for the inhabitants of Belize District, few such options were available to the inhabitants of Toledo until the 1990s, when ecotourism and cultural tourism began to be pursued by the district's Mayan communities.[18]

## Languages of Belize

The myth of a predominantly Afro-descendant, Kriol-speaking population has persisted outside of Belize, but this is only partially true, as can be seen in table 1. Heavy immigration of Belizeans to the United States and England occurred throughout the 1980s and the 1990s. During the same years, Belize experienced waves of emigration from Honduras, Nicaragua, and El Salvador.[19] Yet while some of those immigrants—now in their second and third generation in the country—have continued to speak Spanish, many also speak English and Kriol.[20] Though there are additional varieties of Spanish and of Kriol to be recognized,[21] census data provide a compelling picture of the size and geographic distribution of these linguistic communities in Belize.

English ranks first in terms of sheer numbers of speakers, which are distributed fairly evenly across districts. Spanish ranks second, and its speakers are concentrated in Corozal, Orange Walk, and Cayo. Speakers of Kriol reside primarily in Belize and Stann Creek. Toledo has the lowest proportion of Spanish and English speakers, at 28 percent and 48 percent, respectively, as well as the highest proportion of speakers of Mayan languages, at 68 percent. The second highest number of Mayan-language speakers (16 percent) is found in Stann Creek, which also has the highest concentration of Garifuna speakers (14 percent). These are not the only languages spoken in the country, however; there are also significant numbers of Mennonite Low German (Plautdietsch) and Chinese speakers across all districts.

## Mopan, a Local Language

The three Mayan languages spoken in Belize are Yucatec, Kekchi, and Mopan. According to the 2010 Belize census, there were 2,518 speakers of Yucatec, 17,586 estimated speakers of Kekchi, and 10,649 speakers of Mopan. The highest concentration of Mopan speakers was in Toledo (46 percent), followed by Stann Creek (31 percent) and Cayo (15 percent). The ratio of male and female speakers was balanced, as 49 percent of the speakers of Mopan were male and 51 percent were female. It was a relatively young linguistic community, given that 78 percent of the speakers of Mopan in 2010 were under the age of forty.[22] Between the 1980 and 2010 censuses, the number

**TABLE 1.**

**Speakers of Mayan languages, English, Spanish, and Kriol by district**

| LANGUAGE | TOTALS | PERCENT IN COROZAL | PERCENT IN ORANGE WALK | PERCENT IN BELIZE | PERCENT IN CAYO | PERCENT IN STANN CREEK | PERCENT IN TOLEDO |
|---|---|---|---|---|---|---|---|
| English | 183,90 | 54.4 | 62.2 | 72.5 | 66.7 | 52.0 | 47.9 |
| Spanish | 165,296 | 84.7 | 85.6 | 34.1 | 71.5 | 39.3 | 28.2 |
| Kriol | 130,467 | 18.9 | 16.8 | 63.6 | 39.9 | 67.4 | 47.2 |
| Mayan | 30,748 | 2.5 | 2.3 | 1.2 | 6.2 | 16.3 | 68.4 |

**SOURCE:** Statistical Institute of Belize, *2010 Belize Population and Housing Census Report*, http://www.statisticsbelize.org.bz/dms20uc/dynamicdata/docs /20110505004542_2.pdf.

**NOTE:** Percentages do not sum to 100, as many respondents speak multiple languages.

of Kekchi speakers increased 6 percent, and the number of Mopan speakers *decreased* 3.6 percent.[23] Although both linguistic communities are concentrated in Toledo and are hence subject to parallel socioeconomic conditions, it is Mopan that has come under attention as an endangered language.[24]

Discussions of language endangerment generally involve a local language in contact with a majority language (usually a European language). The most common story sees the local language falling into a precarious state as a result of factors arising from the contact with the majority language, for fairly obvious reasons. Majority languages are used widely, they hold social prestige, and they are used in educational institutions and serve official and governmental purposes. On the other hand, local languages often occupy a disadvantaged social or economic position that causes the language of wider communication to appear more attractive and beneficial.[25] Local languages are also frequently spoken in rural contexts, which are also socioeconomically disadvantaged when compared to urban contexts in the same country or region.[26] These factors are important, as a vast body of research shows that speakers of local languages can be strongly influenced by the general population's perception of their language.[27] The present study considers a variation in this story of contact and language endangerment, however. Specifically, the language shift in question here involves contact between two local languages, Kriol and Mopan, in a multilingual society.

## The Present Study

Our study proceeded in two phases, and we discuss each phase in turn below.

### First Phase: San Antonio in Toledo

The first phase of our study took place in San Antonio, which has approximately eight hundred inhabitants and is widely considered to be the cultural home of the Mopan in Belize. In 1883 Mopan refugees fleeing captivity and enslavement in Guatemala founded San Antonio, Belize. The members of the community briefly returned to their town, San Luis, in Petén, Guatemala, and returned with a statue of San Antonio and church bells, which they installed in the Catholic church they built in their new home.[28] Catholicism continues to be important in the village and is a symbol of tradition for a congregation that continues to hold mass in Mopan. San Antonio is by most accounts the last remaining Belizean place in which Mopan is the primary language.[29]

We collected seventy-eight quantitative surveys (approximately 10 percent of San Antonio's inhabitants) from forty women and twenty men age twelve to seventy-eight in the community. A female native speaker of Mopan who lives in the village administered the surveys in peer fashion, introducing the survey and its goals to participants, who often completed the surveys as a family. She also assisted in translating questions for participants when appropriate. The surveys included demographic questions, statements regarding the Mopan language specifically, and statements concerning Mopan vis-à-vis one other language (English in one half of the surveys and Kriol in the other half of the surveys).[30] There were no differences in the content or structure of the two surveys except for the inclusion of English or Kriol in the relevant statements.

Statements regarding the Mopan language (e.g., "One cannot be considered Mopan if one does not speak Mopan") and statements involving English or Kriol (e.g., "I would like Mopan to replace English as a medium of instruction in our public schools" and "My ability to speak Kriol will assure me a good job as soon as I finish school") were arranged on a Likert scale, with 1 designating "strongly disagree" and 5 designating "strongly agree."

### Second Phase: Punta Gorda Town in Toledo

The second phase of the study took place in Punta Gorda Town. PG, as it is called in Belize, is a town of approximately six thousand people located thirty kilometers (eighteen miles) southeast of San Antonio on the coast. The road that connects the two locations was constructed in the 1930s and resulted in the erosion of the "Mopan/non-Mopan boundary" due to the increasing flow of intercultural transactions between the two sites.[31] Today, a bus line runs from San Antonio to PG, but most villagers do not venture out of the rural community. The exception to this general rule is Mopan youth who take the bus into PG in order to attend secondary school and college on the University of Belize branch campus there.

The Mayan participants for this phase of the study were a subset of those interviewed in a larger study on attitudes toward Kriol.[32] We employed a verbal-guise test to gauge attitudes toward two varieties of Kriol, with participants rating recorded voices on an array of personality characteristics.[33] Participants also completed qualitative questions about Kriol, as well as questions on their own linguistic backgrounds. Interviews took five to thirty minutes per participant, with the length of time determined by anecdotes and stories provided to us freely by participants. We surveyed thirty-eight participants in PG who identified as Maya Mopan, Maya Kekchi, or Maya Mopan-Kekchi. The surveys were anonymous, though we kept track of demographic information such as age, sex, location of interview, native language, and occupation in order to keep our participant pool varied. All the Mayas who were surveyed were college students and provided us with substantial anecdotes to warrant a study of the place of Kriol, English, Spanish, and Mayan languages in their lives.

## Quantitative Data from the First Phase

Our participants from San Antonio Village were quite uniform with regard to socioeconomic status: 77 percent of our participants listed their father's occupation as "farmer," while 91 percent listed their mother's occupation as "housewife." All but two of our participants chose Mopan as their ethnic identification, while one identified as Mopan/East Indian and another as Kekchi/East Indian. The linguistic background of our participants ran parallel to their ethnic identifications: when asked which language they learned as a baby, 95 percent answered Mopan; 2.5 percent answered Kriol; 1.3 percent Mopan/East Indian; and 1.3 percent Kekchi/East Indian.[34] Nonetheless, 95 percent of participants stated that they spoke Mopan well or very well. Notably, the 5 percent who indicated their level of speaking proficiency as "not well" were not among those who indicated Kriol as their first language. These responses tell us less about proficiency itself and more about strong positive attitudes toward the language and target culture.[35] Older participants tended to indicate that they were bilingual (Mopan and English), while younger participants tended to indicate that they were multilingual and spoke several languages, including Mopan, Kekchi, English, Kriol, and Spanish, "very well."

Overt attitudes toward English and Mopan were predictable. In questions that asked if Kriol increased participants' chances of future success, there was no significant difference between younger and older speakers of Mopan. Likewise, there were no significant differences among younger and older speakers of Mopan who were asked if English increased their chances of a successful future. Similarly, there were no significant differences in responses to the questions relating to the implementation of Mopan instead of English in schools, from primary to tertiary levels. However, a significant difference between younger and older generations emerged when participants were asked if Mopan should replace Kriol in educational environments, with the older Mopan speakers far more likely to favor replacing Kriol in schools with Mopan.

Surprisingly, the surveys that contained questions about Kriol had an impact on how participants answered queries about Mopan identity, even when those queries made no mention of another ethnicity. For example, the statement "One cannot be considered Mopan if one does not speak Mopan" resulted in very different results depending on whether the second language foregrounded in the survey was English or Kriol.[36] In table 2 we see dramatically different results for this question depending on whether the comparison language was English (on the right) or Kriol (on the left). Essentially, younger and older participants agreed on the relationship between Mopan language and identity when the comparison language was English. On the other hand, there was much less agreement on this very same question between the younger and older groups when the language mentioned in other questions was Kriol. This suggests that with respect to Mopan, the Kriol language is rising in prestige or desirability among the younger generation. On the other hand, as table 2 suggests, the relationship between Mopan and English is much more static. We found similar dynamics across a range of other linguistic comparisons involving the three languages. In each comparison, the results show the elevated status of Kriol with respect to the Mopan language among younger participants.

In sum, there were no significant differences when the surveys led participants to think about the relationship between Mopan and English. However, surveys that led participants to reflect on Kriol highlighted covert attitudes toward the Mopan language that were quite different for younger

**TABLE 2. Results from questions on Mopan identity**

| MOPAN/ENGLISH SURVEYS | | MOPAN/KRIOL SURVEYS | |
|---|---|---|---|
| Ages 12–25 | Ages 26–73 | Ages 12–25 | Ages 26–73 |
| 3.34 | 3.44 | 2.47 | 3.74 |
| Diff: F = 0.6, P = .8 | | Diff: F = 31.79, P = <.0001 | |

and older generations. It was almost as if weighing the place of Kriol in Belize served as a catalyst for participants to also think of the Mopan language's place in Belize. We supplemented these quantitative results with ethnographic observations and informal, unrecorded interviews with young Mayans. The data suggest important presuppositions that can explain the implicit linguistic hierarchy that operates at an ideological level in Mayan communities in particular but also in Belize more broadly.

## Qualitative Data from the Second Phase

PG is currently one of the most ethnically diverse towns in Belize. The population is composed primarily of ethnic Creoles, Garinagu, Kekchi and Mopan Mayas, East Indians, and Chinese Belizeans in addition to immigrants from neighboring El Salvador, Guatemala, and Honduras. While most speak their respective languages with other members of their group, the language used to communicate across groups is Kriol. This is true as well of the Mennonites and Mayas who leave their villages in the surrounding areas and come to town on market days. Furthermore, we observed that it is also true of the young Mayas who take the buses from their villages into town to attend the University of Belize.

Unbeknownst to us when we designed the surveys, the questions that asked participants to identify the origins of recorded voices became a gateway topic to further conversation about Kriol in Belize. This became a game for many people we interviewed, including the Mayan students, who often completed our surveys in groups. These small groups of friends became spontaneous focus groups in which participants lightheartedly teased each other and openly showed their delight when they saw that there was even a bilingual English/Kriol dictionary that had recently been published.

On our surveys, Mayan students responded that Kriol was spoken with friends, at home, in Belize City, in Belize, and in PG. We observed a high degree of bilingualism during our conversations with them after they completed their surveys. They didn't speak Kriol to us, but it was certainly the language they used with their friends as they joked with and teased each other about who finished the quickest and who guessed the "correct" origin of the speakers. Outside the spontaneous "focus groups," we observed Kriol spoken between Mayan friends while they chatted outside their classrooms and on the grounds of the campus. Importantly, Kriol, like most other creoles, exists on a continuum that ranges from a very strong identification with Standard English (the acrolect form) to a form that diverges sharply from the lexifier language (the basilect form).[37] Although more research is needed in this area, our sense was that the young Mayas we observed in the test situation and ethnographic setting moved with ease in the mesolectal area on the Kriol continuum (table 3).[38] We surmise from their responses to our surveys and the linguistic behavior we observed that many young Mayas in Belize speak Kriol in informal situations and with each other both inside and outside their Mayan villages.

Kriol is a lingua franca spoken across Belize and has been the vernacular language of choice among the inhabitants since the colonial period. "Creolization" ran parallel to the independence movement since at least the 1960s but appears to have been strongest outside of Toledo.[39] The variety of languages spoken in Toledo illuminates the current appreciation for Kriol to a limited extent, since it is possible that coming into contact with speakers of Garifuna, Spanish, English, and different Mayan languages might encourage young speakers of Mopan and Kekchi to value multilingualism. Yet, we did not observe young Mayas speaking Garifuna or Spanish among themselves. Evidently, though other local languages are spoken in the same geographic space, only Kriol emerges as a language with added value.

This appears to be especially true for the newest generation of Belizean Mayas, those whose childhoods were spent post-1981 in the newly independent country. Unlike their parents, the vast majority of whom are farmers incorporated into subsistence agrarian economies or mothers who became housewives and relied on their husbands as breadwinners, they have gained access to higher education and a wider range of employment opportunities. Speaking Kriol provides the younger generation with a comparative advantage that is unmatched by any other language spoken in Toledo, and it is useful in postindependence Belize in a way that it was not for older Mayas when they were in their twenties. Educational success is important in Mayan families, just as serving the community is an important value that elders expect children to uphold. Both in our conversations with elders in San Antonio and in our conversations with younger Mayas, we heard stories

**TABLE 3.** Variational points along the Kriol continuum

| VARIATIONAL POINT | EXAMPLE |
|---|---|
| Basilect | **Di flai dehn mi-di bait laas nait.** |
| Mesolect | Di flies dem mi bitin las nite. |
| | Dem flayz de baytin las nait. |
| | Di flayz-dem de waz baytin. |
| Acrolect | Di mosquitos were bitin las nite. |
| Standard English | The mosquitos were biting last night. |

about young Mayas returning to the village to serve as teachers and cultural workers, occupying positions in nongovernmental organizations and cultural centers. Yet despite the pervasive belief across the country that Kriol is broken English, acrolectal and mesolectal Kriol provides young speakers of the language an option that can be beneficial, particularly if the positions they seek are in the emerging tourist industry in Toledo.

Kriol is an integral part of the daily lives of these young Mayas, while Spanish is useful in other areas of the country but less beneficial closer to home. In Toledo Kriol offers promises of upward mobility and sufficient models to attest to the connection between language and career advancement. Meanwhile, the Spanish speakers we encountered in Toledo were almost uniformly immigrants in low-wage occupations. The only monolingual Spanish speaker we met in San Antonio worked as a cook for a Mopan couple who owned a small business and she spoke English and Mopan with a degree of difficulty. In PG the Spanish speakers we met worked as vendors in shops along the downtown area. Like the newly arrived Chinese in PG, monolingual Spanish speakers live a world apart from Belizeans of all ethnic groups in Toledo.[40] We did not hear Spanish in the courtyard of the University of Belize—Toledo campus, none between the groups of Maya friends waiting outside of class, and none at all during our "focus groups" with Maya participants. The responses to our question about where it was appropriate to speak Spanish reflected this Spanishless context. "Spanish sites" were outside our participants' immediate circle of Mayan friends and beyond their Mayan and PG communities. This might be related to the status of Spanish observed elsewhere in Belize, especially Orange Walk District, where it is negatively perceived even among native speakers of Spanish.[41] We suspect further that Spanish in PG has an even higher stigmatization due to the proximity of Livingston, Guatemala at a distance of just 19.2 nautical miles, and the ongoing threat of annexation to the Guatemalan territory. Furthermore, as we have said elsewhere and as other scholars have stated before us, there remains a negative attitude toward immigration from other Central American nations to Belize.

## Discussion

Intergenerational transmission of a language is the most important indicator of language maintenance, since it is only when intergenerational transmission of a language ceases that it can be said that speakers have shifted to another language.[42] Kriol was the language that our two youngest Mopan participants spoke "as babies," while Kekchi continues to be the first language of many young people born in mixed Mopan-Kekchi households outside of San Antonio.[43] The appeal of another Mayan language is easily explained, as Mayan kinship networks remain paramount to individuals across generations. However, the appeal of Kriol is relatively new and quite striking, since it reveals a turn to a language that appears at first blush to be on equal footing as Mopan.[44]

Indeed, when it claimed independence in 1981, Belize stood as the most ethnically diverse nation in Central America, and its transition into an independent nation-state was predicated on bringing all its ethnic communities into the national fold. As Belize's first history textbook stated, "Our population is made up of Creoles, Mestizos, Garifuna, Maya, Mennonites; and people with Arab, East Indian, Chinese, European, British or other ancestry, and any number of combinations. Each group brings with it a rich heritage and helps to make our national culture."[45] Thirty-five years after independence, young Belizeans continue to be taught to appreciate the rich cultural and ethnic diversity of their nation through Belizean history lessons and cultural festivals celebrated annually throughout the country. Educational policy and positive attitudes, however, are not enough to secure linguistic vitality. As linguist Salikoko Mufwene argues, "We must understand more about the ecologies in which languages are spoken and identify which factors are hospitable or inhospitable to their 'healths,' so to speak."[46] In the case of Mopan, as our research indicates, language shift from Mopan to Kriol appears to be driven by economic factors.

The literature on language endangerment has long focused on language endangerment as a product of the core/periphery relationship between the Global North and Global South and the repercussions of this relationship on local languages outside of Europe and North America. We must nonetheless remember that "at a more local scale, almost every country has its cores and peripheries, and at the boundaries of almost all these, peripheral languages are on the retreat."[47] Our study concurs with the linguistic literature in the field that the driving force of this retreat is not personal or even interpersonal but macro- and microeconomic. After all, what determines the peripherality of a language is not the language itself but the differences in the economies and societies of the people who speak it.[48]

Seen in this light, language shift occurs when linguistic communities in contact "have radically different economic roles: not equal like two groups of forest foragers, and not complementary, like a coastal gatherer meeting an island hunter, but in which the prospects of one party are a superset of the prospects of the other."[49] Although derived from a binary understanding of languages in competition for prominence, the observation is useful for understanding the divergent economic roles of English, Kriol, and Mopan within a single context—in this case, Toledo. As English, Kriol, and Mopan assume different positions in the economic future of Belizean Mayas, the economic utility of these languages is reevaluated by their speakers. At the moment, there are significant socioeconomic incentives for speakers of Mopan to speak English. Speaking the official language opens doors to higher education and the professions, making it possible to achieve a higher standard of living than the previous generation. As the tourist industry moves into Toledo, young Mayans who have attended college are faced with the choice of remaining in their rural communities or leaving to pursue job opportunities in urban contexts like Punta Gorda and Belize City, where the lingua franca is Kriol and Standard English is expected of anyone interested in higher-level professions.

Although the Mopan/non-Mopan "boundary" was breached in the 1930s when the road between San Antonio and PG was first built, as late as 1976 contact between Mopan speakers and non-Mopan speakers was largely limited to economic transactions taking place during brief visits to PG.[50] With the outsiders' cultural influence at such a minimum, the process of linguistic creolization that had spread from Belize to other districts—Cayo, Orange Walk, and Corozal—had not occurred in Toledo until this present generation. Our results indicate that an important change in the ecology of the Mopan language is that Kriol has become a formidable competitor in the linguistic landscape. If Mopan-English bilingualism of the older generation was enough to ensure the economic stability of families and the larger Mopan community, young Mayans today feel that they need Kriol in their linguistic repertoire in order to ensure the economic viability of their kinship networks.

As linguistic research demonstrates, language maintenance depends on many factors, including a community's degree of isolation and/or urbanization; emigration and cyclical migration; the size of the linguistic community; formal and informal opportunities for speakers to use the language, including its use at home and in religious and educational institutions; and whether or not it is transmitted to future generations.[51] Isolation is clearly undesirable, particularly in light of the territorial issues that Mayan communities in Toledo continue to face and for which solidarity and support across ethnic lines are desirable. Yet, urbanization does not have to claim speakers of Mopan languages in the process. As has been observed in the case of Mayan communities in Guatemala, maintaining ties to the homeland, to elders, and to spiritual ceremonies is paramount in cultural and linguistic maintenance. In the case of the Mopan language in Belize, the foundation for that is already in place. Despite the challenges faced by Mayas in the country and the region at large, cultural pride is quite strong, as evidenced by *all* our participants, not just elders.

Languages, of course, hold neither birth nor death certificates. However, we can track the process of language atrophy—and the reverse process of language maintenance—as the number of places in which a language can be used diminishes or rises.[52] At present, the growth of urban centers responding to an increase in tourism on the Belizean Caribbean coast is drawing the youngest members of Mayan communities away from rural hometowns. It is a process that has reduced the number of instances and contexts where speakers of Mopan can still perceive their language as cultural capital. In order for that effect to be reversed, grassroots organizing for the preservation and revitalization of the Mopan language must involve a vision for increasing the number of sites and contexts in which Mopan languages can be spoken. The Tumul K'in Center of Learning in Toledo has made inroads in that respect.[53] By promoting a model of tourism that keeps control of the tourist projects in Mayan hands, it provides an economic incentive for young people to maintain cultural *and* linguistic identity.

## Acknowledgments

This article is part of a larger project that considers the impact of Belizean Kriol on local languages in Belize. It has received generous support from the University of Minnesota system through grants from the Global Programs and Strategy Alliance (GPS Alliance), the Grant-in-Aid Program (GIA), the Institute for Diversity, Equity and Advocacy (IDEA), and the Institute for Advanced Study (IAS). We are grateful to our colleagues for their feedback on previous drafts of this research, and we wish to especially thank our three reviewers at *NAIS* and the audiences at the Linguistic Society of America, the Southeastern Council for Linguistics, and the Chicago Linguistic Society for their thoughtful questions and critical insight. Finally, and most importantly, we honor the San Antonio Mopan community. We will forever be indebted to the two Mopan families who invited us into their homes and church and shared meals and stories with us during our stay in Toledo.

JENNIFER CAROLINA GÓMEZ MENJÍVAR is an associate professor in the Department of World Languages and Cultures at the University of Minnesota Duluth. She is the coauthor of *Tropical Tongues: Language Ideologies, Endangerment, and Minority Languages in Belize* (2018) and is coeditor of *Indigenous Interfaces: Spaces, Technology, and Social Networks in Mexico and Central America* (under contract with the University of Arizona Press).

WILLIAM SALMON is an associate professor in the Department of English, Linguistics, and Writing Studies at the University of Minnesota Duluth. He is the coauthor of *Tropical Tongues: Language Ideologies, Endangerment, and Minority Languages in Belize* (2018).

## Notes

1. In this article we write *Maya* when the word is used as a noun and add the *s* when a subgroup of people of the group are mentioned (e.g., the young Mayas we interviewed). We write *Mayan* when using the word as an adjective. Karl Sapper was one of the earliest ethnologists to conduct linguistic fieldwork on Mayan languages. Since Sapper's presentation of a Chol wordlist at the Congrès International des Américanistes, XVᵉ Session, held in 1907 in Quebec, a plethora of studies have been devoted to the grammar, phonology, and semantics of Mayan languages in Mexico and Guatemala. This body of linguistic literature includes the research conducted in the 1940s by Norman McQuown, in the 1960s by Terrence Kaufman, and, most recently, by Nora England. Since 1992 the discussion of language rights as an aspect of human rights has been a central concern for activists in Guatemala who have fought to protect the rights of Mayan communities in Guatemala. The movement has sought the "official recognition" of Mayan languages and promoted their usage as part of the process of constructing a "multiethnic, multilinguistic and multicultural society." See Ajb'ee Odilio Jiménez Sánchez, "Mayan Languages and the Mayan Movement in Guatemala," paper presented at the Latin American Studies Association, 1998, http://lasa.international.pitt.edu/lasa98/jimenezsanchez.pdf.

2. The Mayan literary movement in Mexico and Guatemala has provided a platform for writers like Humberto Ak'abal, Gaspar Pedro González, Marisol Ceh Moo, and Jorge Miguel Cocom Pech, among others, to advocate for Mayan languages. See Emilio del Valle Escalante's multilingual anthology of Mayan poetry, *U'k'ux Kaj, U'k'ux Ulew: Antologia de poesia maya guatemalteca contemporanea* (Pittsburgh, PA: IILI, 2010). For a critical assessment of the linguistic and cultural repercussions of the movement, see Arturo Arias, *Recuperando las huellas perdidas: El surgimiento de narrativas indígenas contemporáneas en Abya Yala* (Guatemala: Editorial Cultura, 2016). A comparative analysis of the Mayan and Zapotec literary and linguistic renaissances can be found in Gloria Chacón, *Indigenous Cosmolectics: Kawab'awil and the Making of Maya and Zapotec Literatures* (Chapel Hill: University of North Carolina Press, 2018).

3. See, for example, the outstanding accounts of Mayan experience in the United States in James Loucky and Marilyn Moors, *The Maya Diaspora: Guatemalan Roots, New American Lives* (Philadelphia: Temple University Press, 2000); Wayne A. Cornelius, David Scott Fitzgerald, and Pedro Lewin Fischer, *Mayan Journeys: New Migration from Yucatán to the United States* (Boulder, CO: Lynne River Publishers, 2007); and Ann L. Sittig and Martha Florinda González, *The Mayans among Us: Migrant Women and Meatpacking on the Great Plains* (Lincoln: University of Nebraska Press, 2016).

4. See Salikoko Mufwene, *The Ecology of Language Evolution* (Cambridge: Cambridge University Press, 2001), as well as his "What Have Pride and Prestige Got to Do with It?," in *When Languages Collide* (Columbus: Ohio State University Press, 2003), 324–46.

5. See Osmer Balam, "Overt Language Attitudes and Linguistic Identities

among Multilingual Speakers in Northern Belize," *Studies in Hispanic and Luso-phone Linguistics* 6, no. 2 (2013): 247–77; Osmer Balam and Ana Prada Pérez, "Attitudes towards Spanish and Code-Switching in Belize: Stigmatization and Innovation in the Spanish Classroom," *Journal of Language, Identity and Education* 16 (2017): 17–31; and Karl Steven Seitz, "Migration, Demographic Change, and the Enigma of Identity in Belize" (master's thesis, Arizona State University, 2005).

6. The Yucatecan branch is believed to have begun diversifying in AD 950, and Mopan was the first branch of the tree. See Terrence Kaufman, *Proyecto de alfabetos y ortografías para escribir las lenguas mayences* (Guatemala: Proyecto Lingüístico Francisco Marroquín, 1976); and Charles Andrew Hofling, *Diccionario Maya Mopan—Español—Inglés* (Salt Lake City: University of Utah Press, 2012).

7. See "Maya, Mopán," https://www.ethnologue.com/language/mop.

8. The Itzá language status is 8b (nearly extinct). According to Hofling (https://www.ethnologue.com/language/mop), the Itzá in Guatemala have retained ethnic identity, though there were sixty bilingual nonfluent speakers in 1991. Also according to Hofling, the Itzá in Belize now speak Spanish. Charged with overseeing the implementation of the 2003 Law of Mayan Languages, one of the many responsibilities of the ALMG is overseeing funds earmarked for rescuing Mayan languages in danger of extinction. As the ALMG makes clear, not all Mayan languages in Guatemala face the same predicament as Mopan and Itzá (Mam, Kiché, Kaqchikel, and Q'eqchi', for example, are considered the strongest among the twenty-two Mayan languages spoken in the country). See the online radio interview with Jesús Dionicio Felipe, former president of the ALMG: https://emisorasunidas.com/noticias/nacionales/advierten-que-idiomas-mayas-itza-mopan-estan-riesgo-desaparecer/.

9. For more on Spanish contact—induced language change and language shift, see Carol Klee and Andrew Lynch's excellent study *El español en contacto con otras lenguas* (Washington, DC: Georgetown University Press, 2009); and Silvina Montrul, *El bilingüismo en el mundo hispanohablante* (New York: Wiley Blackwell, 2012).

10. While both "Creole" and "Kriol" are used in Belize to refer to the language, we use the spelling adopted by the Kriol language rights movement in this study.

11. In order to secure its position as a future independent nation-state, Belize fortified the adjacency line (which is now the current geopolitical border between the countries) with UN Peacekeepers, maintained its alliance to England, and strengthened its economic and political relationship to the United States. See Assad Shoman, *Thirteen Chapters of a History of Belize* (Belize City: Angelus Press, 1995).

12. Although the spelling Q'eqchi' is common in Guatemala, both Kekchi and Ketchi are used by Mayans in Belize. We employ Kekchi in this article because it was the most prevalent in our surveys. For the sake of clarity, we refer hereafter to Toledo District as simply Toledo.

13. Yuki Tanaka, "Exploring a Heritage Language: Linguistic Ideologies, Identity

and Revitalization of Belizean Mopan," *Proceedings of STILLA*, http://kellogg
.nd.edu/projects/quechua/STLILLA/proceedings.shtml.

14. The map of the disputed territory appeared in an article entitled
"Reclamo territorial" in the January 22, 2013, issue of the Guatemalan newspaper *La Prensa Libre*. The bullet points highlight "differences" between
Belize and the rest of Central America to the Guatemalan readership: "Guatemala claims 12,272 km$^2$ of Belize's territory and about a hundred islands;
Guatemala has claimed this territory for more than 150 years; Belize has a
monarchic system with a Prime Minister; agriculture is the main activity, followed by fishing, construction, transport, and tourism; Belize has 0.74 percent of Central America's population with some 311,000 inhabitants; Belize's
economy is the smallest of the seven countries in the isthmus; and Belize
is Anglophone, but many of its inhabitants speak Kriol. The currency is the
Belize dollar" (translation ours).

15. https://issuu.com/prensalibregt/docs/plmt23012013.

16. See, for example, Greg Gandin, *The Blood of Guatemala: A History of Race
and Nation* (Durham, NC: Duke University Press, 2000) and the many sources
therein.

17. Other important socioeconomic indicators between the two regions
include the following: 93 percent of the inhabitants in Belize City District had
electricity from a public source, compared to 56 percent in Toledo. The proportion of households using a flush toilet was highest in Belize City District (92 percent) and lowest in Toledo (28 percent), and the proportion of households using
a pit latrine was lowest in Belize City District (5 percent) and highest in Toledo
(57 percent). Lastly, 84 percent of the homes in Belize City District had a fixed
bath or shower in the home, compared to 23 percent of the homes in Toledo.

18. The goals of such initiatives over the course of the last decades have
been to preserve and revitalize cultural traditions while ensuring that the
Mayan villages benefit from tourist initiatives instead of turning profit over to
foreign or central government interests. For more on one of the earliest tourist development projects in Toledo, the Maya Village Indigenous Experience, see
Michael K. Steinberg, "Tourism Development and Indigenous People: The Maya
Experience in Southern Belize," *Focus* 44, no. 2 (1994): 17–20. For a project in
operation today, see "Eco-tourism: Tumul K'in Center for Learning," http://
www.tumulkinbelize.org/eco_tourism.html.

19. For more on the demographic effects of emigration and immigration, see
Shoman, *Thirteen Chapters*.

20. See William Salmon and Jennifer Gómez Menjívar, "Language Variation
and Dimensions of Prestige in Belizean Kriol," *Journal of Pidgin and Creole Languages* 31, no. 2 (2016): 316–60.

21. See, respectively, Balam, "Overt Language Attitudes"; Balam and Prada
Pérez, "Attitudes towards Spanish"; and Salmon and Gómez Menjívar, "Language Variation."

22. Statistical Institute of Belize, *2010 Belize Population and Housing Census Report*, 82–83, http://www.statisticsbelize.org.bz/dms2ouc/dynamicdata
/docs/20110505004542_2.pdf.

23. Yuki Tanaka-McFarlane, "Re-examining the Role of Language Documentation as a Medium in Relation to Language Renewal Efforts, 'Purity' Ideologies and Affects among Belizean Mopan Speakers," *Texas Linguistics Forum* 58 (2015): 139—51.

24. See also Christopher Moseley, *Atlas of the World's Languages in Danger* (Paris: UNESCO, 2010); and Tanaka, "Exploring a Heritage Language." Tangential discussion of this concern also arises in Salmon and Gómez Menjívar, "Language Variation."

25. See Lenore Grenoble, "Endangered Languages," in *Concise Encyclopedia of Languages of the World,* ed. E. K. Brown and Sarah Ogilvie (Oxford: Elsevier Ltd., 2009).

26. The research on this topic is immense. For a case study on the Anglophone Caribbean similar to the one at hand, see Janice L. Haynes, "Rural and Urban Groups in Barbados and Guyana: Language Attitudes and Behaviors," *International Journal of Society and Language* 34 (1982): 67—82; and for a case in a Hispanophone context, see Daniela Salcedo, "Defining Andeanness away from the Andes: Language Attitudes and Linguistic Ideologies in Lima, Peru" (PhD diss., Ohio State University, 2013).

27. While the linguistics literature on the subject is, once again, quite extensive, see Donna M. Bonner, "Garifuna Children's Language Shame: Ethnic Stereotypes, National Affiliation, and Transnational Immigration as Factors in Language Choice in Southern Belize," *Language in Society* 30 (2001): 81—96 for a comparable case in Belize; and see Ana Celia Zentella, "Dime con Quién Hablas y Te Diré Quién Eres: Linguistic (In)security and Latina/o Unity," in *The Blackwell Companion to Latina/o Studies, ed. Juan Flores and Renato Rosaldo* (Malden, MA: Blackwell, 2007) for a case involving two European languages.

28. See Shoman, *Thirteen Chapters*, 88—89.

29. Other Mopan villages in Belize have large percentages of Kekchi-speaking and Spanish-speaking inhabitants, as intermarriages have become increasingly common. See Tanaka, "Exploring a Heritage Language"; Tanaka-McFarlane, "Re-examining the Role."

30. We designed the surveys following Federica Guerini, "Multilingualism and Language Attitudes in Ghana: A Preliminary Survey," *Ethnorema* 4 (2008): 1—33.

31. See James Gregory, "The Modification of the Inter-ethnic Boundary in Belize," *American Ethnologist* 3, no. 4 (1976): 683—708.

32. This larger study involved 141 participants and is reported in extensive detail in Salmon and Gómez Menjívar, "Language Variation."

33. See Robert Cooper, "Introduction to Language Attitudes II," *International Journal of the Sociology of Language* 6 (1975): 5—9; Ingrid Huygens and Graham Vaughn, "Language Attitudes, Ethnicity, and Social Class in New Zealand," *Journal of Multilingual and Multicultural Development* 4 (1983): 207—23; and Tore Kristiansen, "Attitudes, Ideology, and Awareness," in *The SAGE Handbook of Sociolinguistics,* ed. Ruth Wodak, Barbara Johnstone, and Paul E. Kerswill (Los Angeles: SAGE, 2011), 265—78.

34. "East Indian" is not a language. We interpret our participants' decision

to state this on the survey as pride in being a descendant of the cultural groups that *both* of his/her parents represent.

35. Maya Ravindranath states in her study on Garifuna, an Afro-indigenous language spoken in Belize: "Instead of taking interviewees' responses to be indicative of their language dominance, which is difficult for anyone to judge even of themselves, I consider their response to this question to be indicative of their language attitudes, following McCarty et al. (2006:38), who recognize 'that self-assessments of language proficiency are complex and problematic [but that] they are nonetheless important indicators of local perceptions of language use and vitality that have implications for language choices.'" See Ravindranath, "Language Shift and the Speech Community: Sociolinguistic Change in a Garifuna Community in Belize" (PhD diss., University of Pennsylvania, 2009).

36. For a discussion of experimental context effects on language attitude test results in general, see Peter Garrett, *Attitudes to Language* (Cambridge: Cambridge University Press, 2010). For a discussion of experimental context effects on attitudes in coastal Belize, see our "Setting and Language Attitudes in a Creole Context," forthcoming in *Applied Linguistics*.

37. See Ken Decker, *The Song of Kriol: A Grammar of the Kriol Language of Belize* (Belmopan, Belize: National Kriol Council, House of Culture, 2005), following Colville Young, "Belize Creole: A Study of the Creolized English Spoken in the City of Belize in Its Cultural and Social Setting" (PhD diss., University of York, 1973); and Geneviève Escure, "Decreolization in a Creole Continuum: Belize," in *Historicity and Variation in Creole Studies,* ed. Arnold R. Highfield (Ann Arbor, MI: Karoma, 1981), 27–49.

38. Ibid.

39. We thank our anonymous reviewers for bringing to our attention Edna Louise Koenig's "Ethnicity and Language in Corozal District, Belize: An Analysis of Code-Switching"(PhD diss., University of Texas at Austin, 1975); and Thomas Brockmann's "Language, Communication and Ethnicity in British Honduras," in *Sociolinguistic Studies in Language Contact: Methods and Cases*, ed. William Mackey (The Hague: Mouton Publishers, 1979), 161–80, both of which explore this phenomenon outside the Toledo District before the country's independence.

40. While the Chinese presence in Belize has not been as well documented as that of other ethnic groups in the country, Belizeans make a distinction between two major waves of Chinese immigration (nineteenth and twenty-first centuries). For more on the subject, see Anne Sutherland, *The Making of Belize: Globalization at the Margins* (South Hadley, MA: Bergin and Garvey, 1998); and St. John Robinson, "The Chinese of Central America: Diverse Beginnings, Common Achievements," *Journal of Chinese Overseas* 5, no. 1 (2009): 91–114.

41. See Balam and Prada Pérez, "Attitudes towards Spanish," who examined the attitudinal data and found a high regard for Kriol among native Spanish-speaking teachers and adolescents.

42. See Joshua Fishman's discussion in *Reversing Language Shift: Theoretical and Empirical Foundations of Assistance to Threatened Languages* (Bristol: Multilingual Matters, 1991).

43. Longitudinal research is needed in order to determine if the youngest generation will transmit Mopan to their children and grandchildren.

44. Belizean education policy in the *Handbook of Policies and Procedures for School Services* reads that "first languages are important vehicles for [children's] transition from home to school." Quoted in Balam and Prada Pérez, "Attitudes towards Spanish," 19.

45. *The Nation We Are Making*, the textbook that was used after Belizean independence to teach the new generations about their history, began with descriptions of a multicultural nation with a strong tolerance for diversity. Please see Jessica Nembhard, *The Nation We Are Making: A Junior History of Belize* (Belize: Ministry of Education, 1990).

46. See Mufwene, "What Have Pride," 333.

47. See Daniel Nettle and Suzanne Romaine, *Vanishing Voices: The Extinction of the World's Languages* (Oxford: Oxford University Press, 2000).

48. For further reading on how these factors have impacted the languages of Belize, see Jennifer Gómez Menjívar and William Salmon, *Tropical Tongues: Language Ideologies, Endangerment and Minority Languages in Belize* (Chapel Hill, NC: Institute for the Study of the Americas, 2018).

49. Nettle and Romaine, *Vanishing Voices*, 130.

50. See James Gregory's excellent account of preindependence San Antonio in his "The Modification of an Interethnic Boundary."

51. See Montrul, *El bilingüismo*.

52. See Mufwene, "How Languages Die," in *Combat pour les langues du monde/ Fighting for the World's Languages: Hommage à Claude Hagege*, ed. Jocelyne Fernandez-Vest (Paris: L'Harmattan, 2006), 377–388.

53. For more on the groundbreaking work done by this grassroots organization, including its high school and program in professional tourism, see http://www.tumulkinbelize.org/.

ROSE MIRON

# Fighting for the Tribal Bible:
# Mohican Politics of
# Self-Representation
# in Public History

**IN 1951** Jim and Grace Davids traveled from Wisconsin to the East Coast of the United States to see the homelands of their ancestors. Jim was an enrolled member of the Stockbridge-Munsee Band of Mohicans,[1] while Grace was from the nearby Oneida reservation.[2] On their trip, they stopped in Stockbridge, Massachusetts, where Jim's ancestors, the Mohicans, lived for twenty-five years in the eighteenth century as a part of the Stockbridge mission settlement, led by the Reverend John Sergeant.[3] Today, the Mission House, where Sergeant and his family lived from 1734 to 1749, still stands and is open daily for tours.

While visiting the museum, Jim and Grace were surprised to recognize a two-hundred-year-old two-volume Bible set and a four-piece pewter Communion set that had previously been held on the Mohican reservation in Wisconsin.[4] Although it had been a while since Jim and Grace had seen the objects in person, it was not until they traveled to Stockbridge that they even realized the objects were missing from the reservation. Most tribal members had heard about the Bible and Communion set from elders, but few had seen them in person. Most assumed they were in a safe place on or near the reservation but would not have guessed that they had been taken from central Wisconsin. Beyond their initial shock that the Bible and Communion set were no longer on the reservation, tribal members still wondered: How had the items ended up in Stockbridge, and what could the Mohicans do to get them back?[5]

In the fifty-five years following Jim and Grace's discovery of the items, the Mohicans began to strategize and then formally asked the Mission House Museum to return the Bible and Communion set to the Mohican people. What started as a request, however, would become nothing short of an all-out battle for possession and control. While a word like "battle" may seem extreme in regard to retrieving objects, I use this and similar terms because the immense struggle the Mohicans engaged in was multipronged, required extensive labor and resources, and took more than three decades following their formal request. What follows is the story of the Mohicans' fight to retrieve their Bible and Communion set, make these items accessible to tribal members, and represent themselves and their histories on their own terms and in their own space.

While a Bible and Communion set may not immediately be conceived as sacred or cultural Indian objects, these items and their place on the Mohican reservation were and continue to be a critical issue for the Mohican people. Material culture theory suggests that groups of people can have myriad attachments to objects based on the groups' cultural background, status, and education.[6] In that sense, different individual Mohicans perceive the Bible and Communion set as important for different reasons. While some find their importance chiefly related to Christianity, for others, they are important because they connect the Mohicans to a specific historical time period. As tribal leader Dorothy Davids noted, "The Bible links the old people to us today. . . . A lot of sweat and spirit is there. . . . The Bible is a chance to bring us together."[7] Given the sacredness of these items, the desire to return them to the Mohican reservation and represent their history in the Mohican tribal museum was paramount. As Amy Lonetree argues, "Objects in museums are living entities. . . . Every engagement with objects in museum cases or collection rooms should begin with this core recognition. We are not just looking at interesting pieces. In the presence of objects from the past, we are privileged to stand as witnesses to living entities."[8] The importance of living entities such as these mandates that American Indian nations should have the right not only to possess these objects but also to choose how and if they are displayed in museums.

Since European American settlers arrived in North America, the rights of Indigenous nations to possess and represent their own sacred items has been mired in paternalism. White collectors who stole objects assumed that American Indians would disappear and items would thus be lost, and, as we will see in the story to come, many museums have repeatedly refused to return items based on racist anxieties that tribes could not care for them. The passage of the Native American Graves Protection and Repatriation Act (NAGPRA) in 1990 gave tribes significantly more authority to retrieve sacred items, but as I discuss later in the article, the law still relegates significant power to museums and other institutions that receive federal funding. As a result of these paternalistic assumptions about who has the right and the ability to house and represent Indigenous items, the fights for these objects required extensive labor, unparalleled determination, and grit. The Mohicans' fight for their Bible and Communion set illustrates the significant barriers many tribes faced both before and after NAGPRA was passed, as well as the significant labor these battles for possession still require.

In this article, I use the Stockbridge-Munsee Mohicans' fight for their historical items to examine the central place of self-representation in Native political action.[9] In this context, I understand self-representation to describe the act of Mohican peoples representing their own history by possessing their own historical and cultural objects. Native histories have long been represented by non-Native peoples in non-Native spaces without consent, collaboration, or consultation with Native peoples themselves. The act of working to shift the representation of Native histories back to Native peoples thus resists the ongoing notion that Native histories and objects are open to public presentation and consumption without consent from Native peoples.

By intervening in this standard practice, the Mohicans also importantly resist the myths perpetuated by these representations. For the Mohicans, the common practice of non-Native museums housing and displaying Native items without consent and collaboration is especially detrimental because of the myths presented in James Fenimore Cooper's *The Last of the Mohicans*.[10] As a result of the novel and countless other popular culture representations that followed, it does not take much for non-Native museumgoers to recognize the Mohican name on an object label, see no reference to living Mohicans, and thus assume the object is a relic of a now-dead culture. Fighting for their Bible and Communion set enables the Mohicans to resist the common notion of their disappearance by giving them a platform to say that they are still here and have a right to tell their own stories and represent their own histories. Thus, I argue that the Mohican fight to retrieve their Bible and Communion set exemplifies the important place of self-representation in Native political action and resistance.

As a non-Mohican and non-Native person, I examine Mohican resistance and self-representation without claiming to participate in Mohican self-representation myself. Instead, I center Mohican voices by primarily consulting and citing sources created by the tribe and tribal members and focusing on *their* actions in this story. I have worked closely with the Mohican Nation since 2011, and I received consent from the Mohican Historical Committee and the Tribal Council before publishing this piece. By collaborating with and receiving consent from the tribe to conduct and publish this research, I seek to contribute to and stress the importance of ethical research practices that center and privilege Indigenous voices and perspectives.

## A Case of Missing Objects: History of the Bible and Communion Set

The Stockbridge-Munsee Band of Mohicans is a federally recognized American Indian Nation in central Wisconsin. Before European contact, their homelands covered both sides the Mahicannituck (Hudson) River and included land in what are now the states of New York, Vermont, Massachusetts, and Connecticut.[11] As Lisa Brooks notes, Mohican homelands were part of an extensive Indigenous network of diplomacy and waterways, even after Europeans arrived on the Algonquian coast.[12] Yet as the European presence in Algonquian and Iroquois homelands grew, the Mohicans, like many other Indigenous peoples, were forced to move west. As a result of seven different removals between 1734 and 1936,[13] the Mohicans now live on their reservation in the townships of Bartelme and Red Springs in Shawano County, Wisconsin, which lies on the southern border of the Menominee Indian Reservation.[14]

One of the first significant changes in Mohican lifeways occurred when the Mohicans agreed to the establishment of a Christian mission in their village Wnahktukuk in 1735, what Brooks calls "an experiment in cooperative

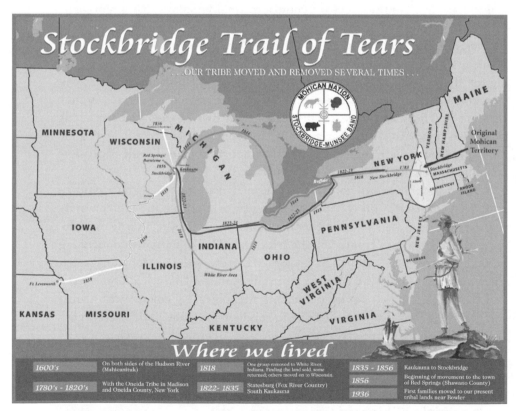

**FIGURE 1.** A historical poster produced by the Stockbridge-Munsee Mohican Nation to depict the tribe's numerous removals between their ancestral homelands and current reservation in central Wisconsin. Poster courtesy of the Arvid E. Miller Library-Museum.

living between Natives and colonists."[15] As Linford D. Fisher argues, Indian nations had numerous reasons for accepting missionization projects, and it is imperative that we do not overlook the "broader social and cultural contexts" of these decisions.[16] For the Mohicans, accepting a mission at Wnahktukuk was primarily influenced by the desire for Mohican children to learn to read and write in English.[17] The mission was led by John Sergeant, who renamed the village Stockbridge. As more tribes began to join the Mohicans here, it became not only a mission but also a significant meeting place that fostered ongoing diplomatic relationships between the Mohicans, the English, the Mohawks, and the Abenakis.[18] In other words, the mission at Stockbridge played a significant role in Mohican history, and this place remains important to the Mohicans not only as their Wnahktukuk but also as a place that fostered literacy, diplomatic relations, and peace in the Housatonic River Valley.[19]

It was also at Stockbridge that the Mohicans acquired the gold-lettered two-volume Bible set. (The Communion set was not given at the same time; the tribe acquired it when they lived in upstate New York in the early 1800s.)[20] In 1745 Francis Ayscough, the chaplain or spiritual advisor to the Prince of Wales, heard of the mission at Stockbridge and was captivated. He decided to give the congregation of Indians the two-volume Bible set, which was the same edition of the Bible the Prince would use at his coronation.[21] Ayscough inscribed the first volume with instructions on the care of the Bible:

> To the used [sic] of the Congregation of Indians, at or near Houstonnoc in a vast wilderness part of New England; who are at present, under the Voluntary Care and Instruction of the Learned and Religious Dr. John Sergeant, and is to remain in the use of the Successors of those Indians, from generation to Generation; as a testimony of the said Doctor's Great Regard for the Salvation of their souls
> London. 31st day of December, 1745[22]

The Mohicans cherished the Bible as both a sacred religious item and a treasured gift. The Mohicans and other Algonquians often see gift giving as a gesture of alliance and even a way of binding relationships.[23] Though there is no official agreement suggested in the inscription of the Bible, Ayscough likely meant the gift as a gesture of goodwill, and since the gift was given in the midst of King George's War, it was also potentially a subtle gesture of peace and alliance. Likewise, as Kevin McBride argues, Native communities often perceived Bibles as powerful objects, even though they were outside their own spiritual traditions.[24] In the context of missionization and as a historical object, the Bible was and continues to be important to the Mohicans for myriad reasons.

**FIGURE 2.** The two-volume Bible and four-piece pewter Communion set. Photograph courtesy of the Arvid E. Miller Library-Museum.

As the Mohicans were forced to move west beyond what is now New York beginning in the early 1800s, they carried their Bible and Communion set with them in an oak chest they built and kept the Bible and Communion set on the reservation until the mid-twentieth century. Many of the Mohicans maintained their Christian traditions throughout these removals, and according to tribal member Elaine M. Jacobi, the Bible and Communion set were "preserved, and always placed on the altar wherever they [the Mohicans] settled in a new home and a new church."[25] However, in the early twentieth century, numerous non-Native churches and museums began to inquire about how they could acquire the items. As one newspaper noted, "An effort has been made to place the volume in a library without success," and "the Indians have turned down offers [to sell the Bible] of several thousand dollars on several occasions."[26] Still, the tribe and especially Jamison Quinney, the tribal leader who was charged with caring for the items, worked to keep the Bible within the tribe.[27] In spite of their efforts, the Mohicans were not able to prevent their Bible and Communion set from being stolen by insidious white collectors, and the story that follows reveals the paternalistic assumptions that motivated this theft.

In March 1929 Jamison Quinney, the tribal leader responsible for caring for the items, passed away, leaving the Bible and Communion set under the care of his wife, Ella Quinney, in their home on the reservation.[28] It was at this time that a local religious leader, Reverend Frederick G. Westfall, illegally entered the Quinney home while Ella was away and seized the Bible and Communion set.[29] Westfall was the leader of the John Sergeant Memorial Church, a congregation located near the Mohican reservation in Wisconsin. Though it was named after the same missionary who led the Mohicans in Stockbridge, Massachusetts, it was not founded by the tribe, and sources suggest the church's congregation was largely non-Indian.[30] Still, since there were still a few tribal members who belonged to the church, and since the items in question were Christian, Westfall paternalistically assumed that the safest and most logical place for them would be his congregation.

The year 1929 was also when Reverend Westfall began corresponding with three women on the East Coast, each of whom is crucial to understanding the ultimate sale of the Bible and Communion set. In October 1929 Revered Westfall replied to a letter from a Virginia Baughman, a resident of Berkshire, Massachusetts, who was interested in learning more about the Mohicans.[31] Westfall indicated that the Mohicans did indeed have the historic Bible set she asked about and that he had placed it, along with a pewter Communion set, in a bank vault in Shawano, Wisconsin, about thirty miles east of the Mohican reservation.[32] Within weeks of Baughman's letter, Westfall also received a letter from a Mabel Choate, an acquaintance of Baughman's who was assembling a museum about Stockbridge, Massachusetts, and was interested in historical items related to the Mohicans and Sergeant.[33] Over the next six months, Choate continued to correspond with Westfall and worked to acquire Mohican items for her museum. She even paid Ruth Gaines, who was employed by the Heye Foundation's Museum of the American Indian in New York City, to travel to Wisconsin in November 1929 to see what other items the Mohicans might be willing to sell. Gaines also corresponded with Westfall during this time and bought items on behalf of Choate and the Museum of the American Indian. Between November 1929 and May 1930 Choate and Gaines purchased photographs of the Bible and Communion set, papers from a Mohican tribal member, a book that included "Cherokee characters," a beaded necklace, baskets, photographs and daguerreotypes of tribal members, two kettles, a cornucopia, and deerskin leggings. They also purchased a bowl, a pipe, a cane, and a brass bell that all belonged to tribal leader John W. Quinney. Some of these objects ended up in the Mission House Museum, while others went to the Museum of the American Indian in New York, where they remain to this day.

Both Gaines and Choate corresponded with Westfall during this period and indeed used his perceived influence with the Mohicans in their quest to collect items.[34] In one letter Gaines noted that "Mr. Westfall told me that the Indians would believe anything he told them, and do as he told them. If so, he can tell them that we aim to be the living point of contact between the histories of our people; that we are in a sense the logical guardians of your Indian treasures."[35] In that sense, Westfall, Gaines, and Choate erroneously presumed that Indians were disappearing and unable to care for their historical items and that it was white collectors' duties to preserve Indian history, or to become "the living point of contact" between Indians and non-Indians in public history spaces.

Throughout these six months, Choate never forgot about the items she hoped would become the crown jewel of her collection, the Bible and Communion set. As Westfall's letters to her grew increasingly ominous in early 1930, suggesting that it was only a matter of time before the tribe and the John Sergeant congregation would no longer exist, Choate seized the opportunity and offered to buy both the Bible and Communion set for $1,000.[36] Throughout her correspondence with Westfall, Gaines, and Baughman in 1929 and 1930, Choate was subtle but clear throughout that her ultimate goal was to purchase the Bible and Communion set. In her letters, she expressed her concern that other dealers might persuade the Indians to sell the items and that she would not want them to be forced to do so out of a need for money. Yet, she had no hesitation about indicating that "naturally, I should like to be the purchaser if the things are going to be sold, and perhaps they might give me first chance."[37]

When Westfall stole the Bible and Communion set from the Quinney home in 1929, he claimed possession of these items for the church upon Quinney's death without seeking permission or a legal title from the Mohican Nation.[38] Aside from the few individual tribal members who were still part of the congregation at this time, Westfall did not consult the tribe before selling the Bible and Communion set, meaning the majority of the Stockbridge-Munsee people were not aware of the sale of the items.[39] Instead, they likely assumed they were still in the Quinney home or the bank vault in Shawano.[40] Astoundingly, Westfall failed to mention that he had not consulted the tribe in his letters to Choate and Gaines and even admitted in a letter to Gaines that he had misrepresented the Mohicans' interest in having their items sold to Choate: "I am afraid that my first impression that the Stockbridge Indians were to have some sort of tribal interest in her [Choate's] collection at Stockbridge was erroneous. But however that may be, I am personally more interested in it."[41] In that sense, Westfall never had a legal title or permission from the owners of the items, nor does it seem the Mohicans were at all interested in parting with the Bible and Communion set, given their lack of interest in Choate's museum and the previously described devotion to the items. Ultimately, when Westfall wrote the deed of sale in May 1930, he was clear that the church owned the items and the church received the payment, and he admitted in a letter to Choate that he was not sure "if such an exchange is legal."[42] Westfall did what was in his own interest, and the sale of the Bible and Communion set to Choate was illegal, given its lack of legal title.

Westfall's prediction that the church would cease to exist did, in fact, materialize shortly after the sale, and Westfall left Wisconsin for Michigan City, Indiana, days after finalizing the sale of the items. However, his assumption that the tribe would also cease to exist was utterly false. In 1948 Choate gifted the Bible and Communion set to the Trustees of Reservations,[43] a preservation agency in Massachusetts that was taking over control of the Mission House and the objects in it.[44] The Trustees, founded in 1891, is the nation's oldest regional nonprofit conservation organization and works to preserve and protect the natural and historical resources of Massachusetts, including the Bible and Communion set.[45] It was not until 1951 that the Mohicans discovered that the Bible and Communion set were no longer in their possession, twenty-one years after Westfall sold the items to Choate.[46]

## Fighting for the Bible: Resistance, Repatriation, and Self-Representation

The tribe began to officially petition for the return of their Bible and Communion set in 1975. While twenty-four years may seem like a long time to wait before engaging in a formal request, the Mohicans' appeal for their Bible and Communion set was directly connected to a larger project the tribe had started in 1974, the Arvid E. Miller Library-Museum (hereafter referred to as AEM Library-Museum).[47] The creation of the museum and archive was the first major project within a larger effort led by the newly formed Mohican Historical Committee, which sought to gather Mohican history, make historical materials more accessible to tribal members on the reservation, and, more broadly, shift the right to represent Mohican materials and histories back to the Mohicans themselves. Recovering the Bible and Communion set was important because these items provided a direct link to a significant time period in Mohican history, and many Mohicans still understood them as sacred religious items.[48] However, these objects were also important because their placement in the Mohican tribal museum was a crucial aspect of the tribe's larger self-representation goals.[49]

The tribe's initial request for the Bible and Communion set in 1975 was denied. In the summer of 1981 they again pursued the subject, this time citing extensive historical evidence that proved the items were rightfully theirs.[50] The Trustees of Reservations of Stockbridge, Massachusetts, the preservation agency Choate gave the Bible to, again refused, reaffirming their legal responsibility to Choate. However, they agreed to consider the evidence the Mohicans mentioned.[51] Unfortunately, the Trustees' alleged interest in new evidence and willingness to find a solution were soon found to be insincere. Beginning in 1981, the Mohicans continually pressed the Trustees to meet in person, offering to present the evidence the Trustees claimed they were willing to consider. Unfortunately, the Trustees largely ignored this request and often refused to communicate with the tribe directly, opting to primarily contact the tribe's lawyer instead.

By October 1981 the tribe had become frustrated and decided to simultaneously both seek legal counsel and pursue an extensive public campaign, which materialized in a pamphlet titled "Documents Relating to the Recovery of the Stockbridge Bible by the Stockbridge Indians."[52] The pamphlet, printed in November 1981, was circulated nationwide through the help of the Indian Information Project and other Mohican contacts.[53] A brief history of the Bible and Communion set accompanied the pamphlet, as did an explanation of the Indian Religious Freedom Act, which the Mohicans used to argue that their Bible and Communion set were integral in their right to religious freedom. Though the importance of the Bible has always been framed through its connection to a specific place and time in Mohican history, many of the Mohicans are Christian, so these items were also sacred religious objects. The pamphlet also included a final paragraph asking that readers write to the Trustees and urge them to return the Bible and Communion set to the Mohicans.[54]

This letter-writing campaign continued throughout the Mohicans' fight for the items, and hundreds of letters from across the United States were sent to the Trustees, demanding that they return both the Bible and the Communion set to the Mohican people.[55] Newspapers and TV stations began calling the Mohican Historical Committee for more information, and the tribe continued to reach out to countless media sources to raise awareness for their cause. As a whole, the massive public campaign drew national attention to this important issue. As Dorothy Davids, a leader in the fight for the items noted, the Mohicans "hope[d] the Trustees of Reservations [would] 'get the message' and agree to negotiate directly with the Stockbridge Indian representatives."[56]

Instead, the Trustees mostly remained silent throughout 1981 and 1982. In spite of the tribe's multiple requests that a delegation of Mohicans meet with the Trustees directly, the Trustees continually ignored the request to meet in person, opted to only communicate with the tribe's lawyer, and insisted the Mohicans send *copies* of the historical evidence the Mohicans had mentioned.[57] Since the Mohicans had already agreed to provide a description of evidence, they were quite hesitant to send copies of this evidence, fearing that if they did so, the Trustees would ignore their request to meet in person altogether. As Davids argued in a letter to the tribe's lawyer regarding this, "We are not in litigation; we have asked to present evidence in person; the evidence is a result of our research; we have received little evidence that the Trustees are interested in a mutual resolution of the matter."[58] After multiple frustrating exchanges, the Mohican tribal president contacted the Trustees directly in May 1982, articulating that the Tribal Council "has *not* designated [Howard Bichler, the tribe's lawyer] to be the liaison, negotiator or spokesperson for the Stockbridge people in the matter of the Bible and Communion set."[59] He also emphasized that the Mohican people were "eager to establish a meeting date with the Trustees so that [they] can come and personally present what evidence [they] have that the Bible is rightfully [theirs]."[60] The Trustees never responded to this letter.

For the next four years, advocates for the Mohicans from across the country sent letters to the Trustees to no avail. From what the public historical record shows, the Trustees remained silent.[61] Yet the internal communications between Trustee board members tell a very different story. Though the Trustees publicly claimed they were interested in hearing additional evidence from the Mohicans, internally, they were incredibly concerned about the possibility of losing the items, given their central place in the Mission House Museum. The fact that a museum about Indigenous conversion fought so hard to prevent Indians from accessing a Bible and Communion set is an irony that should not be lost on us.

In an attempt to keep the items and maintain their story of conversion, the Trustees came up with countless ways and excuses to avoid returning them to the tribe. The Trustees were concerned with getting involved in a lengthy and expensive legal battle that would leave them with what one of their lawyers called "a public relations black eye."[62] Though they briefly considered the possibility of suing the tribe for ownership of the Bible and Communion set in 1976, they soon decided this would not be advantageous to them after one of their lawyers combed through the original sales agreement and realized that it gave *possession* of the Bible and Communion set to Choate but never actually used the words "buy" and "sell."[63] In other words, not only would a legal battle have been costly and reflected poorly on the public image of the Trustees, but they would also have likely lost if the case had been tried in court. Of course, this was a detail they kept to themselves.

The Trustees also began to consider the possibilities for a co-ownership agreement on the Bible and Communion set, in which the items would spend time in both Stockbridge, Massachusetts, and Bowler, Wisconsin, on the Mohican reservation. Yet this discussion revealed additional concerns, including the paternalistic assumptions Trustee board members had about the Mohicans' ability to take care of the Bible. Even though the Mohicans had cared for the Bible and Communion set for 186 years before they were stolen and then sold, Trustee board members consistently wondered, "How straight is this Indian group—will we ever see the Bibles again?" and expressed, "I'm not convinced [the] Indians have good faith in their interest in the Bible and don't even want to sell it."[64] One board member remarked that "co-ownership makes me shiver. Until somebody's been out there [the Mohican reservation] and seen their operation, we don't know where things stand or who they are."[65] Others agreed and insisted on gathering as many "character witnesses" as possible to learn more about the Mohicans themselves.[66] In the midst of these concerns, the Trustees agreed to ignore communication from the tribe throughout the early 1980s and instead gather information about the Mohicans, including from larger entities like the National Endowment for the Humanities, the Smithsonian National Museum of Natural History, the Department of Anthropology at Williams College, and more local institutions like the Milwaukee Public Museum, to determine what a co-ownership agreement with the Mohicans might look like and how disadvantageous such an agreement might be for the Trustees.[67]

The Mohicans were discouraged by the lack of communication and cooperation from the Trustees and did not contact them again until 1986. In this four-year interim, the tribe maintained but did not continue to expand their public campaign and considered their next move. The issue was reignited in January 1986, when the Mohicans again contacted the Trustees, urging them to reconsider their position on the Bible especially. This time they also included an article that discussed the "moral and legal obligations surrounding the use of Indian artifacts in Museums [sic]."[68]

Much like the Mohicans, the Trustees were also aware of the growing national focus in the late 1980s on American Indian human remains and sacred items being held by non-Native institutions. Though tribes fought for their remains and objects throughout the twentieth century, the catalyst for this national movement occurred in 1986, when representatives from the Northern Cheyenne Nation discovered that the Smithsonian had possession of nearly 18,500 human remains. In 1987 Senator Daniel E. Inouye (D-HI) led the effort to pass Senate bill S. 1722, the National American Indian Museum and Memorial Act. Though it never passed, similar legislation, the National Museum of the American Indian Act, did in 1989.[69] Likewise in 1990 the Heard Museum in Arizona hosted a yearlong dialogue on repatriation, producing a panel report that would eventually serve as a blueprint for the Native American Graves Protection and Repatriation Act (NAGPRA), which passed later that year.[70]

As a federally funded institution, the Trustees were cognizant of this national discussion, which is clear in the evidence they collected in the late 1980s while they were determining whether or not to return the Bible and Communion set to the Mohicans. The Trustees archived newspaper articles about a sacred pole returned to the Omaha tribe, a state law passed by the New York Assembly that allowed the New York State Museum to permanently loan wampum belts to the Onandogas, and a section of a textbook that summarized the Denver Art Museum's decision to return what it termed "a Zuni War God" to the Zuni people. They also spoke directly with a representative from the Smithsonian about a recent case Trustee board members had seen in the newspaper.[71] In addition to these records, internal communication between Trustee board members also show that the Trustees were concerned about not only how these returns might affect their own organization but also how their decision about the Bible and Communion set might set a precedent for other institutions holding American Indian items and remains. Trustee board members discussed this concern throughout their correspondence and meetings, and their lawyer used it as a rationale to keep the matter out of court, stating, "I spoke with a friend in the legal counsel's office at the Metropolitan Museum and a lawyer in the Smithsonian's legal office. Both were terribly concerned that any litigation in this area might lead to bad case law for museums generally."[72] They were not only aware of the national debate over who should own and represent American Indian items but also actively following it, engaging in it, and seeking information about it from other museums.

In June 1989, eight years after the Mohicans originally requested an in-person meeting, the Trustees of Reservations finally agreed to meet with representatives from the Mohicans in Stockbridge.[73] Though the Mohicans were forced to travel for the first meeting, members of the Trustees also visited the AEM Library-Museum in Bowler to meet with additional tribal members for a follow-up meeting in July. While the matter of the Bible and Communion set was not decided in either of these two meetings, they indicate a major turning point in the issue. Stanley Piatczyc, one of the leaders of the Trustees who attended both meetings, referenced letters between Mabel Choate and Reverend Westfall that suggested the Stockbridge Indians had approved of the sale. He noted, "I have been opposed to the return of the Bibles all these years because I have been going on documentation that we have at hand, letters written by Rev. Westfall and Mabel Choate primarily. Westfall writes of a 'happy consummation' in the sale, approved by both the Indians and himself."[74] After hearing evidence from Davids to the contrary and noting that the church was in need of money at the time and that the items were placed in the church under questionable means, Piatczyc said,

"We want to find a solution to this dilemma. Our sense of urgency has been greatly heightened by this meeting with you."[75] Surely, the urgency would have been "heightened" much earlier if over the last eight years the Trustees had answered the numerous requests from the tribe to meet and present evidence in person.

Mohican supporters across the nation continued to send letters to the Trustees, and pressure from within the organization grew.[76] As a result of the Mohicans' ongoing commitment to the Bible and the growing national conversation about the place of American Indian sacred items in museums, the Trustees were increasingly concerned about potentially negative publicity. The Mohicans were relentless in keeping this issue in the press, resulting in a steady stream of articles covering the Bible and Communion set regularly published by local newspapers around the Stockbridge area. One Trustee member wrote:

> This is a highly emotional issue on two counts: first dealing with indians [sic] and second dealing with religion. The Trustees are in a no win situation. Either we break the trust of guardianship of these books [the Bible], or we will incurr [sic] a landslide of negative press for apparently opposing the abused red man and and [sic] his colonial christian [sic] roots. This may cloud the name of the Trustees for years and there [is] still a good chance we would lose the bibles [sic] in the end.[77]

Similarly, Trustee meeting minutes from the late 1980s are peppered with concerns over a "media blitz" and "bad publicity" surrounding the Trustees' refusal to return the items, and Trustee board members emphasized throughout that "careful planning and serious consideration must be given to make certain that the utmost public relations benefit is obtained while minimizing the adverse reaction."[78] The Trustees were aware of the growing number of sacred items being returned to tribes, and they considered the publicity of their organization critical. If they were going to have to return the Bible eventually, it made more sense for them to do so as a token of goodwill than being forced by legislation. They finally voted to return the Bible in August 1989.[79]

On April 19, 1990, the Trustees of Reservations officially signed an agreement with the Stockbridge-Munsee Band of Mohicans indicating they would return the Bible to the tribe.[80] However, this was only signed under the condition of four additional agreements. First, the tribe would make "appropriate custodial arrangements" for the Bible, including a security system and fireproof vault storage. Second, *after* the tribe had successfully installed these systems, the Trustees would apply for a court sanction that allowed them to return the Bible. Third, if this court sanction did not occur within one year of the agreement, the entire agreement would be void. Fourth, a new inscription describing the transfer would be added to the front of the Bible, and it would be delivered back to the tribe.[81]

While this agreement was certainly exciting for the Mohicans, who had worked for the past fifteen years to see their Bible returned, the paternalistic requirement of a security system was troubling. Of course, the Mohicans also wanted *their* Bible protected, but the requirements from the Trustees not only assumed the Mohicans were unable to care for the Bible but also were absurd, considering the Bible's true ownership. Moreover, the fact that the Trustees, who were given the Bible after an illegal purchase by Choate and theft by Revered Westfall, were the party insisting on a security system so the Bible could not be stolen a second time is incredibly ironic. For the Mohicans, this demand was not only insulting but also seen as another method to delay the transfer of the Bible. Most importantly, since the Bible was the property of the Mohicans, there is no reason the Trustees should have been allowed to dictate the terms of its storage at the AEM Library-Museum, which is on the sovereign land of the reservation. As Bernice Miller Pigeon, founder of the AEM Library-Museum, argued, "They're our bibles [sic], how we take care of them is our business."[82]

Still, the Mohicans were committed to having their Bible returned, and they had the security system and fireproof vault installed in the fall of 1990.[83] As promised in the agreement, the Trustees applied for a court order allowing them to release the Bible, and the transfer was approved and signed by Justice William Highgast on December 19, 1990.[84] A plan to transfer the Bible was set for March 1991.[85] The successful agreement was a huge success for the Stockbridge-Munsee people, who had been fighting to have this Bible returned for the last fifteen years. This continued perseverance demonstrates the unyielding commitment the Stockbridge-Munsee Mohicans hold to serve as their own agents of preservation and representation rather than being forced to allow others to house items that are important to the Mohicans' tribal history.

Ten members of the Mohican tribe traveled to the East Coast to collect the Bible, and former tribal president Leonard E. Miller accepted the Bible set on behalf of the tribe. Additionally, tribal leader Dorothy Davids and the founder of the AEM Library-Museum, Bernice Miller Pigeon, gifted a wrought-iron statue of the tribe's "Many Trails Symbol" to the Trustees. Miller Pigeon said the statue was a symbol of the tribe's "strength, endurance and hope for a long-suffering proud and determined people." She continued, "Because it hurts to part with it, we know it is a meaningful gift. We are giving you a part of ourselves."[86] The ten members who traveled east were greeted back in Bowler by an excited crowd of tribal members. Upon their return, tribal vice chairman Dave Besaw blew into a conch shell, described as a "historic way of calling tribal members to worship or witness an important event."[87] Miller Pigeon stated, "When we met those people, then I felt like crying. We've been after [the Bible] for such a long time, I don't know what to say."[88]

The Mohicans' fight for their Bible illustrates the significant barriers many tribes faced before legislation on repatriation was passed, as well as the power that museums and other institutions held over American Indian sacred items and human remains. NAGPRA was passed in November 1990, just six months after the Trustees signed an agreement to return the Bible and six months before the Bible was actually transferred to the Mohicans.[89] While NAGPRA has been widely hailed as a victory for American Indian nations, many scholars argue that it still presents significant barriers for tribes working to retrieve sacred items and human remains.[90]

In its simplest definition, NAGPRA requires that all institutions that receive federal funding repatriate Native American human remains, associated and unassociated funerary objects, sacred objects, and objects of cultural patrimony in their collections to "culturally affiliated" Indian tribes and Native Hawaiian organizations.[91] It also requires these same federal institutions to work with Indian tribes and Native Hawaiian organizations if Native American human remains, associated or unassociated funerary objects, sacred objects, or objects of cultural patrimony are found and/or removed from federal or tribal lands.[92] Yet these requirements are to some extent overstated. They do not require federally funded institutions to immediately begin returning items and remains; instead, they require them to complete inventories of human remains and cultural items in their collections and send a copy of these assessments to the federally recognized tribes that these institutions determine might be culturally affiliated with the items. From there, the task of conducting significant historical research to establish and prove this cultural affiliation falls almost entirely on tribal nations themselves.

Human remains and associated funerary objects are typically returned upon receiving a request from a lineal descendant, Indian tribe, or Native Hawaiian organization that can show that they are "more likely than not" culturally affiliated with the remains or objects (though certainly this is not always the case). However, the process for the repatriation of unassociated funerary objects, sacred objects, and objects of cultural patrimony is significantly more complicated and arduous. For these items to be repatriated, the claimant (tribes), must (1) show that the item is an unassociated funerary object, sacred object, or object of cultural patrimony; (2) demonstrate that the object was previously owned by the tribe; and (3) present evidence to show that the institution in possession of the object did not have the "right of possession" when it obtained the object, meaning it did not secure the item with "voluntary consent" of the party that had authority over the item previously.[93] On the other hand, museums must only compile evidence if they believe they had "right of possession" to an item. This process is laborious, time-consuming, and frequently complicated, and though NAGPRA offers grants, consulting, and training for tribes, this process has not always been successful or led to collaborative efforts.[94] NAGPRA does little to lessen the significant labor and historical research tribes were required to do prior to NAGPRA, as shown in the fifteen-year fight for the Mohican Bible. This extensive amount of work to provide documentation substantiating repatriation claims persists.

NAGPRA requires institutions that receive federal funding to communicate with tribes and consider historical research and evidence tribes present, but the institutions themselves retain the authority to make decisions about whether tribes are culturally affiliated with the items and remains that they claim, as well as whether the items constitute sacred objects.[95] In this sense, unless disputes eventually come before the NAGPRA Review Committee, museums and other institutions that receive federal funding, as opposed to tribes themselves, still retain the authority to decide what is Indian and what is not, as well as what is sacred and what is not.[96] Likewise, the immense number of claims for objects, the continual negotiation between colonial ideologies and Native worldviews, and the lack of federal oversight to enforce timely communication between tribes and institutions means that these processes still take time. Though NAGPRA certainly would have required the Trustees to consider evidence sooner and communicate more directly with the Mohicans after their initial request for the Bible and Communion set in 1975, even if NAGPRA had been in place, the Trustees still would have had the ultimate legal power to decide whether these items were indeed culturally affiliated with the Mohicans or not. This would have been difficult for them to do, given their organization's focus on the Stockbridge-Munsee Mohicans in the Mission House museum, yet Trustee board members consistently questioned in their internal communication whether the group asking for the Bible was *really* Mohican, and they required the Mohicans to obtain evidence of federal recognition from the BIA at one point after questioning whether this was *the* Mohican Nation.[97] In other words, with or without NAGPRA, institutions hold significant power when it comes to accepting and enacting repatriation requests.

Still, NAGPRA was significant for the Mohicans in retrieving other items they had long been fighting for, such as their Communion set, which they received in 2006, sixteen years after NAGPRA passed. The four-piece set, which includes a flagon and two goblets from the early to mid-1800s, as well as a charger from the mid- to late 1700s, was sold to Choate at the same time as the Bible, and as a result of its cultural and religious significance, it qualified as an object of cultural patrimony under NAGPRA.[98] However, while NAGPRA was a key factor in this repatriation, the fact that it still took sixteen years exemplifies that pursuing the return of objects through NAGPRA can still often be an exhausting fight. After the passage of NAGPRA, museums were overwhelmed with the number of remains and objects they had to categorize while they scrambled to understand how the law would affect their institutions. Simultaneously, tribes were inundated with inventories, and they often lacked the staff to respond to and gather the required historical evidence to substantiate their cultural affiliation to items.[99] The process of receiving inventories, gathering evidence, and establishing consistent communication between tribes and federal institutions still takes significant time. Even in the case of the Communion set, where the Mission House museum had an established relationship with the tribe (one that was actually quite good after the museum eventually did return the Bible) and where the documentation required (that it is an item of cultural patrimony, that it was previously owned by the Mohicans, and that neither Reverend Westfall, Mabel Choate, nor the Trustees of Reservations ever had right of possession) was nearly identical to that of the Bible, it still took sixteen years to officially notify the Mohicans of this item, for the Mohicans to provide the required documentation, and for the Trustees to formally transfer the items.[100]

## On Resistance: Why Self-Representation?

Self-representation is not usually considered a mode of resistance. However, for American Indian people, who have been forced again and again to assert their ongoing presence and identities as Indigenous peoples, self-representation opposes and intervenes in the frequent practice of non-Native people representing Native people without consent and collaboration. This is particularly true in public history settings, since many conceptualize museums as very Western, white spaces—places for ancient Indian "artifacts," not living Indian curators. By retrieving and housing their own objects, the Mohicans defy the notion that they are unable or unwilling to represent themselves and instead assert their rights as the rightful owners of their Bible and Communion set. In this way, the act of self-representation is a political one.

For the Mohicans, fighting for the right to represent the Bible and Communion set not only defied the practice of non-Native museums holding Native objects but also changed how Mohican history is represented in one specific museum—the Mission House in Stockbridge. The Mission House focuses on the history of John Sergeant and his family, and it displayed the

Bible and Communion set before 1990 and 2006, respectively. The home turned museum is run by the Trustees of Reservations.[101] Visitors walk through the two-story building and learn about the clothing its inhabitants wore, their religious rituals, and their cultural practices. Largely missing from the narrative presented in the Mission House, however, are the Stockbridge Indians, distinctly asserting that this is not an Indian place but rather one for European Americans.

In fact, the one mention of the tribe within the museum is an open, empty shelf, with a sign indicating that it was the previous location of the two-volume Bible and the Communion set. Since Christianity is a main theme within the Mission House's exhibits, these items were significant pieces in the narrative they present about missionization and Stockbridge as a significant site of conversion. Leaving an empty shelf not only communicates how symbolic these items are in the presented missionization narrative but also might convey that a significant part of the museum was taken, that the museum is even perhaps grieving a loss and memorializing these items with a notable absence. When I visited the museum in 2012, our tour guide addressed the vacant space, stating, "This is where we used to keep two Bibles and a Communion set that were given to the Indians as a gift. But a few years ago the Stockbridge Indians asked for them back. We just couldn't say no to such a sweet request. So now the Bibles are in Wisconsin on the reservation."[102] As is evident from the thirty-one-year fight that the Mohicans engaged in to retrieve their Bible and Communion set, recovering these items was by no means a situation in which the Trustees simply "couldn't say no to such a sweet request." Describing it as such and emphasizing the loss and absence of these items by continuing to display an empty shelf is yet another instance in which white settlers are deemed generous and Indians are relegated to "sweet" recipients. In the initial story of the Mohicans receiving the Bible as a gift, the non-Native museum displays of Native objects across the country, and the current display of absence at the Mission House, the narrative is the same: white collectors are generous gift givers or saviors of objects, and Indians are the recipients of these gifts. These narratives continue to paint white collectors and museums as benevolent and to obscure their, at best, complacency with housing Native objects and, at worst, their role in actively taking these objects from Indigenous communities. Moreover, these narratives dismiss the activism, labor, and all-out battles for these sacred objects that American Indian nations have led. These are the narratives the Mohicans are pushing back against by fighting to represent their own histories.

Exiting the back door of the Mission House, visitors are invited to visit the Indian Museum, a small building behind the Mission House that tells the story of the village's other previous inhabitants, the Stockbridge Indians. The museum was constructed in 1929 by Mabel Choate and underwent renovation in 1987. Though it is mostly filled with items collected by Choate in the 1930s, it also includes two newer posters contributed by the Mohicans that discuss NAGPRA, as well as historic preservation projects on the reservation in Wisconsin. The tribe also created a seven-minute video for the museum that provides additional information about the Mohicans today.

The NAGPRA and historic preservation posters were likely added within the last ten or eleven years, based on a photo in the poster about NAGPRA that shows the Communion set in its location within the AEM Library-Museum. Since these objects were not returned to the tribe until 2006, the posters and the video are rather recent additions. With this in mind, it is important to consider what kind of narrative this museum presented before their addition. According to the 1987 renovation plan for the Indian Museum, exhibits included an "Assimilated Indian" section with a map showing the forced removal of the Mohicans, an "artifact wall" where the proposed takeaway was that "the Stockbridge Indian was a viable culture," and another space to recognize John Sergeant (in addition to the Mission House itself). It also included a "Kids Corner" where children were invited to try on headdresses, apply makeup "to duplicate warpaint [sic] symbols," and "view themselves as the Stockbridge Indians did in an adjacent puddle/basin of water-mirror." Not shown on the blueprint but detailed in the complete renovation plan was one small section titled "Modern Indian," which featured three photographs of present-day Stockbridge-Munsee Mohicans.[103]

Though some of these exhibits have been updated, others have not, and it's critical to consider what kind of an assertion a museum filled with "assimilated Indians" and "artifacts," as well as opportunities for children to don redface made prior to the addition of the Mohican posters. While acknowledging the current location of the Mohicans in Wisconsin through maps and three photographs, earlier versions of the museum did little to discuss the current Stockbridge-Munsee Mohicans and instead contributed to the ongoing erasure of Indians from the New England landscape. In the context of museums and other public history institutions, these misrepresentations and outright racist depictions are especially detrimental, since the visitors who visit and view museum exhibits are conditioned to understand the information produced there as correct, impartial, and knowledgeable. Museums are also frequented by a wide range of visitors, including legislators, which means these representations of Indians existing firmly in the past can have significantly damaging effects for tribes as they continue to assert their rights as sovereign nations.[104]

**FIGURE 3.** A view from inside the Indian Museum. The left side of the picture shows a more current version of the "Kids Corner" (which does not give children the option to don redface). The wall on the left contains two maps (the "Assimilated Indian" section) and the two posters (in orange) added by the tribe, as well as a spot where visitors can view a seven-minute video created by the tribe. The back wall is the "artifact wall," which contains some of the "Indian items" Choate collected. Photograph by the author, 2012.

As Jean O'Brien and Amy Den Ouden note, the myth of Indian disappearance is especially prevalent in New England, where there are very few federally recognized tribes. This myth is perpetuated in places like the Indian Museum and has had hugely detrimental effects for New England tribes as they continue to contest claims that they are not "real Indians."[105] The more the public is presented with the notion that Indians have disappeared from New England, the harder it is for tribes to win federal recognition cases. The persistence of these myths has also made NAGPRA in New England an extremely complicated matter. Though the Mohicans are federally recognized and their reservation is now in Wisconsin, other unrecognized Indian nations with ties to New England have little power when it comes to recovering their human remains and sacred objects. Tribes must show "cultural affiliation" in order to provide evidence of their connection to remains and objects, but in order to do so, they must also have federal recognition.[106] Though there have been instances where federal institutions have still agreed to return remains and sacred items to unrecognized tribes, non—federally recognized tribes are largely prevented from recovering remains and sacred items under NAGPRA. Instead, the items frequently become categorized as "culturally unidentifiable," meaning they remain in the possession of non-Native institutions. This is especially common in New England because of the significant number of tribes who do not have federal recognition.[107] In that sense, the persistence of the myth of disappearance in New England, which is perpetuated in public history spaces like the Indian Museum, significantly affects New England tribes' abilities to make claims through NAGPRA by way of federal recognition.

Though this myth has not prevented the Mohicans from maintaining their federal recognition or recovering numerous items through NAGPRA, the romanticized narrative of Indians in New England has still plagued the Mohicans' ability to have their histories accurately represented. Though the relationship between the town of Stockbridge and the Mohicans has improved significantly since the repatriation of the Bible and Communion set, one of the challenges the Mohicans faced when fighting for these items was the continual misrepresentation of the Mohicans. As Davids observed in 1983, "Some of the Christian inhabitants of the village have place[d] the Mahicans in a romantic niche in their village history."[108] In other words, residents of Stockbridge celebrated what they considered the cherished history of the Stockbridge Indians, in which Native people were peacefully Christianized, fought for the colonists in the Revolutionary War, and quietly disappeared west as white settlement expanded. This narrative erased the long history of violence that accompanied dispossession and missionary projects and allowed non-Native residents of Stockbridge to remember the Mohicans as merely a chapter in their town's history rather than acknowledging the fact that the existence of their town and all the history that has come after were made possible by the forced removal of the Mohican people.

Given the state of the Mission House and the Indian Museum before the more recent additions, as well as the Mohican engagement with the Indian Museum since then, it is clear that the fight for the Bible and Communion set resulted in not only the return of the items but also significant changes in how Mohican history was represented (and by whom) in Stockbridge and on the Mohican reservation. These changes represent how repatriation can sometimes actually produce positive outcomes that create possibilities for future dialogue and exchange. In spite of the extended battle for the Bible and Communion set, the relationship between the Trustees and the Mohicans has significantly improved, and the groups often collaborate on projects together. To this day, the Mohicans continue to represent themselves at the Mission House and in the Stockbridge Library in their own exhibits, and tribal members return to the town year after year, often giving public presentations about Mohican history and culture. By recovering items so important to Mohican history and continuing to represent themselves and their histories through these objects, the new additions to the Indian Museum, and public presentations in Stockbridge today, the Mohicans engage in a politics of self-representation to resist a narrative that locates their importance in the past.

## Conclusion

For different tribal nations, the goals of repatriation are different. While some tribes hide, bury, or destroy sacred objects that were never meant to be seen or displayed in the first place, others like the Mohicans put them back in museums. However, instead of being housed and shown by non-Native museums, these items are held by Native people in *their own* tribal museums. Moreover, the Bible and Communion set are not only displayed as important historical and sacred objects, the placement of these items in the AEM Library-Museum also communicates the important story of the fight for the items, exemplifying their importance in Mohican tribal history, as well as the remarkable story they tell about self-representation and resistance.[109] This decision is more than a preservation goal; it is a political act. By intentionally using tools like museums that have historically served to produce dominant narratives of disappearance, the Mohicans are reclaiming their histories and repurposing these tools to tell their stories. The recovery of the Bible and Communion set and their placement in the Mohican tribal museum exemplify these concepts and the larger resistance against a narrative of disappearance. By actively fighting to obtain their historical objects, the Mohicans are demonstrating that they not only have persevered despite settler-colonial violence and disappearance claims but also are an active sovereign tribal nation that has the right to preserve and represent their own history.

As the Bible and Communion set are now displayed at the AEM Library-Museum on the Mohican reservation, they continue to be sacred to the Mohicans not only as religious and historical objects but also as an example of the tribe's resilience and unrelenting fight for self-representation. The fight for these objects set an important precedent for the subsequent repatriation requests the Mohicans have made under NAGPRA. The placement of all these items in the AEM Library-Museum and the reburial of repatriated human remains in Mohican ancestral homelands are a testimony to the continual resistance and self-representation the Mohicans participate in. For every visitor, Native or non-Native, who enters the AEM Library-Museum, the Bible and Communion set are not only presented as sacred religious and historic objects. They are important because they tell a story of resistance, a story of a tribe that has refused to be complacent with the way they are represented by others. The Mohicans have consistently strived to represent their own histories, and in doing so they disrupt the common practice in which non-Native peoples represent Native peoples without consent and collaboration. This struggle for the Bible and Communion set is a clear example of Mohican engagement in historical preservation and demonstrates the important place of self-representation in Native political action.

ROSE MIRON is an independent scholar based in Minneapolis, Minnesota. She completed her dissertation, entitled "Mohican Archival Activism: Narrating Indigenous Nationalism in Public History," in June 2018.

## Notes

1. The name Mohican refers to the union of three tribes in the seventeenth century: the Mahicans (sometimes spelled Mahikan), the Wappingers, and the Housatonic, who lived in the Hudson River Valley. Both Mahican and Mohican are derived from the name Muh-he-con-neok, which means People of the Waters That Are Never Still, referring to the Mahicannituck (Hudson) River, beside which this tribe lived within their ancestral homelands. The names Mohican and Mahican should not be confused with the name Mohegan, which refers to an entirely different tribe whose homelands are in eastern Connecticut. Although it is true that some members of the Mohegan tribe fled west to join the Mohicans at Stockbridge after the Pequot War, the Mohegans and Mohicans are still two distinct tribal nations. The name Munsee refers to another tribe of American Indians that was part of the larger Delaware group and lived along the Mahicannituck (Hudson) River in the Catskill Mountains. The Munsees lived with the Mohicans starting in the early eighteenth century, and until 1856 the government referred to the group as the Stockbridge and Munsee Tribes of Indians, suggesting two separate groups. However, in 1856 the United States hyphenated the name, and the entire group became the Stockbridge-Munsees. As for the name Stockbridge, this refers to the name of the village the Mohicans lived in during the eighteenth century after white settlers encroached upon their homelands in the Mahicannituck (Hudson) River Valley. When John Sergeant came to live with the Mohicans as a missionary in 1734, he named their mission village along the Housatonic River Stockbridge after a village in England. From this point on the group that lived here was known as the Stockbridge Indians or the Stockbridge-Munsee Band of Mohicans. Throughout Mohican historiography, the names Mohicans, Mahicans, Stockbridge Indians, Stockbridge-Munsee Indians, and Stockbridge-Munsee Mohicans are used interchangeably unless referring to the tribe before these groups formed a confederacy. Thus, in this article I will primarily refer to the Stockbridge-Munsee

Band of Mohicans as simply the Mohicans or the Stockbridge-Munsee, but I may also use the previously mentioned terms interchangeably throughout my work. Each name refers to the same group of people unless otherwise stated. For more on this, see James Oberly, *A Nation of Statesmen: The Political Culture of the Stockbridge-Munsee Mohicans, 1815–1972* (Norman: University of Oklahoma Press, 2005); Dorothy W. Davids, *A Brief History of the Mohican Nation Stockbridge-Munsee Band* (Bowler, WI: Stockbridge-Munsee Historical Committee and Arvid E. Miller Memorial Library-Museum, 2001); and Brad D. E. Jarvis, *The Brothertown Nation of Indians: Land Ownership and Nationalism in Early America, 1740–1840* (Lincoln: University of Nebraska Press, 2010).

2. Dorothy W. Davids, "Brief History of The Stockbridge Bibles: A Stockbridge-Munsee Perspective," 1 April 1981, Historical Records, Arvid E. Miller Library-Museum, Bowler, WI (hereafter cited as AEMLM); enrollment information from a personal phone conversation with Molly Miller, September 11, 2015.

3. Shirley Dunn, *The Mohican World 1680–1750* (Fleischmanns, NY: Purple Mountain Press, 2000).

4. Throughout these endnotes the Bible and Communion set are referred to in a number of different ways. Because the Bible is made up of two volumes, it is sometimes referred to as "Bibles" and sometimes as "Bible," depending on the document. Also, between 1975, when the tribe requested the Bible and Communion set be returned, and 1991, when the Bible was repatriated, some of the letters refer only to the Bible and not the Communion set. In some cases, the author of a letter or document is really only referring to the Bible, while in other cases, we can assume that person is referring to both the Bible and the Communion set but shortened them to simply "Bibles."

5. Davids, "Brief History"; Dorothy Davids to Daniel Mandell, 14 February 1983, box 5, Dorothy "Dot" Davids Collection II, AEMLM.

6. Michelle A. Hamilton, *Collections and Objections: Aboriginal Material Culture in Southern Ontario* (Montreal: McGill-Queen's University Press, 2010), 11.

7. Margaret E. Guthrie, "The Return of a Pious Gift," *Milwaukee Journal*, 2 June 1991, Historical Records, AEMLM.

8. Amy Lonetree, *Decolonizing Museums: Representing Native America in National and Tribal Museums* (Chapel Hill: University of North Carolina Press, 2012), xv.

9. In my dissertation I examine self-representation as a political action by also connecting self-representation to larger efforts to change the way Mohican history is written and taught. For the purpose of this article, however, I focus strictly on self-representation to exemplify the significant role it plays in the Mohicans' motivations behind the fight for these objects.

10. James Fenimore Cooper, *The Last of the Mohicans: A Narrative of 1757* (New York: Thomas Y. Crowell & Co. Publishers, 1826). For examples of other authors who claim the Mohicans disappeared, see W. H. Carpenter, *The History of Massachusetts: From Its Earliest Settlement to the Present Time* (Philadelphia: Lippincott, Grambo & Co., 1853); Codman Hislop, *Albany: Dutch, English, and American* (Albany: Argus Press, 1936); "Last Mohican Is Living Here," *Milwaukee*

*Journal*, 1 February 1931, series 5, box 4: Stockbridge Connections, Stockbridge Library, Stockbridge, MA (hereafter SL); Richard Nunley, "Cooper—Ugh!," *Our Berkshires*, 19 November 1992, series 5, box 4: Stockbridge Connections, SL; For a more complete analysis of disappearance narratives, see Jean O'Brien, *Firsting and Lasting: Writing Indians out of Existence in New England* (Minneapolis: University of Minnesota Press, 2010).

11. There are multiple different spellings of Mahicannituck that occur throughout literature, but I've chosen to rely on the spelling used by the Mohicans on their tribal website, "Origin and Early History," Stockbridge-Munsee Community, accessed 15 March 2017, http://mohican-nsn.gov/origin earlyhistory/.

12. Lisa Brooks, *The Common Pot: The Recovery of Native Space in the Northeast* (Minneapolis: University of Minnesota Press, 2008).

13. The final removal in 1936 was from the town of Red Springs to the current location of the reservation in Bartelme (a distance of about ten miles). While parts of the reservation still border the town of Red Springs, the tribe lost the majority of this land and the rest of their reservation land through the Act of 1871, which sold fifty-four sections of pine-forested reservation land "for the relief of the Stockbridge-Munsee Indians" and the subsequent General Allotment Act in 1887. Through the Indian Reorganization Act, the Mohican Nation was able to regain fifteen thousand acres in Bartelme (the western portion of their original reservation designated by the Treaty of 1856) after it had been clear-cut by pine loggers. For the Mohicans, this is the seventh removal, because they moved ten miles west from the little remaining land they had in Red Springs to this new land in Bartelme. Moreover, only twenty-five hundred of these fifteen thousand acres were placed in trust for the tribe at this time, and the remaining acres were not placed in trust until 1972. See Davids, "Brief History."

14. Oberly, *A Nation of Statesmen*.

15. Brooks, *The Common Pot*. Again, I've chose to rely on the spelling found on the Mohican tribal website rather than the spellings Brooks uses; see "Origin and Early History."

16. Linford D. Fisher, *The Indian Great Awakening: Religion and the Shaping of Native Cultures in Early America* (New York: Oxford University Press, 2012), 8.

17. Ibid., 47.

18. Brooks, *The Common Pot*, 44–48.

19. For more on this period of Mohican history and the mission at Stockbridge, see Shirley Dunn, *The Mohicans and Their Land 1609–1730* (Fleischmanns: Purple Mountain Press, 1994); Patrick Frazier, *The Mohicans of Stockbridge* (Lincoln: University of Nebraska Press, 1994); Dunn, *The Mohican World*; Shirley Dunn, *The River Indians: Mohicans Making History* (Fleischmanns: Purple Mountain Press, 2009); Drew Lopenzina, *Red Ink: Native Americans Picking Up the Pen in the Colonial Period* (Albany: SUNY Press, 2012); David J. Silverman, *Red Brethren: The Brothertown and Stockbridge Indians and the Problem of Race in Early America* (Ithaca, NY: Cornell University Press, 2010); Rachel Wheeler,

*To Live upon Hope: Mohicans and Missionaries in the Eighteenth-Century North-east* (Ithaca, NY: Cornell University Press, 2013); Hilary E. Wyss, *English Letters and Indian Literacies: Reading, Writing, and New England Missionary Schools, 1750–1830* (Philadelphia: University of Pennsylvania Press, 2012).

20. Timothy McKeown, "Notice of Intent to Repatriate a Cultural Item: The Trustees of Reservations, Beverly, MA," memorandum, 2 February 2006, Historical Records, AEMLM.

21. Davids, "Brief History."

22. Ibid.

23. Michael Witgen, *An Infinity of Nations: How the Native New World Shaped Early North America* (Philadelphia: University of Pennsylvania Press, 2012).

24. Kevin A. McBride, "Bundles, Bears, and Bibles: Interpreting Seventeenth Century Native 'Texts,'" in *Early Native Literacies in New England: A Documentary and Critical Anthology*, ed. Kristinia Bross and Hilary E. Wyss (Amherst: University of Massachusetts Press, 2008), 137. For more on the importance of Bibles to Native communities in early New England, see Phillip Round, *Removable Type: Histories of the Book in Indian Country, 1663–1880* (Chapel Hill: University of North Carolina Press, 2010); Ann Marie Plane, "'To Subscribe unto GODS BOOK': The Bible as Material Culture in Seventeenth-Century New England Colonialism," *Journal of the Bible and Its Reception* 3, no. 2 (2016): 303–29.

25. Elaine M. Jacobi, "Our Great Spirit, Mohican Creator, 'Putahmowus,'" *Reflections on the Waters That Are Never Still* 1 (2015): 46.

26. "Has 198 Year Old Bible at Presbyterv [sic] Session" *Milwaukee Sentinel*, October 1915, folder 20, box 4, Stockbridge Indian Collection, SL.

27. Davids, "Brief History."

28. Frederick Westfall to Ruth Gaines, 31 January 1930, Mission House Stewardship Files, Archives and Research Center, Sharon, MA (hereafter cited as ARC).

29. Ibid.

30. Davids, "Brief History."

31. Baughman indicates in an earlier letter to Mabel Choate that her cousin previously taught the Stockbridge Indians in Wisconsin. He is likely the one who informed her of the Bible and Communion set. See Virginia Baughman to Mabel Choate, 6 August 1929, folder 16, box 1, Mabel Choate Papers, ARC; Frederick Westfall to Virginia Baughman, 22 October 1929, Mabel Choate Papers, ARC.

32. Westfall to Baughman, 22 October 1929.

33. Mabel Choate to Frederick Westfall, 31 October 1929, folder 58, box 2, Mabel Choate Papers, ARC.

34. Correspondence between Mabel Choate and Frederick Westfall, folder 58, box 2, Mabel Choate Papers, ARC; correspondence between Ruth Gaines and Frederick Westfall, folder 58, box 2, Mabel Choate Papers, ARC.

35. Ruth Gaines to Mabel Choate, 20 January 1930, folder 42, box 1, Mabel Choate Papers, ARC.

36. Mabel Choate to Frederick Westfall, 2 May 1930, folder 58, box 2, Mabel Choate Papers, ARC; Frederick Westfall to Mabel Choate, 23 September 1929, folder 58, box 2, Mabel Choate Papers, ARC.

37. Mabel Choate to Virginia Baughman, 31 October 1929, folder 16, box 1, Mabel Choate Papers, ARC.

38. Webb Miller (a Mohican tribal member) was elected as the new custodian of the items, but the church, not the tribe, made this decision, and I have not found any correspondence between Choate and Miller. See "Notes of EOM about Bible," undated, Mission House Stewardship Files, ARC.

39. Davids, "Brief History"; Larence M. Channing to Gordon Abbott, 27 October 1975, box 4, Dorothy "Dot" Davids Collection II, AEMLM.

40. Between 1929 and 1951, when the Bible and Communion set were discovered in the Mission House Museum, most tribal members thought the items were being held in the Quinney home. Eventually, many tribal members found out that the Bible and Communion set had been moved from the Quinney home and placed in a Shawano bank vault, but until tribal members met with the Trustees in 1989 and were able to view the actual letters between Westfall, Choate, and Gaines, many did not realize that Westfall had actually entered the Quinney home and taken the items. They assumed that Quinney himself placed the items in the church for safekeeping and that Westfall eventually moved them to the bank vault. See Dorothy Davids to Polly Pierce, 25 December 1989, Stockbridge Indian Collection, SL.

41. Frederick Westfall to Ruth Gaines, 25 February 1930, Mission House Stewardship Files, ARC.

42. Deed of Sale, 4 May 1930, Mabel Choate Papers, ARC; Frederick Westfall to Mabel Choate, 12 May 1930, Mabel Choate Papers, ARC.

43. Throughout this article the Trustees of Reservations are also referred to as simply the Trustees and the Board of Trustees.

44. Mission House Tour, Stockbridge Mission House, Stockbridge, MA, 5 August 2012.

45. Michael Kelley, "Historical Communion Set Finally Returned to Stockbridge's Mohicans at Museum," *Berkshire Record*, 29 September 2006, Historical Records, AEMLM.

46. Guthrie, "The Return."

47. Ibid.; Channing to Abbott, 27 October 1975.

48. Hamilton, *Collections and Objections*.

49. Jon Schedler to Richard Koenig, 7 April 1975, folder 2, Mission House Stewardship Files, ARC.

50. "Resolution No. 0739," memorandum, 14 February 1981, Tribal Minutes, Resolutions and Directives, AEMLM.

51. Dorothy Davids to Leonard E. Miller, memorandum, 3 November 1981, box 4, Dorothy "Dot" Davids Collection, AEMLM.

52. Ibid.

53. "Mohican Tribe Resumes Efforts to Acquire 'Stockbridge Bible,'" *Berkshire Eagle*, 1 February 1982, series 4, box 3, Tribal Affairs, Stockbridge Indian Collection, SL.

54. "Help Return the Stockbridge Bibles," "Tribe Seeks Return of Treasured Bible," and "Stockbridge Bible Controversy," all in box 4, Dorothy "Dot" Davids Collection, AEMLM.

55. For examples of these letters, see Maudlin to Trustees, Uraneck to Trustees, Russian to Trustees, Krefs to Trustees, Larrabee to Trustees, McClellan to Trustees, Richardson to Trustees, Swan to Trustees, Foudau to Trustees, Amundson to Trustees, Freed to Trustees, Comstock to Trustees, Kenote to Trustees, Ganley to Trustees, all in box 4, Dorothy "Dot" Davids Collection II, AEMLM.

56. Dorothy Davids to Polly Pierce, 26 April 1982, box 4, Dorothy "Dot" Davids Collection II, AEMLM.

57. Dorothy Davids to Ned Depew, 10 November 1982, Leonard E. Miller to Trustees of Reservations, 14 May 1982, Howard J. Bichler to Daniel A. Taylor, 29 April 1982, and Howard J. Bichler to Gordon Abbott Jr., n.d., all in box 4, Dorothy "Dot" Davids Collection II, AEMLM.

58. Dorothy Davids to Howard Bichler, 14 May 1982, box 4, Dorothy "Dot" Davids Collection II, AEMLM.

59. Miller to Trustees, 14 May 1982, emphasis in original.

60. Ibid.

61. The only external communication I can find from this time is in responses to letters sent from Mohican supporters. It seems that in some cases, the Trustees responded vaguely to letter writers, indicating that this was a matter the Trustees were still considering and that they were in contact with the Mohican tribe.

62. Daniel Taylor to Unknown, 4 June 1983, folder 5, Legal, Mission House Stewardship Files, ARC.

63. Laurence Channing to Gordon Abbott, 12 February 1976, and Mr. Katz to Mr. Kahn, memo, 10 March 1976, both in folder 4, Legal, Mission House Stewardship Files; Taylor to Unknown, 4 June 1983.

64. Trustees of Reservations Meeting Minutes, 17 June 1982, folder 5, Legal, Mission House Stewardship Files, ARC.

65. Ibid.

66. Rush Taggart, memorandum, 12 October 1982, folder 5, Legal, Mission House Stewardship Files, ARC.

67. Trustees Meeting Minutes, 17 June 1982; Rush Taggart to William Merrill, 27 October 1982, and Rush Taggart to Michael Brown, 1 December 1982, both in folder 5, Legal, Mission House Stewardship Files, ARC.

68. Leonard Miller to Trustees, 30 January 1986, folder 5, Legal, Mission House Stewardship Files, ARC.

69. Dorothy Davids to Daniel E. Inouye, 9 November 1987, box 5, Dorothy "Dot" Davids Collection, AEMLM; Jack F. Trope, "The Case for NAGPRA," in *Accomplishing NAGPRA: Perspectives on the Intent, Impact, and Future of the Native American Graves Protection and Repatriation Act*, ed. Sangita Chari and Jaime M. N. Lavallee (Corvallis: Oregon State University Press), 19–54.

70. Trope, "The Case for NAGPRA."

71. Mission House Stewardship Files, ARC.

72. Daniel A. Taylor to Davis Cherington, 28 July 1989, folder 6, Legal, Mission House Administration Files, ARC.

73. R. C. Miller to Asher E. Treat, 10 October 1989, box 4, Dorothy "Dot" Davids Collection II, AEMLM.

74. "Meeting with Trustees of Reservations" minutes, July 17, 1989, box 4, Dorothy "Dot" Davids Collection II, AEMLM.

75. Ibid.

76. Asher E. Treat to R. C. Miller, 19 October 1989, box 4, Dorothy "Dot" Davids Collection II, AEMLM.

77. Henry Flint to Stan Piatczyc, 5 July 1989, folder 6, Legal, Mission House Stewardship Files, ARC.

78. Trustees of Reservation Meeting Minutes, 26 September 1989, and Trustees of Reservations Meeting Minutes, 1989, both in folder 6, Legal, Mission House Stewardship Files, ARC.

79. Trustees of Reservation Meeting Minutes, 2 August 1989, folder 6, Legal, Mission House Stewardship Files, ARC.

80. Exhibit A in *The Trustees of Reservations v. Attorney General*, Trial Court Essex County Division (1990).

81. Ibid.

82. Jody Ericson, "The Latest of the Mahicans," *Berkshire Magazine*, January 1991, Historical Records, AEMLM, 26; Guthrie, "The Return."

83. R. C. Miller to Daniel A. Taylor, 3 October 1990, box 4, Dorothy "Dot" Davids Collection II, AEMLM.

84. *The Trustees of Reservations v. Attorney General*.

85. Guthrie, "The Return."

86. Amy Pratt, "Bible of Stockbridge Indians Evidently Going back to Them," *Berkshire Eagle*, 21 March 1990, Historical Records, AEMLM.

87. Joan Sousek, "Tribe's Bible Comes Home," 15 March 1991, series 4, box 3, Tribal Affairs, Stockbridge Indian Collection, SL.

88. Guthrie, "The Return."

89. Trope, "The Case for NAGPRA."

90. While I won't be discussing all the critiques that have been lodged against NAGPRA in this article, the main arguments have been that NAGPRA prevents non–federally recognized tribes from claiming human remains and sacred objects, relegates the significant labor of establishing a historical connection/cultural affiliation to tribes themselves without significant support, offers little support for the financial requirements of repatriation, does not mandate a record of items that have been returned, often forces tribes to manage items that have been poisoned by toxic chemicals, leaves little room for flexibility and time for reconsideration when more than one tribe can establish cultural affiliation with remains of objects, and is significantly time-consuming and bureaucratic. It's important to note that though NAGPRA provides grants and consultation services for tribes, these resources are often insufficient for the sheer volume of repatriation notices and claims. For more perspectives on NAGPRA and a more thorough description of these critiques, see Michael F. Brown and Margaret Bruchac, "NAGPRA from the Middle Distance: Legal Puzzles and Unintended Consequences," in *Imperialism, Art, and Restitution*, ed.

John Henry Merryman (Cambridge: Cambridge University Press), 193–217; Chari and Lavallee, *Accomplishing NAGPRA*.

91. The only federally funded institution that is excluded from NAGPRA is the Smithsonian, because the National Museum of the American Indian Act, which was passed in 1989, already included repatriation regulations for the Smithsonian. See Trope, "The Case for NAGPRA." As defined by the act itself, cultural affiliation means "a relationship of shared group identity which can be reasonably traced historically or prehistorically between a present day Indian tribe or Native Hawaiian organization and an identifiable earlier group" (25 U.S.C. 3001 [2]). According to the National Park Service NAGPRA website, NAGPRA recognizes "Alaska Native villages that are recognized by the Bureau of Indian Affairs" as falling under the larger category "Indian tribe." For the full definition, see National Park Service, "Frequently Asked Questions: Who may claim Native American cultural items under NAGPRA," National NAGPRA, https://www.nps.gov/nagpra/INDEX.HTM.

92. Sangita Chari and Jaime M. N. Lavallee, introduction to Chari and Lavallee, *Accomplishing NAGPRA*, 7–18.

93. Trope, "The Case for NAGPRA," 37.

94. Brown and Bruchac, "NAGPRA from the Middle Distance"; Trope, "The Case for NAGPRA."

95. It should be noted that the NAGPRA Review Committee can also resolve disputes between parties, and tribes can appeal to the committee if an institution denies their cultural affiliation claim. See Trope, "The Case for NAGPRA."

96. Eric Hemenway, "Finding Our Way Home," in Chari and Lavalee, *Accomplishing NAGPRA*, 83–98.

97. Trustees Meeting Minutes, 17 June 1982; Trustees of Reservations Meeting Minutes, 30 June 1982, folder 5, Legal, Mission House Stewardship Files, ARC; Francis Fawin [illegible handwriting] to Reginald Miller, 4 January 1990, folder 6, Legal, Mission House Stewardship Files, ARC.

98. Kelley, "Historical Communion Set"; "Notice of Intent to Repatriate a Cultural Item: The Trustees of Reservations, Beverly, MA," n.d., Historical Records, AEMLM.

99. Hemenway, "Finding Our Way Home."

100. Though it's possible that the return of the Communion set under NAGPRA was especially difficult because of its associations with Christianity, there is no hard evidence to support this theory. Throughout my research I was unable to locate any other Christian objects such as Bibles and Communion sets that have been repatriated to or claimed by tribes. It's not clear if this has ever been a factor that has prevented the repatriation of objects. The Eliot Bible is of course a notable example of a Bible that is significantly important to American Indian nations, but I have not found information about any attempts to have copies of the Eliot Bible repatriated.

101. "About the Mission House," Trustees of Reservations, accessed 24 July 2015, http://www.thetrustees.org/places-to-visit/berkshires/mission-house.

102. Mission House Tour.

103. Photos of Indian Museum Exhibit, 1987, Exhibitions/Research, Mission House Stewardship Files, ARC.

104. For more on the power of museum representations, see Susan Crane, ed., *Museums and Memory* (Redwood City, CA: Stanford University Press, 2000); Richard Handler and Eric Gable, *The New History in an Old Museum: Creating the Past at Colonial Williamsburg* (Durham, NC: Duke University Press, 2012); Mary Lawlor, *Public Native America: Tribal Self-Representation in Museums, Powwows and Casinos* (New Brunswick, NJ: Rutgers University Press, 2006); Lonetree, *Decolonizing Museums*; Susan Sleeper-Smith, ed., *Contesting Knowledge: Museums and Indigenous Perspectives* (Lincoln: University of Nebraska Press, 2009); Daniel J. Walkowitz and Lisa Maya Knauer, eds., *Contested Histories in Public Space: Memory, Space, and Nation* (Durham, NC: Duke University Press, 2009).

105. Amy E. Den Ouden and Jean M. O'Brien, introduction to *Recognition, Sovereignty Struggles, & Indigenous Rights in the United States: A Sourcebook*, ed. Amy E. Den Ouden and Jean M. O'Brien (Chapel Hill: University of North Carolina Press, 2013), 1–34.

106. Joanne Barker, "The Recognition of NAGPRA: A Human Rights Promise Deferred," in Den Ouden and O'Brien, *Recognition*, 95–113.

107. Ibid.; Brown and Bruchac, "NAGPRA from the Middle Distance."

108. Davids to Mandell, 14 February 1983.

109. Yvette Malone, email message to the author, 3 February 2016.

JOSHUA HOROWITZ

# Tatanga Ishtima hinkna Iyá Waká:
# Sleeping Buffalo and Medicine Rock
# and Assiniboine Dislocation
# and Persistence

*On the crest of a ridge near Cree Crossing of the Milk River is a group of glacial boulders which from a distance resemble a herd of sleeping buffalo. They were held sacred by the Indians and one in particular was thought to be the leader. It is now part of this monument. . . . The tribes have legends of the herds' origins, and long before the white men came sacrificed possessions to the Sleeping Buffalo.*

A PERSON READING THESE WORDS, inscribed on a plaque that was created by the National Register of Historic Places in 1995 and placed at a National Park Service site called the Sleeping Buffalo and Medicine Rock on Highway 2 in northern Montana, for the first time might assume the buffalo and local Indigenous peoples have vanished from the area. As the plaque mentions briefly, these two boulders were relocated from their original site, where they once sat among a herd of buffalo rocks at a place that Assiniboine people call Cree Crossing.[1] What the plaque does not state is that they were moved at various times in the twentieth century, eventually being confined to the current site in the 1980s and then inducted into the National Historic Registry in 1995. As a result of settler displacement, the rocks survived three forced migrations. Settlers first removed them from their original resting place during a development project on private property in the late nineteenth and early twentieth centuries.[2] At that time, they were placed in a local city park. Then, twice later, in the late twentieth century, they were moved again to open locations along the interstate highway.

An additional plaque at the site quotes a local Indigenous view of the two rocks. On it, Pat Chief Stick is quoted as saying, "These rocks are sacred, just like our old people. The mountains, the rocks, earth, water, all the mountains, all the ecology, and Indian religion. They are all connected."[3] An important distinction between these two excerpts is that Chief Stick uses present tense, whereas the previous quote describes "Indians" and their practices in the past tense. Local Indigenous peoples continue to revere the Sleeping Buffalo and Medicine Rocks.

Sites such as the Sleeping Buffalo and Medicine Rocks, held sacred by Assiniboine people and other local Indigenous peoples, have helped to keep bodies of cultural and environmental knowledge alive despite colonization, settlement, national borders, and reservation systems. Sleeping Buffalo and Medicine Rocks' original location during the prereservation era was important not only to the Assiniboine but also to other tribes such as the Cree, Blackfeet, Chippewa, Gros Ventre, Crow, Northern Cheyenne, and Sioux.[4] Assiniboine people's well-being depends on their abilities to interact with the Makoche Wakan (Sacred Mother Earth), including rocks, springs, plants, animals, stars, and the weather. For the Assiniboine, sacred sites inform how they see themselves as a community belonging to a homeland. Heard primarily through Assiniboine voices, Assiniboine relationships to places retain significant cultural and historical meaning, as well as remain sources of medicine and spiritual power. The relationships between sacred sites such as the Sleeping Buffalo and Medicine Rocks, with animals such as the buffalo, and between Assiniboine people demonstrate a mutual interdependence and parallel histories, as both Assiniboine people and these two sacred rocks faced similar consequences of American and Canadian colonization, settlement, relocations, and confinement. Subsequently, Assiniboine people express a responsibility not only to their own sense of community but also to the lands they inhabit, to animals, and to sacred sites.

Assiniboine people's relationships to places remain integral to their own sense of existence as a distinct people. By focusing on the Sleeping Buffalo and Medicine Rocks as an example of a central and important Assiniboine sacred site, I illustrate how dispersed Assiniboine communities across several reservations share a sense of commonality, kinship ties, and identity through their relationship to ancestral lands. Sacred sites link Assiniboine people between communities and their relationships to places, animals, plants, weather, stars, rocks, and water, despite the geopolitical constructions of reserves in Canada and reservations in the United States. Rather than using Indigenous nationhood as a categorical concept to discuss this shared collective identity and relationship to lands, I draw on Daniel Heath Justice's construct, "peoplehood." In "Kinship Criticism and the Decolonization Imperative," Justice states that "Indigenous nationhood is more than simple political independence or the exercise of a distinctive cultural identity; it's also an understanding of a common social interdependence within the community, the tribal web of kinship rights and responsibilities that link the People, the land, and the cosmos together in an ongoing and dynamic system of mutually affecting relationships."[5] Justice further defines people-hood as "the relational system that keeps the people in balance with one another, with other peoples and realities, and with the world. Nationhood is the political extension of the social rights and responsibilities of people-hood."[6] Weaving Justice's concept of peoplehood with Linda Tuhiwai Smith's ideas about Indigenous relationships with ecological phenomena clarifies Assiniboine sensibilities with the environment. Smith discusses the differences between "Western" concepts and Indigenous concepts about environmental knowledge: "A human person does not stand alone, but shares with other animate and, in the Western sense, 'inanimate' beings, a relationship based on a shared 'essence' of life. The significance of place, of land, of landscape, of other things in the universe, in defining the very essence of a people, makes for a very different rendering of the term essentialism as used by indigenous peoples."[7] Putting these ideas together, I use a related concept in this article, territoriality, which signifies the various relationships between sacred places and Assiniboine people.[8] I define Indigenous territoriality as a complex network of relationships, including human and nonhuman, to sacred sites. These relationships provide a sense of belonging to places and a way of being in the world where animals, plants, rocks, and natural features in the land and waters of the earth are viewed as relatives. Sacred beings help to keep bodies of cultural and environmental knowledge alive for Indigenous communities, such as the Sleeping Buffalo and Medicine Rocks do for Assiniboine communities.

Mountains, rocks, lakes, and trees inform Assiniboine identities, influencing the world in meaningful ways. For many Indigenous peoples, a mountain or a rock sustains a certain body of knowledge: sacred sites bear and protect knowledge. In contrast, sacred Indigenous sites are often interpreted within Western frameworks about landscape or environmental knowledge. In addition, these non-Indigenous-derived concepts fall within jurisdictions of government land management systems, including the National Park Service. All too often, sacred sites are desecrated for tourism, resource extraction, pipelines, highways, or development. In *Hunters and Bureaucrats: Power, Knowledge, and Aboriginal-State Relations in the Southwest Yukon*, Paul Nadasdy correctly argues that Western forms of knowledge documentation and data collection about Indigenous environments cannot fully comprehend Indigenous relationships to their lands and often corrupt those relationships.[9] Nadasdy deconstructs the unequal power of Canadian bureaucracy and the effects on Kluane traditional practices in relating to their territory, such as in the practice of subsistence hunting. For the Kluane, as for the Assiniboine, the animals they hunt, such as moose, are "relatives," whereas for Canadian government officials and environmental scientists, animals are just another wildlife species to manage. Assiniboine people, like other Indigenous nations, map, create atlases, manage wildlife, and store data about their territories and resources in a manner that is akin to a Western archival land management system.[10] For example, Fort Peck Assiniboine and Sioux Reservation maintains tribal lands within their jurisdiction through a complex and bureaucratic Tribal, Fish and Game Department, the Global Positioning System, tribal laws, statistical documentation, data management, and so on. This way of managing lands and archiving information about land and natural resources may be useful when driven by Indigenous peoples themselves rather than through a state or national apparatus, yet it is far different from the relational process of sustaining ceremonial relationships to sacred sites.

Of course, not all Assiniboine narratives about their original homelands are told in the same way, and not all share the same content. Assiniboine oral histories, including the twenty-two interviews I conducted, are fragments and angles of particular visions about a collective sense of Assiniboine territory, belonging, and identity. Furthermore, in all the narratives that I have reviewed, there does not seem to be any moral imperative that every Assiniboine person understands or shares regarding places. At the same time, however, residents of various reservations, including Fort Peck, Fort Belknap, Carry the Kettle, Pheasant Rump, and White Bear, while describing different perspectives about locations, also reveal a shared sense of "original territory." All my consultants acknowledge the Sleeping Buffalo and Medicine Rocks site as an important stopping place to offer prayers and seek protection when traveling west, east, north, or south.[11]

## Makoche Wakan (Sacred Earth)

The Assiniboine call the earth Makoche Wakan, which means Sacred Earth. Like Mecca for Muslims, specific places inform Assiniboine identities, allowing for connections between bands, kin relationships, histories, and spatial understandings, all of which transgress reservation, state, or national boundaries. For Assiniboine people, then, sacred sites are more than symbolic landscapes: sacred sites are *wakan*, which means "powerful," "holy," or "energetic." Sacred sites are knowledge-keepers with power, especially the Sleeping Buffalo and Medicine Rocks.

Sacred sites as keepers of knowledge can be seen in how Assiniboine describe their territories. I witnessed the significance of sacred sites as keepers of knowledge on the small reserve of Pheasant Rump when I interviewed Armand McArthur in his home.[12] Not far from his home a sweat lodge frame sits by a beautiful small blue lake. A barely visible track from it leads up to a sacred hill called Calf Hill, where the grass shines an emerald green in July. After my interview with Armand, he took Robert Four Star and me up in his navy blue Chevy Silverado pickup to an ancient sacred rock site at the peak of this hill. In the center lay a large pile of boulders, about the size of buffalo skulls, on which weathered blue, red, yellow, and white cloth offerings had been placed. From this vantage point, one could see a 360-degree panorama, with cumulus clouds adorning a lapis horizon. Smaller stones radiated out from the center in four directions within a larger concentric circle. McArthur explained that this represented Assiniboine territory. As McArthur described it, starting in the south, he pointed to Devil's Tower in Wyoming; then he pointed west and described the Canadian Rocky Mountains and Stoney Park; then north to Edmonton; then east to Lake of the Woods; and then back to the center. Altogether, this was Assiniboine territory, which was outlined by sacred sites.

A week later, in one of my interviews with Robert Four Star when discussing sacred sites, he stated that the site that Armand McArthur showed us "was a site put together by First Boy, when he came there. . . . The stones to me resemble the original Lodge, Medicine Lodge," and further, "that was about 1100. . . . It tells you where these sacred sites are . . . like boundaries. . . . That doesn't mean that's the only land we occupied. . . . At that time the sacred people that put those there . . . that was the territory they operated in."[13] According to Four Star, sacred sites, especially with stones and petroglyphs like these, are places where prayers go directly to Wagandowa Makoche Gaka (One Above Earth Creator). My interviews with Four Star, McArthur, and others show a collective sense of Assiniboine territory, belonging, and identity.

The Sleeping Buffalo and Medicine Rocks' original location was on a ridge above the Milk River, a place called Cree Crossing. According to Assiniboine, the Sleeping Buffalo, which was the largest boulder at the site, was the leader of a herd of stone buffalo. They were believed to be diversions from hunters, who at first sighting might have assumed the rocks were the animal form of buffalo; and the Indigenous peoples of the region respected them as moral guides and as directional markers. The herd of stone buffalo that dotted the hills around Cree Crossing marked the location where Assiniboine people and other Indigenous peoples would ford the Milk River, moving north or south as they followed animal buffalo herds in Big Bend country, which is today the US-Canadian border.[14] The buffalo rocks and other rocks with petroglyphs throughout this area are deemed highly sacred, placed there specifically by spirit beings.

Many Assiniboine cultural practitioners respect the view that petroglyphs and pictographs are imbued with spiritual power and that they were placed there by spirit beings. I had the great honor of interviewing a very important cultural leader named Gil Horn in July 2012, an elder Assiniboine World War II veteran who remembered visiting Cree Crossing and the Buffalo Rock and Medicine Rocks before their relocations and to the present.[15] I traveled to visit him with the late Robert Four Star, who had adopted me as a son, and was welcomed into his home at Fort Belknap by his daughter, Sis. Robert Four Star was an adopted son of Gil Horn, which helped me gain permission to interview Gil Horn. At ninety-four years of age, with short black-and-gray hair that still covered his head, he sat and laughed and joked with Robert Four Star. He was hard of hearing, so Sis helped to translate. Gil Horn confirmed the spiritual power that the rocks still emanate when he spoke with me in 2012. Horn stated that even when the sacred rocks were north at Cree Crossing and to this day at their present location, when local Indigenous people would visit the sacred rocks they would offer prayers in Assiniboine or their Indigenous language, offer tobacco, and ask for guidance, safe travel, courage, and strength. This ritual practice of praying to the Sleeping Buffalo and Medicine Rocks as the representative leader of buffalo herds has continued to the present day despite the rocks' relocations. The Spirit of the Buffalo remains central in Assiniboine prayers for continued life, even though they do not currently depend on buffalo for sustenance and live on reservations with small buffalo herds managed by Tribal Fish and Game.

Regarding the historical importance that the Sleeping Buffalo holds for local tribes, during the National Historic Registry documentation, Carl Fourstar attested, "All these things that we are hearing, what these people are talking about is not centuries old. What they're talking about is a way of life that exists today and will exist as long as there are Indian people. We'll never be anything else."[16] Carl Fourstar's statement gives strong credence to an important Assiniboine perspective, one that sees sacred sites as keepers of cultural knowledge. Another elder, Bill Tallbull, a Northern Cheyenne man, explained the significance of Cree Crossing: "The ridge itself is like a church and the buffalo is like an altar. When the buffalo was moved, it was like taking the altar from the church."[17] While some would like the rocks returned to their original site, they still keep knowledge alive for Indigenous people at their present location. The sacred rocks' persistent importance, despite their forced migrations, parallels Assiniboine people's endurance in the face of the pain they experienced when they were dispossessed of their territory by the US government when it created the national, state, and reservation borders.

## The Confinement of Reservations

The causes and consequences of reservation boundaries reveal a traumatic history of buffalo destruction for Indigenous peoples of the Northern Plains, including the nine Assiniboine reservations spread out between north-western Alberta and northeastern Montana. By the mid-nineteenth century, as the fur trade escalated into the Northern Plains region, Assiniboine communities had established long-standing networks and influence in the broad territory as described by Armand McArthur at Pheasant Rump. Henry Youle Hind, a Canadian geologist, confirms this in his book *North-West Territory,* which is an illustrated cartographic account of the area written after an expedition through this region in the late 1850s.[18] Hind wrote the name "Assiniboia" to describe the region, from present-day Lake of the Woods, west to the Saskatchewan River, and south to the Yellowstone River.[19] At that time, the British and American governments were competing to build connections across the continent in an effort at national expansion and settlement.

In the United States, a few years after the Treaty of Fort Laramie in 1851, the Treaty of October 17, 1855, established hunting and trading areas primarily for Gros Ventre, Piegan (Blackfeet), and Assiniboine peoples that extended from northern Wyoming to the eastern slopes of the Rocky Mountains, to the Yellowstone River into North Dakota, and north to the US-Canadian border.[20] As Dennis Smith, an enrolled Assiniboine of Fort Peck, discusses, during the 1851 Fort Laramie Treaty, under the authority of "Crazy Bear, chief of the Girl's Band, and The First Who Flies, chief of the Stone Band and brother of The Light . . . Assiniboine agreed to a tribal boundary for Assiniboine bison hunting lands."[21] By this time, the Assiniboine had suffered smallpox epidemics and increased conflicts with other tribes, which were also being pushed from place to place by settler incursions. These peoples included several Sioux tribes, Crow, Blackfeet, Gros Ventre, and various others.

In order to cripple Indigenous peoples of the Northern Plains who were dependent on bison for their existence, American policies of assimilation and national expansion in the late nineteenth century drove an intentional destruction of bison herds. Native peoples also engaged in the decline of the bison, as they, too, supplied the market with bison hides. Nevertheless, the increase in technology and the explicit destructive intent by European American expansionists were the most significant factors. As Jeffrey Ostler argues, "In the early 1870's, however, the political economy of bison destruction underwent a significant transformation when capitalists who controlled new tanning technologies opened up new markets for hides.

. . . [N]on-Indian hunters invaded the Plains, armed with large-bore rifles equipped with telescopic sights and a range of several hundred yards."[22] In conjunction with this overhunting, the construction of the railroads, the lust for Black Hills gold, and conflicts over the Bozeman Trail had the effect of bringing the buffalo to near extinction by 1880.[23] As American forces decimated buffalo herds and as many Indigenous peoples faced starvation, reservations were established.

In the United States, with the Executive Order of July 5, 1873, a multiple tribal reservation that included Assiniboine territory within present-day Montana was reduced, its southern border pushed north and placed at the Missouri River. Then, in the Agreement of May 1, 1888, the three separate present-day reservations at Fort Belknap, Blackfeet, and Fort Peck were established.[24] At Fort Peck, Assiniboine shared the reservation with Sioux and Cree from Turtle Mountain; and at Fort Belknap, they lived among Gros Ventre and Cree-Métis. Gold mining and railroad rights-of-way in the Little Rocky Mountains reduced the southern boundary of Fort Belknap in 1895, thus ceding even more Assiniboine and Gros Ventre territory. Small-scale agriculture programs, such as gardens and cattle ranching, and the provision of rations were set up on the reservations in response to mass starvations, becoming the main source of Indigenous food.[25]

Perhaps the most significant and the most detrimental impact to free access on and off reservation land in the United States was the enforcement of the 1887 Dawes Act in the 1920s, which established large regions of privately owned land designated with barbed-wire fences.[26] Into the early twentieth century in Montana, Assiniboine people subsisted on a combination of rations and small gardens and fields for farming until individual allotments were distributed between 1909 and 1913 at Fort Peck and in 1921 at Fort Belknap. Starting in 1902, the majority of land was leased to settler cattle companies on both reservations. At Fort Peck, lands that had not been allotted were opened to settlers for homesteading in 1917, whereas at Fort Belknap, in 1921, all reservation land was allotted to tribal members.[27] At both Fort Peck and Fort Belknap the discovery of oil in the 1950s led to economic opportunity for tribes. At the same time, the US government only approved leases for individual landowners.[28]

Assiniboine stories about lands they have inhabited for generations share a common theme about original homelands that predate treaties and reservations. They each point to similar boundary markers in order to outline Assiniboine territory during that earlier historical period. This area extended from what is now called the Cypress Hills, Saskatchewan, in the north, south to the Yellowstone River in southern Montana, east to the White Earth River near Fort Union in North Dakota, and west to the

Big Belt Mountains and Sweet Grass Hills of western Montana. Assiniboine descriptions about their original territory show the connections that the Assiniboine have maintained to certain places, despite reservation, state, and national boundaries.[29] Since the time of precontact, before the worst aspects of US colonialism, to the early twentieth century, Sleeping Buffalo and Medicine Rock sat in their place of origin in the heart of Assiniboine territory, a midpoint between all the directions, north, south, east, and west.

How the two boulders were forcibly relocated after three site changes tells a parallel story not only about the boulders' persistence as knowledge bearers but also about the integral importance of Assiniboine people's and other Indigenous peoples' relationships to sacred sites despite forced relocations and land dispossession. The following history of the forced migration of Sleeping Buffalo and Medicine Rocks in the twentieth century and their isolation from their original location and herds demonstrates the violence inflicted on the land itself, the buffalo, and Assiniboine people.

## Settler Views of the Sleeping Buffalo and Medicine Rocks

In the 1860s Granville Stuart, an American pioneer in Montana, gave the first written settler account of the Sleeping Buffalo and the sacred rocks along the Milk River in "Life and Customs of the Indians," which is a chapter in the 1925 book of his journals, *Forty Years on the Frontier*. Stuart describes how local Native peoples of northern Montana would leave "shrines" of cloth, sage, meat, or tobacco offerings on trees and rocks "to invoke the aid of the Great Spirit." Stuart was particularly impressed with the Sleeping Buffalo: "In the big bend of Milk river thirty miles east of Fort Belknap is a big gray granite rock resembling a buffalo lying down. This rock was greatly reverenced by the Blackfeet and River Crows and in passing they always placed on it some talisman. Many of them made long pilgrimages to this sacred rock for the sole purpose of making offerings."[30] Stuart's journals are quite thorough in his descriptions of places that were and still are sacred to local Indigenous peoples.

An article in the October 2, 1958, *Phillips County News* entitled "Sleeping Buffalo at Plunge Turn-Off Revered by Early Day Indian Tribes" quotes Granville Stuart's account, but it also gives other important Indigenous history about the spiritual significance of the sacred rocks. This article states that the rock "was left on the Cree Crossing ridge at least 200 million years ago," and further, "stories told by the Assiniboines date their arrival in the upper Missouri River country at about 1700." The article concludes with the earliest land developer's observations of Cree Crossing: "Henry Hedges and H. G. Robinson who came into northern Montana in 1892 and established ranches in the area of the Cree Crossing told of seeing beads and pieces of cloth on the stone, indicating that until fairly recently the Indians believed in the powers of the 'Sleeping Buffalo.'"[31] Thus, the article reveals the assumption that local Indigenous beliefs regarding the sacred power inherent in the rocks had died off by the 1950s. Yet, tragically, in the 1930s settlers removed the Sleeping Buffalo from this original location on what would later become three forced migrations throughout the twentieth century.

The Sleeping Buffalo was first separated from the herd of other buffalo boulders at Cree Crossing in 1932. It was relocated to a city park in the small town of Malta, Montana. A local newspaper story in the *Phillips County News* dated August 27, 1931, entitled "Sacred Buffalo to Sit on Pedestal in Park" states that "plans are being formulated for the construction of a cement pedestal upon which the Sacred Buffalo will be permanently set in the city park on Front Street." According to this article, the Commercial Club instigated this forced migration. What is clear when reading this three-paragraph article is that there was a strong non-Indigenous desire to publicly archive historical sites. For example, the article states, "Henry Hedges, who for many years has been interested in historical matters in this section of the state, has offered to paint the rock with red and blue colors as it was when he first saw it in 1893." Hedges had seen it in its original location "on the H. G. Robinson ranch at the Cree crossing of [the] Milk River. The rock overlooked a wide level flat to the south upon which ground the Indians held their sports and games."[32] The exact reasons why the Sleeping Buffalo was removed are unclear; however, we can assume that non-Native private landowners desired to claim and control Indigenous territory, and they were the ones who displaced the ancient Sleeping Buffalo to the center of a young Montana town. Perhaps this was a way for Montanan settler descendants to claim an appropriated form of cultural inheritance. Thus, one of the most sacred artifacts, a sentient being, in many Indigenous views, was removed, possessed, and placed on display in a non-Indigenous public space.

A short time after the disturbances reported in Tafton Park, Malta, in 1932, the local American Legion chapter relocated the Sleeping Buffalo and Medicine Rocks to a location east of Malta along Old US Highway 2, where they remained for several decades.[33] At that time, engineers working for the Farm Security Administration built a tall monument of stone and mortar between the rocks. An article entitled "Gifts Left at Buffalo Rock as by Indians in Olden Times," written in 1937, stated that travelers at that time left pennies on the buffalo's back and on the Medicine Rock instead of traditional tobacco, cloth, or meat offerings. The article speculates about the curious transnational phenomenon of pennies: "In all about 300 pennies have been left at the two Indian rocks. One-third of them have been

Canadian coins which may indicate that Canadians are more superstitious or that they believe in following ancient traditions or merely that a great many Canadians visit the Legion plunge." This article also reported an interesting lunar cycle: "Clyde Ferris, project engineer, has observed that more coins are left during the full moon than at any other time."[34] Though this article gives some interesting physical accounts of coin currency in the 1930s, and Canadian tourists are discussed in a humorous tone, local Indigenous peoples seem to have vanished altogether in this narrative, replaced by the customs of obscure "motorists" and the "passerby." Again, after the second forced migration, the Sleeping Buffalo and Medicine Rocks seem to have been claimed by local settlers.

Moving the boulders from the town park in Malta to this location at the junction of Old US Highway 2 and the Malta Legion Plunge Road was strategic. This junction was a few miles from the Malta American Legion Health Plunge, a natural hot springs that the Works Progress Administration had expanded.[35]

## Local Indigenous Views on the Forced Migrations of the Sleeping Buffalo and Medicine Rocks

In both written texts and oral histories, Assiniboine people describe the Sleeping Buffalo and Medicine Rocks in situ, before their removal. In *Land of Nakoda* (1942), First Boy (James Long) devotes ten pages to the importance of the buffalo, specifically, the Sleeping Buffalo, for Assiniboine people. Long confirms their importance: "In the buffalo country is a rock, which resembles a buffalo lying down. It was held sacred by the tribe. . . . [W]henever a band passed by they always camped at some suitable camping place near the rock. Then the people placed offerings around it; some were thanksgiving for things received or for good health enjoyed by their families. . . . The medicine men, who had the Spirit Buffalo for their helper, made their sacrifices for the welfare and prosperity of the people."[36] Fire Bear (William Standing), the illustrator for *Land of Nakoda*, drew a picture of men praying with the Sleeping Buffalo.

In one of Long's interviews, Duck, who was seventy-nine years old at the time, tells two powerful moral stories about the buffalo rock, "handed down through the generations of our people."[37] The first story Duck tells describes how a war party of Assiniboine originally thought that they had discovered a small slumbering herd of buffalo rather than boulders and thus how the boulders became the sacred protectors of the buffalo in animal form. The party leader determined that "this place is sacred," enacted a pipe ceremony of thanksgiving, and offered prayers for sustaining people through hard times. The second story Duck tells describes how a very young couple stranded from their band was saved from starvation during a time when Assiniboine people in the area faced famine. At the time, there were no buffalo in sight, and they thought they were going to die. After the young man offered prayers to the Sleeping Buffalo, Thunder Beings came and with lightning and thunder diverted three buffalo toward the couple's small willow lodge. With the man on the woman's back, since his legs were too weak to walk, he was able to muster enough strength in his arms to kill one buffalo with his bow and arrow. The next morning, the woman found her band, and they were able to hunt the other two buffalo, living to tell the story. There are many stories like this among other tribes of the area that explain the moral importance of taking only what is necessary to live from the buffalo.[38] This is both heard and seen in the oral histories and the written records about these sacred rocks.

## How the Sleeping Buffalo and Medicine Rocks became a "Historic Place"

In the 1990s the fact that the sacred rocks had been forcibly relocated three times to reshape the land for the expansion of settler society presents an awkward irony. People in the non-Indigenous public, travelers of Highway 2, and the federal and state governments seemed to claim the Sleeping Buffalo site for their own and displace prereservation Indigenous culture, specifically Assiniboine culture, into the past. In contrary view, Assiniboine and other tribal memories and practices related to this sacred site were still very much alive. In 1995 Chere Jiusto, a non-Indigenous person who worked for the Montana State Historical Preservation Office (MSHPO), consulted with and interviewed eight elders from six different regional tribes in order to evaluate the impact of the rocks' displacements. Each tribe considered the elders who were consulted regarding the nomination of the Sleeping Buffalo and Medicine Rocks as part of the National Historic Register as spiritual leaders. These interviews and meetings were conducted to determine whether or not the Sleeping Buffalo and Medicine Rocks should be designated as a "Historic Place" on the National Park Service's National Historic Register and thus protected as a public site. In addition to the interviews held in Billings and Great Falls, Montana, over the course of 1995, Jiusto also documented the elders' statements from various communities throughout northern Montana at a discussion meeting at Sleeping Buffalo Hot Springs Resort in November 1995.

The meeting exemplified the complex relationship between the rocks, local Indigenous peoples, the public's interest as represented by the

National Park System and the state's transportation agency, and a small private resort. The owners of the resort, Jon Cantway and Roger Ereaux, were strong supporters of the Indigenous elders' views. The elders at the meeting argued that the sacred rocks' exposure along a national interstate highway for decades presented a significant offense to local Indigenous peoples. Nevertheless, relocating them to their original location at Cree Crossing also was not a viable option for two reasons. First, the rocks originated from privately held ranchland. Second, it would be a major obstacle for elders to visit the location given the current roads and fences in place. It is significant that Jiusto's National Register of Historic Places document, recorded on paper and as digital data, includes the elders' memories, which arc back to both the time before and the time after the forced migration of the Sleeping Buffalo and Medicine Rocks. As cultural knowledge keepers in the Indigenous sense, the elders show their reverence for the rocks' sacredness as protectors in their own right and stress that their historical knowledge should not be undervalued.

Out of the eight tribal consultants interviewed by the MSHPO, three were Assiniboine elders: Leslie Fourstar, Carl Fourstar, and Gil Horn. In 1995 Leslie Fourstar was the oldest tribal member of the Fort Peck Assiniboine and, according to Jiusto, the last remaining fluent speaker in the "old Assiniboine language." Leslie Fourstar, while attesting to the power of the boulders, told one story about how one of his daughters was originally born dead; however, after he prayed to the "Buffalo Rock," she began crying ten minutes after her birth. Leslie Fourstar also declared, "We Assiniboines consider that Sleeping Buffalo the most sacred thing." He went on to tell another story of how some Assiniboine first came upon the Sleeping Buffalo in its original location, which was a story passed down from his grandfather's grandfather, and "other old timers [who] told the same story, identical."[39] The elders obviously remembered the time when they were children before the rocks were displaced from Cree Crossing.

In deep time, the Sleeping Buffalo and Medicine Rocks etched a living memory in these elders that predated the rocks' first removal in 1932 and subsequent relocations. Pat Chief Stick, a Chippewa-Cree, tells the story about how the Sleeping Buffalo was moved for road construction and then returned by its own volition.[40] Pat Chief Stick heard the story from a "Canadian Indian" at Waterton Park, Alberta, which sits on the border of Glacier Park in Montana. According to the story, road workers asked for assistance from a local medicine man, who then performed a pipe ceremony for the mysterious rock, which had moved itself back to its original position. After the ceremony, the medicine man declared, "That rock is sacred. It doesn't want to be removed. Let it sit where you found it." Representing a collective view held by all the consultants, Pat Chief Stick also stated the importance of the original location at Cree Crossing: "The Cree Crossing comes from the time of long time ago. When they were hunting buffalo this is where they used to come."[41] Moving parties, bands, and groups that crossed the Milk River at this point to hunt buffalo or make exchanges with other tribes considered this site sacred. According to all eight tribal consultants, the original site of these boulders at Cree Crossing remains historically significant for all the tribes of the greater Northern Plains.

John "Buster" Yellow Kidney, a Blackfeet elder and spiritual leader, also affirmed the importance of being instructed in cultural and historical knowledge at this pre-relocation ancient sacred site. In his February 17, 1995, interview with Chere Jiusto, Don Wetzel (Blackfeet), and Paul Putz in Great Falls, Montana, Buster tells how as a young boy his grandfather used to take him to Cree Crossing and the Sleeping Buffalo before its relocation to instill the importance of this place as a living archive. Buster remembers, "When my grandfather was alive, he took me to these places, he showed me this is what happened here. He took me to the Crossing. . . . They used to move there and they'd spend two–three days there, nothing but ceremonies involving the buffalo."[42] Jiusto also referenced A. L. Kroeber's ethnographic records that describe Gros Ventre practices in relation to the buffalo rocks at the turn of the twentieth century.[43]

Several elders interviewed by Jiusto recorded memories of the sacred rocks' first removal from Cree Crossing to the town of Malta. After the move in 1932, local Indigenous elders stated that the Sleeping Buffalo did not like its home in Trafton Park, Malta. Donovan Archambault, a member of the local Gros Ventre of Fort Belknap, relayed some interesting history about Sleeping Buffalo to Don Wetzel (Blackfeet) during a phone interview in November 1995. Wetzel was then working with Chere Jiusto for the National Register of Historic Places. According to Archambault, people of the town reported that the Sleeping Buffalo would change directions, moving at night, suggesting it wanted to return to its original location: "The people in Malta at night would hear these buffalo bellowing, and they didn't know where it was coming from. So they wanted them out of there."[44] Leslie Fourstar confirmed this history: "One night, one of the city patrol heard a cow bellowing and wondered if it was coming from this rock. He got scared and told the other patrol, the police. And they came over and it bellowed again. So they brought it back down to that place where they moved it from."[45] From Assiniboine and other local Indigenous peoples' view, the Sleeping Buffalo's reported volition was not unexpected. According to Assiniboine oral tradition and worldview, human beings are quite similar to buffalo in terms of social behavior and how they raise their young. In this sense, humans and buffalo are both social animals with hierarchies and specific role relationships, and they move together in kin groups. So from Assiniboine people's perspectives, it would make sense that the Sleeping Buffalo would feel unnaturally out of place, alone, and restless.

In 1967 the Montana Highway Transportation Authority constructed the new Highway 2 approximately two miles north of the old highway. At the time of this change, the Sleeping Buffalo was moved for the third time, to where it sits in its present location, a highway right-of-way on the north side of the highway; unfortunately, the Medicine Rock was left at the Old Highway 2 site.[46] This made the Sleeping Buffalo highly accessible to local Indigenous people and the general public on a heavily traveled interstate highway, but it also left the Sleeping Buffalo unprotected and separated from the Medicine Rock.

Twenty years later, in 1987, Jon Cantway and Roger Ereaux, owners and operators of the Sleeping Buffalo Resort, formerly the Legion Plunge, now named after the sacred rock, petitioned the Montana Highway Department to build a protective structure for the rock and volunteered to be the caretakers of Sleeping Buffalo. Tribal councils from Fort Peck, Fort Belknap, and Rocky Boy, as well as the Phillips and Valley Counties Historical Societies, all supported the construction of a "shrine" for the Sleeping Buffalo. In addition, they suggested that it be nominated for the National Register of Historic Places, a petition that was unsuccessful until a decade later, in the 1990s.[47] Consequently, at the junction of US Highway 2 and the small road that leads to the Sleeping Buffalo Resort, today one can see the shelter constructed out of wood and stone discussed at the beginning of this article. To mark the completion of this shelter, the first Sleeping Buffalo Days Celebration was held in September 1987. A temporary arbor was built where members from local tribes performed dance ceremonies.

More importantly, because of consultations held with local Native elders, the Medicine Rock also was moved for a third time, this time migrating from the Old Highway 2 location, where it had been left behind, to again join the Sleeping Buffalo. At this ceremonial event, local spiritual leaders Ken Ryan (Assiniboine), Max White (Assiniboine), and Donovan Archambault (Gros Ventre) conducted a pipe ceremony.[48] According to some local people, this was an improvement because it provided the elderly and the physically challenged a more convenient location. Cultural practitioners from multiple tribes that know the history of these sacred rocks stop to give prayers and offerings. In addition, the maintenance by the owners of the Sleeping Buffalo Resort helps to protect the rocks, which also present an interesting tourist attraction for visitors.

Despite the Indigenous reverence for the sacred rocks, as Chere Jiusto points out in her description, the Sleeping Buffalo and Medicine Rocks' "exposure to the public leaves them vulnerable to desecration and vandalism. Many days, trash, broken glass and other things are mixed with the offerings, defiling the site and the buffalo rock."[49] Unfortunately, I have observed the same condition. It is quite painful for an Assiniboine cultural practitioner to see broken beer bottles scattered around these sacred rocks. In sum, then, the present shelter for the Sleeping Buffalo and Medicine Rocks provides both protection from and exposure to the public as a designated National Historic Registry site.

On May 17, 1996, the location of Sleeping Buffalo and the adjacent Medicine Rock were designated a ceremonial site by the National Register of Historic Places. There was a great deal of local controversy over this designation.[50] The Native elders who were interviewed were from seven different tribes, but all shared a common history with the Buffalo Rock. These tribes included the Blackfeet, Assiniboine, Gros Ventre, Chippewa, Cree, Northern Cheyenne, and Crow. Several of those consulted were Assiniboine relatives of some of my interviewees, while others were people whom I had known personally. Some individuals wanted the rocks returned to their original location; some wanted them to remain because of their appeal to tourists; and some wanted to keep them at this site as easy access for elderly Indigenous peoples. All the Indigenous consultants considered these rocks imbued with sacred power.

Finally, after this consultation with local elders, the National Park Service officials signed the nomination form and listed the rocks as a "Historic Place" in April 1996. Even though no one owns the rocks as private property, today they reside under the jurisdiction of the Montana Department of Transportation. Jiusto affirmed in the introduction to the nomination form that "in assessing the integrity of ceremonial objects such as the Sleeping Buffalo Rock, those most qualified to gauge the level of integrity are the traditional users themselves. The rocks have a strong presence of their own . . . . The continued relationship and ceremonial use of the Sleeping Buffalo Rock by the traditional community is evidence of their perception that the rocks maintain their power, significance and meaning. . . . The integrity of the rock itself and its cultural link to the native peoples of the high plains remains unbroken."[51] In a larger frame of reference, the Sleeping Buffalo and Medicine Rocks represent the issue of sacred sites as keepers of knowledge for Indigenous peoples. Many of these sacred sites, and the Indigenous groups that sustain relationships to them, were able to survive land dispossession, starvation, and reservation and national boundary designations. For Indigenous peoples of the Northern Plains, the Sleeping Buffalo and Medicine Rocks are sentient beings—keepers of knowledge—who help them perpetuate their territoriality; they also represent the survival of the buffalo. In acknowledging this continuity, Jiusto asserted that "despite tremendous changes during the historic period, tribal groups on the Northern Plains today continue to trace an uninterrupted affiliation with their aboriginal territories and a continuance of the cultural fabric, although some of their lifeways have changed and adapted to new conditions. To them, the power of the Sleeping Buffalo remains undiminished."[52] As a result of the recognition on the National Register of Historic Places in 1996, it was decided that the Sleeping Buffalo and Medicine Rocks would remain at their present location and that the owners of the Sleeping Buffalo Resort would be caretakers.

## Conclusion

Reservation, state, and national boundaries are imaginary lines drawn onto political maps; yet they have had real effects on Assiniboine lives. On the other hand, borders do not limit the Assiniboine people. Routes predating European American contact have been conduits for trade in goods and bodies of cultural knowledge across the vast stretches that Assiniboine people have long considered their homelands. Assiniboine people have always been on the move, dwelling in places and gaining knowledge from sacred sites that span a massive region, from the Rocky Mountains to the Great Lakes and from the Yellowstone River in Montana to the Athabascan River in Alberta.

The Sleeping Buffalo and Medicine Rocks are just one example of how sacred sites have sustained bodies of cultural knowledge. As discussed above, there are many other examples of important sites from which Assiniboine draw meaning and power. While some sites are within reservation boundaries, others span the wide breadth of Assiniboine ancestral territories. Deep in the heart of Fort Belknap, I had the honor of staying with Teddy Bell, Robert Four Star's adoptive brother. Teddy lives in what is called the Iron Cradle, a pristine environment of pine forests, limestone, shale, and sandstone cliffs that form a kind of cradle at the north side of the Little Rockies. Parts of the Little Rockies were excluded from the reservation, and they were the location where the company Landusky and Zortman Mines contaminated the land while reaping millions in profit, none of which the tribes ever saw. In Assiniboine, the Little Rockies are called Iyagheh Widana (Rock Island). Teddy stated that there are a lot of elk, mountain lions, bear, and deer that live around his home. Like many residents of reservations in Montana, people hunt many of these animals for subsistence, not for trophies. Even so, Teddy does not allow any hunting, as he sees himself as a caretaker of the land; as he said, "Living in harmony with nature" is a quiet and yet deep belief, not just a cliché.[53] His name, Inkmu Yahaza, means Mountain Lion Protects Him.

As the Sleeping Buffalo and Medicine Rocks kept knowledge alive from the late nineteenth century through the twentieth century, even when settlers removed them from their original home, the period of established reservations and assimilation programs failed to destroy Assiniboine connections to their original territories. Similar to the rocks' continued existence as sentient beings along Highway 2, now sheltered in a National Historic Registry shed, Assiniboine have adapted to modern economic systems and international boundaries to fit their own purposes, and now many tribes maintain small herds of buffalo.

The Sleeping Buffalo and Medicine Rocks and other sacred sites protect local animals and plants, as well as the continuity of Assiniboine sense of peoplehood in relation to their homelands. Sacred sites for Assiniboine keep cultural knowledge alive through relationships of mutual interdependence. In the Northern Plains of America, settlers decimated the buffalo and imposed the reservation system on the Assiniboine. This forced them to adapt their practices to small-scale ranching and government bureaucracy. Today the Assiniboine have their own herds of buffalo and a tribally managed Fish and Game Department (FGD).[54] Even though Assiniboine people, buffalo herds, and the Sleeping Buffalo and Medicine Rocks have been displaced by forced migrations to reservations and reorganized by government structures through the late nineteenth century to the present, the Assiniboine view of buffalo and rocks as living relatives and keepers of sacred knowledge remains strong.

Assiniboine ties to their ancestral homelands as seen with sacred sites such as the Sleeping Buffalo and Medicine Rocks exemplify an ongoing Indigenous resistance to settler, state, and corporate dominance over Indigenous homelands globally. As Gerald Vizenor states in "Aesthetics of Survivance," "The practices of survivance create an active presence, more than the instincts of survival, function, or subsistence." Vizenor defines survivance from a Native perspective as "the action, condition, quality, and sentiments of the verb *survive*, 'to remain alive or in existence,' to outlive, persevere with a suffix of *survivancy*."[55] For many Indigenous peoples, such as the Assiniboine, survivance largely depends on unfettered relations with the nonhuman world, such as animals, rocks, and undeveloped lands. With the example given in this article, the relationship between the sacred site known as the Sleeping Buffalo and Medicine Rocks and the Indigenous peoples of the Northern Plains lives on despite the ongoing settler, nation-state, and corporate treatment of land as commodity.

**JOSHUA HOROWITZ** is a lecturer and program manager at San Francisco State University. He earned a PhD in history from the University of British Columbia in 2014. He is working on a manuscript from his dissertation, "Nakona Wasnonya Yuhabi / Assiniboine Knowledge Keepers: Indigenous Archiving from the 19th into the 21st Centuries." His next project will focus on local Indigenous cultural practitioners in the San Francisco Bay Area whose work helps Indigenous communities globally keep their bodies of knowledge alive for future generations.

## Notes

1. According to the Assiniboine elders whom I learned from, the Assiniboine are a First Nations / Native American tribe of the Nakona (plural, Nakonabi) or Nakoda or Nakota, all of which translate to the Friendly People. The late Robert Four Star taught me that the correct spelling and pronunciation of the word is Nakona, and most Assiniboine I interviewed agree; nonetheless, different people on different reserves have their own opinions on the matter, which are sometimes hotly debated. Throughout this article I use the name Assiniboine, a Cree word that means Stone Boilers, according to some Assiniboine oral history; however, linguists debate this issue. For a summary of this issue, see Raymond J. DeMallie and David Reed Miller, "Assiniboine," in *Handbook of North American Indians*, ed. William C. Sturtevant, vol. 13, *Plains*, part 1 (Washington, DC: Smithsonian Institution Press, 2001), 590—92. I am part Seneca on my mother's side and was involved in the Student Alliance of North American Indians and Native American Studies at the University of California at Santa Cruz for many years. The late Rudolph Oliver Archdale, a brother of the late Robert Four Star, introduced me to the Sleeping Buffalo Rock the first time in the summer of 1996. I first met Archdale, a powerful Assiniboine medicine man (*pejuta wichasha*, or "plants man"), in June 1996 on the Fort Peck Assiniboine and Sioux Reservation in Wolf Point, Montana. Jeff Cummins, an Assiniboine tribal member, had invited me to drive with him to attend the Medicine Lodge, held annually in June after the first full moon on the Fort Peck Reservation. I knew Jeff as a sweat brother from the University of California at Santa Cruz, and we were fellow members of the Student Alliance of North American Indians. Cummins was also one of the interviewees for the oral history research for my dissertation. I discuss Archdale and my induction into Assiniboine societies further in the introduction to my dissertation; this article draws from chapter 4 of my dissertation. In the fall of 2016 I went to Wolf Point on the reservation to honor and pay homage to my late *ade* (father; it is not customary to say "adopted," according to Assiniboine tradition), Robert Four Star (Tatanga Hunga Dobah Naji, Chief Buffalo Stops Four Times), and helped his family for their one-year memorial giveaway ceremony. I reflected on the many pilgrimages west on Highway 2 with Robert Four Star when we stopped at the Sleeping Buffalo and Medicine Rocks to give offerings and prayers for safe travel for all our relatives and to give thanks for the great privilege it is to walk this Makoche

Wakan. This great honor I owe to the Assiniboine people who first introduced me to the Sleeping Buffalo and Medicine Rocks, Oliver Archdale and his brother, Robert Four Star.

2. Chere Jiusto, "Recent History of the Sleeping Buffalo Rock," MSHPO, NPS/NRHP, file number 96000548, sec. 8.

3. Pat Chief Stick statements and discussion, Sleeping Buffalo meeting, November 30, 1995, Sleeping Buffalo Hot Springs, Saco, MT, Chere Jiusto, MSHPO, NPS/NRHP, file number 96000548, sec. 8, p. 4.

4. Chere Jiusto, "Sleeping Buffalo and Medicine Rocks," Montana State Historical Preservation Office, Phillips County, Montana, May 17, 1996, National Park Service Archives, file number 96000548, sec. 8. According to this document, members of these other tribes also consider the Sleeping Buffalo and Medicine Rocks as sacred helpers.

5. Daniel Heath Justice, "Kinship Criticism and the Decolonization Imperative," in *Reasoning Together: The Native Critics Collective,* by Janice Acoose, Craig S. Womack, Daniel Heath Justice, and Christopher B. Teuton (Norman: University of Oklahoma Press, 2008), 151. Justice draws on Amanda Cobb's concept "*peopleness*" (unpublished manuscript in the collective's possession, 1986).

6. Justice, "Kinship Criticism," 152.

7. Linda Tuhiwai Smith, *Decolonizing Methodologies: Research and Indigenous Peoples* (London: Zed Books, 1999), 74.

8. I draw from Mishuana Goerman's work *Mark My Words: Native Women Mapping Our Nations* (Minneapolis: University of Minnesota Press, 2013), on the differences between settler-colonial concepts of territory and Indigenous concepts of territory.

9. See Paul Nadasdy, *Hunters and Bureaucrats: Power, Knowledge, and Aboriginal-State Relations in the Southwest Yukon* (Vancouver: UBC Press, 2003).

10. For an example of an Assiniboine interpretation that utilized two-dimensional cartography, see a map of the Fort Peck Reservation produced by Donald "Ducky" La Vay, a Bureau of Indian Affairs employee in 1983, which shows the principal waterways in bold thicker lines that look very much like a bird's-eye view of an outline of a buffalo; David Miller, Dennis Smith, Joseph R. McGeshick, James Shanley, and Caleb Shields, *The History of the Assiniboine and Sioux Tribes of the Fort Peck Indian Reservation, Montana, 1800–2000* (Helena: Montana Historical Society Press, 2008), 481. For an interesting discussion that contrasts Indigenous and European American styles of mapping territory, see Renée Fosset, "Mapping Inuktut: Inuit Views of the Real World," in *Reading beyond Words: Contexts of Native History,* ed. Jennifer Brown and Elizabeth Vibert (Peterborough, ON: Broadview Press, 2003), 111–32.

11. Not by coincidence, it is an image and description of the Sleeping Buffalo and Medicine Rocks that Brenda Farnell uses to begin her sixth chapter: "Chapter 6: Storytelling and the Embodiment of Symbolic Form," in *Do You See What I Mean? Plains Indian Sign Talk and the Embodiment of Action* (Lincoln: University of Nebraska Press, 2009), 174.

12. Armand McArthur had called me requesting this interview. I had visited with him while he was leading the Medicine Lodge at Carry the Kettle, and he had requested Robert Four Star to sing at the lodge. I helped Robert sing and had traveled on all these trips with Robert as my navigator, guide, and consultant. After this interview at his home, Armand asked Robert for songs, and after Robert recorded them, Armand gave Robert a very sacred Eagle Feather headdress he had been given previously when he had been a band chief. This was an excellent example of exchanging songs and regalia as a way of archiving.

13. Interview with Robert Four Star in the home of Larry Smith, July 9, 2012.

14. Historical placard at the Cree Crossing as photographed by Phil Konstantin in 2003 at the website www.americanindian.net/2003w.html, accessed March 5, 2012.

15. Gil Horn interview (with Robert Four Star and Sis Horn present) in his home at Fort Belknap, Montana, July 5, 2012.

16. Carl Fourstar's statements and discussion, Sleeping Buffalo meeting, November 30, 1995, 5.

17. William Tallbull's statements and interview with Don Wetzel and Chere Jiusto, November 2, 1995, Billings, MT, Chere Jiusto, MSHPO, NPS/NRHP, file number 96000548, sec. 8, p. 5.

18. Henry Youle Hind, *North-West Territory, British North America: Reports of Progress Together with a Preliminary and General Report on the Assiniboine and Saskatchewan Exploring Expedition, Made under Instructions from the Provincial Secretary, Canada* (London: G. E. Eyre and W. Spottiswoode, 1860), B2. I could argue here that this exemplified imperial anxiety about the growing Metis "problem."

19. "Assiniboia" first appears in ibid., 127; Hind points out that Assiniboine is from "'assini' a stone—Cree" word. See also maps in S. J. (Simon James) Dawson, *Report on the Exploration of the Country Between Lake Superior and the Red River Settlement: And Between the Latter Place and the Assiniboine and Saskatchewan* (Toronto: J. Lovell, 1859).

20. For a focused discussion of events leading up to the creation of the Fort Peck reservation, see Dennis Smith, "Convergence: Fort Peck Assiniboine and Sioux Arrive in the Fort Peck Region 1800–1871," in Miller et al., *The History*, 55.

21. Ibid., 46.

22. See Jeffrey Ostler, *The Plains Sioux and U.S. Colonialism from Lewis and Clark to Wounded Knee* (New York: Cambridge University Press, 2004). I discuss this in more depth in my introductory chapter to my dissertation when I discuss the Azanzana and prereservation and contemporary Nakona historicity. For an excellent discussion of the transformations of Plains Indian cultures caused by equestrian, beaver-to-bison fur trade transitions, and European American expansion, see Pekka Hämäläinen, "The Rise and Fall of Plains Indian Horse Cultures," *Journal of American Indian History* 90, no. 3 (2003): 833–62.

23. The Bozeman Trail was a route used by settlers to migrate through Indigenous territories from southeastern Wyoming Territory to the gold fields of present-day Montana in the 1860s. The US military set up forts along this trail to try to protect these settlers from Indigenous tribes that attacked settlers.

For a discussion of this trail's significance during this period of US imperialism in North Plains Indigenous territories, please see Pekka Hämäläinen, *The Comanche Empire* (New Haven, CT: Yale University Press, 2008), 321; also see Ostler, *The Plains Sioux*, 45.

24. DeMallie and Miller, "Assiniboine," 585. Also see Loretta Fowler, *The Columbia Guide to American Indians of the Great Plains* (New York: Columbia University Press, 2003), 87, and map 7 on p. 54.

25. DeMallie and Miller, "Assiniboine," 585–86.

26. In an excellent study of the tragedy of land dispossession, see Melissa Meyer, *The White Earth Tragedy: Ethnicity and Dispossession at a Minnesota Anishinaabe Reservation, 1889–1920* (Lincoln: University of Nebraska Press, 1999). Also, the Industrial Survey Records done by the Office of Indian Affairs in the 1910s and 1920s show photographs and notes regarding families' "progress" with small-scale farming and livestock, such as numbers of chickens, donkeys, and cattle at Fort Peck and Fort Belknap: archival research conducted in June 2010, Industrial Survey Records, Reports of Industrial Surveys, 1922–1929, Fort Belknap and Fort Berthold, box 10, PI-163, entry 762, RG 75, National Archives I, Washington, DC.

27. DeMallie and Miller, "Assiniboine," 586.

28. Loretta Fowler, *Shared Symbols, Contested Meanings: Gros Ventre Culture and History, 1778–1984* (Ithaca, NY: Cornell University Press, 1987), 107.

29. For maps that show Assiniboine original territory and then their subsequent reservations, see Fowler, *The Columbia Guide*, 27, 31, 33, 54. Also, see my favorite artistic map by Assiniboine artist William Standing on the inside cover of James L. Long, *Land of Nakoda: The Story of the Assiniboine Indians, from the Tales of the Old Ones Told to First Boy (James L. Long) with Drawings by Fire Bear (William Standing), under Direction of the Writers' Program of the Work Projects Administration in the State of Montana* (1942; Helena, MT: State Publishing Company, 2004). The 2004 edition includes an introduction by James Shanley.

30. Granville Stuart and Paul C. Phillips, *Forty Years on the Frontier as Seen in the Journals and Reminiscences of Granville Stuart, Gold-Miner, Trader, Merchant, Rancher and Politician* (Lincoln: University of Nebraska Press, 1925), 15, 41. Also, Stuart describes the "Sundance" and medicine men in a way that matches current descriptions (41–45). In his introduction see the information about his envoy and "minister plenipotentiary" to Uruguay and Paraguay— his journals contain "much information about the copper, nitrate, and other resources of that continent" (17). Stuart is also quoted in the article "Sleeping Buffalo at Plunge Turn-Off Revered by Early Day Indian Tribes," *Phillips County News*, October 2, 1958.

31. "Sleeping Buffalo at Plunge Turn-Off," cited in Diane Smith's ("The Rock Whisperer") picture-book, which is titled *The Sleeping Buffalo Rock and Other Petroglyph Features in Phillips County Montana* (n.p.: self-published, 2007), 21.

32. "Sacred Buffalo to Sit on Pedestal in Park," *Phillip County News*, August 27, 1931. I found this as a photocopy in Smith, *The Sleeping Buffalo Rock*, 17.

33. Jiusto, "Recent History," 4.

34. "Gifts Left at Buffalo Rock as by Indians in Olden Times," *Great Falls Tribune*, December 9, 1937, cited in Smith, *The Sleeping Buffalo Rock*, 17.

35. Gladys Costello, "Sleeping Buffalo Revered by Indians for Centuries," *Phillips County News*, September 1962, cited in Smith, *The Sleeping Buffalo Rock*, 25.

36. Long, *Land of Nakoda*, 81.

37. Ibid.

38. See the chapter "Buffalo—Staff of Life," in ibid., 74–85.

39. Leslie Fourstar's statements and discussion, Sleeping Buffalo meeting, November 30, 1995, 1.

40. See similar accounts regarding rock volition for Musquem in Vancouver in Susan Roy, *These Mysterious People: Shaping History and Archeology in a Northwest Community* (Montreal: McGill-Queen's University Press, 2010).

41. Pat Chief Stick, statement, November 30, 1995, as documented by Jiusto, "Sleeping Buffalo and Medicine Rocks," 2.

42. John "Buster" Yellow Kidney's statements in interview with Don Wetzel, Chere Jiusto, and Paul Putz, Great Falls, November 17, 1995, MSHPO, NPS/NRHP, Chere Jiusto, file number 96000548, sec. 8, p. 1.

43. Chere Jiusto, MSHPO, NPS/NRHP, file number 96000548, sec. 8, p. 2. Jiusto cites A. L. Kroeber, *Ethnology of the Gros Ventre*, Anthropological Papers of the American Museum of Natural History 1, pt. 4 (New York: American Museum of Natural History, 1908), 281.

44. Donovan Archambault, telephone interview with Don Wetzel, November 1995, Chere Jiusto, MSHPO, NPS/NRHP, file number 96000548, sec. 8, p. 3.

45. Leslie Fourstar's statements and discussion, Sleeping Buffalo meeting, November 30, 1995, 3.

46. Jiusto, "Recent History," 4.

47. Ibid.

48. Ibid.

49. Ibid.

50. From National Park Service form; narrative description prepared by Chere Jiusto in "Sleeping Buffalo and Medicine Rocks." I thank John Byrne, National Register database manager, National Park Service, for sending me this file on March 7, 2012.

51. Chere Jiusto, "Narrative Description," MSHPO, NPS/NRHP, file number 96000548, sec. 7, p. 1.

52. Chere Jiusto, "Oral Accounts of the Sleeping Buffalo," MSHPO, NPS/NRHP, file number 96000548, sec. 8, p. 3.

53. Teddy Bell, interview in his home, Fort Belknap, MT, July 7, 2012.

54. Along with the Inter-Tribal Bison Cooperative, Assiniboine and Sioux of Fort Peck and Gros Ventre and Assiniboine of Fort Belknap have fostered a small herd of buffalo originally from Yellowstone Park since about 1997.

55. Gerald Vizenor, "Aesthetics of Survivance: Literary Theory and Practice," in *Survivance: Narratives of Native Presence, ed.* Gerald Vizenor (Lincoln: University of Nebraska Press, 2008), 11, 19.

## KAITLIN REED

*Native Space: Geographic Strategies to Unsettle Settler Colonialism*
by Natchee Blu Barnd
Oregon State University Press, 2017

WHEN THE STRESSES OF MY GRADUATE PROGRAM become overwhelming, I lace up my running shoes, escape my hectic schedule, and explore the residential streets of Davis, California. I run up Washoe Street and down Ohlone Street until I make it to Hoopa Place. Amused, I wonder if there has ever been a Hupa Indian in this seemingly grandiose and manicured cul-de-sac before. Natchee Blu Barnd argues, "In non-Native (largely White) communities, the production of Indian-themed spatial markers expresses a colonial ideology and physically marks out the consequences and legacy of anti-Indian spatial practices. . . . [These] signs stand in place of and to some extent even deny tribal survival and indigenous geographies" (24). And so I keep running.

*Native Space* explores how Native communities and individuals have reclaimed Indigenous spatialities and asserted Indigenous geographies. Barnd explores diverse articulations of Indianness in settler spatialities while simultaneously centering Native space-making practices. In so doing, Barnd interrogates relationships between race, space, Indigeneity, whiteness, and colonialism.

Indian street names—branded and sold as clusters by development companies—proliferated in the mid-twentieth century amid termination era policies. The spatial equivalent of playing Indian, Indian street names consistently locate whiteness. Why street signs? Mundane, yes; but Barnd is interested in the mundane. He argues that mundane practices normalize colonialism, that street signs are "mundane spatial markers" that "materially stand as labels for the world" (73, 21). Moreover, "street names remain unquestioned as modes of hegemonic cultural production that operate at the intersection of colonialism, identity, race, and space" (73). Street signs perform the ideological labor of settler colonialism; they denote colonized space.

Barnd contrasts spatial markers in exclusive settler spaces with those within Indigenous communities. The differences between Indian street signs in Indian versus white communities include language, community, and cultural context. Barnd argues that using street signs with Indigenous language and cultural representation promotes community health and produces a tribal geography, and, most importantly, that control over geographic expression is "mirror[ed] [in] other regained aspects of self-governance and self-determination: language, education, health, and economic development" (52).

Barnd considers history and settler memory through compelling case studies. One example centers on Set-tainte, a nineteenth-century Kiowa warrior and political figure who dedicated himself to protecting Kiowa lifeways and fighting white oversettlement. He jumped to his death from a prison window. Barnd explores the way Set-tainte is both memorialized and spatialized. Barnd juxtaposes the town of Satanta, Kansas, and a Kiowa community descended from Set-tainte located in Oklahoma, and he does so to demonstrate the ways in which "the production of space (dominant, indigenous, both, or otherwise) is constituted by intersections and overlappings of race, gender, indigeneity, Whiteness, and everyday acts of colonialism" (80).

Every year for the past half century, the predominantly white community of Satanta congregates for the Satanta Ceremony, during which two high school seniors dressed in regalia take center stage: the male senior holds a peace pipe up to the sky, smokes from it, and passes the pipe to the male junior. The male senior then removes his headdress and transfers it to the male junior. The female senior transfers her shawl, necklace, and ring to the female junior. This appropriative example of playing Indian aims to unmake Native space while narrating white innocence in the process. However, despite the fact that Satanta is "an active neocolonial space" (82), the process of unmaking Native space is never complete. For Set-tainte descendants, Kiowa ancestral territory "remain[s] part of an imagined, traditional Kiowa geography. This also means that Satanta and many other places necessarily exist as overlapping indigenous and colonial geographies. While remade, they have not been fully unmade as Native space" (83).

*Native Space* considers how Indigenous artists and activists contest settler place making in daily practice. Native artists interrogate colonial space and, in turn, reassert Native spaces. Barnd examines artists such as Jaune Quick-to-See Smith, who employs maps as mediums, redeployed to subvert colonial outcomes. These works, in differing and complementary ways, engage Native dispossession, presence, and mobility in a neocolonial nation.

Provoking, self-reflective, and at times poetic, this text is an important contribution to Indigenous geography and Native American studies. This book demonstrates the ways in which Native peoples actively confront the US settler colonial nation, as well as the ways in which settler colonialism continues to spatially erase Indigenous presence. Barnd advocates for Indigenous frameworks of relationship and responsibility toward land; such a recentering can hopefully facilitate a reimagining of colonial geographies based on conquest.

KAITLIN REED (Yurok/Hupa) is a Native American studies doctoral candidate at the University of California, Davis.

# DAVID KRUEGER

*Spirit in the Rock: The Fierce Battle for Modoc Homelands*
by Jim Compton
Washington State University Press, 2017

**JIM COMPTON'S** *Spirit in the Rock: The Fierce Battle for Modoc Homelands* offers a thoughtful and well-researched account of the context, course, and outcome of the Modoc War. Fought from 1872 to 1873 in the vicinity of Tule Lake on the border of California and Oregon, this conflict is mostly remembered for the brutal fighting that took place in the cave-pocked lava fields of Captain Jack's Stronghold, where outnumbered Modoc defenders inflicted embarrassing losses on the advancing ranks of the United States Army and state volunteers. When Modoc leaders met with a party of army officers to negotiate an end to the fighting, Captain Jack (Chief Kientpoos) was pressured by militant followers into killing General Edward Canby, believing it would demoralize and disperse the besiegers. Instead, it smothered any lingering sympathy for the Modoc and ignited a national campaign to avenge Canby's murder.

*Spirit in the Rock* recounts this familiar confrontation and the course of the campaign masterfully, but, more importantly, it places it within the greater context of Indian-settler interaction in the mid- to late nineteenth-century Pacific Northwest. It locates the origins of the conflict in a familiar mélange of muddled treaties, acquisitive settlers, and reciprocal violence, identifying the scheming of the Applegate family to monopolize local water rights as a critical factor in escalating retaliatory raiding into open warfare. But just as the threat of dispossession and removal gave the Modoc no room for retreat, the murder of Canby at the height of the war left the army with a mandate to pursue justice. Compton approaches the subsequent capture and execution of Captain Jack with deliberate fairness, mobilizing a variety of sources to argue that despite the flaws and prejudices of the court-martial, the chief had committed a crime and was punished accordingly. The treatment of his band in the aftermath of the campaign rightly receives a more critical assessment as the narrative follows the efforts of Modoc families to survive and create a meaningful existence in Indian Territory after being forcefully relocated far from their kin and homeland.

An accomplished journalist, Compton displays an eye for interesting and powerful quotations that allow the war's participants to reveal their own motives and observations as events unfold. These are woven into relatively short and briskly paced chapters that strike an effective balance between context and content, advancing a lively narrative that is informative but not overburdened with analysis. The author's passion for the people, history, and geography of the region proves to be a strength throughout, as he is able to draw on Modoc oral histories, interviews, visits to sacred sites, and a wealth of local scholarship to craft a sympathetic but balanced interpretation of the campaign and its consequences. The included maps and photographs can occasionally feel unpolished or unnecessary but are nonetheless interesting and attractive supplements to the already detailed in-text descriptions of locations and events.

Historians and readers familiar with late nineteenth-century reservation policies or warfare in the American West may wish for a more serious engagement with a broader historiography, but *Spirit in the Rock* keeps a tight focus on its subject and relies on extensive primary source research rather than theoretical scaffolding for its framework. This discipline serves to contain the scope of the project but at times limits its claims and leaves relationships and connections between the Modoc and other experiences of warfare, dispossession, and resettlement largely unexplored. Of particular interest might be investigating the composition, motivations, and interactions with the Indian scouts who fight alongside the United States Army in this campaign and are critical to tracking Captain Jack's band and compelling its surrender. The passing of Mr. Compton prior to the manuscript's publication will sadly deny us his future voice and scholarship on these issues; nonetheless, his balanced treatment of both Modoc and army leaders provides a careful and welcome nuance to a history that can invite polemics, highlighting a conflict as often marked by fear and cultural misunderstanding as greed or hatred.

DAVID KRUEGER is an instructor of history at the United States Military Academy and PhD candidate in American history at Harvard University.

# ANNETTE KOLODNY

*Memory Lands: King Philip's War and the Place of Violence
     in the Northeast*
by Christine M. DeLucia
Yale University Press, 2018

**IN THE WORDS OF HISTORIAN** Christine M. DeLucia, King Philip's War, the conflict that from 1675 to 1678 raged up and down the Connecticut River Valley, "traumatically entangled the region's diverse Algonquian communities with expansionist New England colonizers" and "constituted one of the most devastating periods in the history of the early American Northeast" (xi). Galvanized by the Pokanoket Wampanoag leader Metacom (or Metacomet), whom the English called King Philip, this unprecedented multitribal uprising left in its wake a region transformed by the brutal dispossession of its original Indigenous inhabitants. Despite all the books and articles that have previously examined this war and its aftermath—work that DeLucia knows well and builds upon—*Memory Lands: King Philip's War and the Place of Violence in the Northeast* adds significantly to the story.

Eschewing the conventional chronological organization of most academic histories, this book moves back and forth across time and place in order to weave together a dense and wide-ranging reconstruction of the war and its many continuing consequences. In so doing, the book makes two principal arguments. First, *Memory Lands* confirms William Faulkner's observation that the past is never really past. Even today, King Philip's War hangs like a shadow over both the region and the descendants of all those involved. Following the end of the war, moreover, the power dynamics inherent in the logics of settler colonialism endured, establishing the patterns of political disenfranchisement, cultural repression, and land loss that still continue to impose themselves on Native peoples. Second, in what is perhaps its most original aspect, *Memory Lands* insists upon the *materiality* of memory. As DeLucia puts it in her introduction, the "remembrance of historical violence *takes place*: understandings of contested pasts take shape in relation to particular landscapes, material features of the world, and politically defined territories" (2). It is those particular "spots on the land" and their attendant artifacts that, as a New Englander, DeLucia knows well and reads as an archive of events and stories, or what she terms "memoryscapes."

No less important for her purposes are those other archives, the miscellaneous holdings of New England's many public libraries, its sometimes out-of-the-way local historical societies, tribal museums, and esteemed repositories like the American Antiquarian Society in Worcester, Massachusetts. Indeed, she opens her preface with a minister's 1815 gift of a charred kernel of corn and a chunk of quartz to that same newly founded society. In examining "memorial touchstones" like these, DeLucia probes how such artifacts are chosen to memorialize specific events, by whom they are chosen, and for what purposes. In this instance, objects donated by an Anglo-American Christian minister to a culturally specific European American institution during the nation's formative years "appeared to signify the terrifying savagery of Indigenous opponents, as well as their eventual resounding defeat" (xi). Urging us to view them from the vantage point of Native peoples, however, DeLucia asks us to consider by what ethical measure "these unsettling mementos deserved to be removed from their original contexts, collected, possessed, and venerated" (xi).

Acknowledging Gerald Vizenor's concept of "survivance," DeLucia suggests that "the most crucial dimension of this study may be its assessment of how memories of devastation exist *relationally* alongside those of regeneration" (22). By way of example, she offers the Sacred Run and Paddle ceremony undertaken by tribal members and their supporters on October 30, 2010. Commemorating the forced removal of Native people from their homes to the desolate Deer Island in Boston Harbor during the winter of 1675–76, runners set out before dawn from South Natick, Massachusetts, headed for Boston. At the same time, alongside crew teams from local colleges, three *mishoonash* were being paddled on the waters of the Charles River. "These were wooden dugouts fashioned by Wampanoags from burnt, hewn tree trunks, and perhaps not since the violent days of King Philip's War had such vessels" been seen on that river (29). Rather than merely "maritime curiosities," DeLucia argues that in tandem with the dawn runners, the dugouts "were politically charged agents of decolonization, making a provocative statement to Boston in reaffirming the city's urban heart as Native space" (29).

Similarly, on St. David's Island in Bermuda, under the auspices of the St. David's Island Indian Reconnection Committee, the history of Native peoples enslaved and shipped to Bermuda for sale in the aftermath of King Philip's War is now being recovered. Through visits and various ceremonies, "certain [Algonquian] tribal community members and St. David's islanders have mutually extended their circles of belonging" (313). Alongside the Sacred Run and Paddle ceremony, this recovery of Bermuda's Indigenous memoryscapes stands as another example of the ongoing legacy of King Philip's War too often left unstudied or even unremarked. DeLucia brilliantly breaks that silencing.

**ANNETTE KOLODNY** formerly served as dean of the College of Humanities at the University of Arizona in Tucson and is currently College of Humanities Professor Emerita of American Literature and Culture.

# MELANIE K. YAZZIE

*Prairie Rising: Indigenous Youth, Decolonization, and the Politics*
   *of Intervention*
by Jaskiran Dhillon
University of Toronto Press, 2017

JASKIRAN DHILLON'S *Prairie Rising* is an ethnography of the state that tracks and uncovers the multiple technologies of colonial governmentality, such as participation, care, and rescue, that gain legibility through the disciplining of Indigenous bodies. The book's theorization of state power is a major focus that has been discussed at length by other reviewers. I would thus like to shift the focus of my comments to another major theoretical contribution of the book, what I call a politics of materiality. This politics of materiality has three dimensions in the book: colonial gender violence, the carcerality of everyday life, and the here and now of contemporary Indigeneity.

Dhillon draws from Indigenous and antiracist feminism to define the parameters of a material politics of colonial gender violence. "The settler state of Canada has something very material to gain," she writes, "with a continuation of colonial gender violence. And it is made real through a number of cunning technologies of governance" (182). Pointing out that these technologies of governance disproportionately target Indigenous women and girls, Dhillon argues that "an awareness of the material, everyday violence that is a core feature of being an Indigenous woman or girl in Canada . . . calls for a suturing together of the microdynamics of daily life with macropolitical struggles for land" (249). This suturing together of bodies with land, of the everyday exercise of power enacted through the disciplining of bodies with the structural exercise of power enacted through the dispossession of land, points us toward a conceptualization of materiality that emphasizes the relationality between human and other-than-human relatives like land. Land/body relationality has been a central theme of Indigenous feminism, and *Prairie Rising* makes a significant contribution to this work.

This Indigenous feminist understanding of what constitutes the political also frames Dhillon's analysis of the carcerality of everyday life. Throughout the book she repeatedly demonstrates how the technologies of governance that bring colonial governmentality alive find their most potent influence in the caging, surveillance, and control of the bodies and movement of Indigenous youth. For Dhillon, carcerality describes the way Indigenous youth experience settler colonialism and state power in their everyday lives; it describes their very ontology as Indigenous youth: "The persistent sensation of being hunted, of monitored movement, of freedom being truncated through institutional caging is central to the daily reality of being an Indigenous youth" (106).

For all its far-reaching influence, however, carcerality is a material configuration that emerges from, targets, and ensnares specific bodies in specific spaces. She includes in the book's introduction a brief section entitled "Saskatoon: The Here and Now of Place." That *Prairie Rising* takes place in Saskatoon, Saskatchewan, is no trivial detail that should take a backseat to the book's complex and sophisticated theories of state power and materiality. Carcerality and colonial gender violence emerge from the specific context of urban life for Indigenous youth in a space that quite literally defines contemporary state power and Indigeneity in Canada. As Dhillon notes, Saskatoon is behind only Winnipeg in having the largest Indigenous population of any Canadian city, and the majority of this population is under thirty-five. And in Saskatchewan, an astounding 88 percent of youth in custody are Indigenous (108). It is thus important to highlight the specific context of Saskatoon not only because this is where Dhillon situates her ethnography but because this is where the majority of Indigenous people today live, experience, and contest settler colonialism. The urban landscape of east Saskatoon, with its large population of Indigenous youth, describes the here and now of Indigeneity, which helps to explain why colonial governmentality has turned its panoptic gaze toward Indigenous youth in this city. As Dhillon argues in the book's conclusion, "Through their existence as Indigenous youth, these young people constitute a direct threat to an already existing settler social order" (106). Where Indigenous futures are manifest by sheer fact of high numbers and future generations, colonial governmentality will certainly follow.

What this also means is that urban Indigenous youth, as the literal majority and materiality of Indigenous futures, must be at the center of our decolonial efforts. In the book's conclusion Dhillon asks, "How does decolonial praxis shift when we put Indigenous youth at the centre of our political strategies for radical social transformation?" (237). By offering a politics of materiality derived from the lived experiences of urban Indigenous youth caught in the teeth of colonial violence, *Prairie Rising* offers productive ground for an effective decolonial praxis.

MELANIE K. YAZZIE (Diné) is assistant professor of Native American studies at the University of New Mexico.

# SIERRA WATT

Network Sovereignty: Building the Internet across Indian Country
by Marisa Elena Duarte
University of Washington Press, 2017

MARISA ELENA DUARTE'S *Network Sovereignty: Building the Internet across Indian Country* offers a reconceptualization of what the spread of and access to information and communication technologies (ICTs) mean for Native communities across the United States. Through case studies of contemporary programs from tribes throughout the country, as well as intertribal government agencies and organizations, she deconstructs the false dichotomy separating Indigenous peoples from technological development. Drawing upon numerous fields, including library science, information technologies, Native American studies, decolonizing methodologies, and tribal governance, Duarte puts forth an argument that ICTs constitute yet another form tribal communities utilize to continue the work of sovereignty and self-determination.

Duarte employs both the applied and theoretical, shifting effortlessly between normative arguments and empirical case studies. Chapter 1 breaks down the fallacy of technology as antithetical to Indigeneity, the dichotomy becoming intertwined with the narrative of Native disappearance, particularly through tribal dispossession of lands contemporary with the spread of telegraph and railroad lines during western expansion (10). Chapter 2 defines her methodology as "reframing" and presents the necessity of acknowledging the relational nature of ICTs for tribal communities, in that they are tools for implementing shared community goals rather than marks of "progress" (29, 33). Chapter 3 explores the relationship between tribal sovereignty and ICTs through interviews with contemporary programs, including the Pascua Yaqui and Hopi tribal radio stations; Tohono O'odham and their use of various ICTs, including two-way radio; and intertribal groups, in particular Native Public Media (38, 45, 47, 50). Likewise, chapter 4 deals with the challenges to implementing ICTs by analyzing Internet service providers, including Southern California Tribal Technologies, and tribes that have implemented service, including the Coeur d'Alene, Cheyenne River Sioux, and Navajo Nation (59, 68, 77, 83). Chapters 5 and 6 focus on the way ICTs relate to self-determination and sovereignty, respectively, noting that ICTs are not end goals in their own right but a step in a series of goals that tribes hold for themselves. In this way, ICTs remain steeped in a history of colonialism. Just as they do with water, land, and mineral rights, tribes must contend with corporate entities and the extreme emphasis on individualist, private property rights encoded in US legal systems to ensure that their communities' rights to assert the ICTs of their choice, in accordance with tribal knowledge, remain upheld. Applying these tools to tribal goals requires acknowledging the continued struggle for self-determination and sovereignty. Duarte concludes in chapter 7, reiterating the need to rethink and remove the "nationalist progress" message imbedded in ICT rhetoric and discontinue equating "premodern"—Indigenous peoples—with "antitechnological" (122, 132).

*Network Sovereignty* states that information flows like water between relationships of all kinds: familial, intertribal, legal, and economic; so, too, moves her subtle, radical argument (12). She is at her best when combatting conventional views of tribes as backward and, worse, vanishing. She asserts the fluid use of ICTs to further Indigenous desires as counternarrative. For tribes, ICTs are not conclusions but utensils (89). ICT build-out into Indian Country is not foreign to it but can be likened to traditional trade networks and intertribal policy learning, such as the proliferation of gaming, among other economic developments; digital environments are yet another space in which tribes must navigate as the third sovereign among competing government and economic interests.

Duarte speaks power to our tribal communities, where the practical is also always cultural. From the Hopi prophecy of Spider Woman weaving the world together to the way the Kumeyaay took strategic advantage of a wildfire that made space among sacred manzanita plants to lay foundation work for a tower, tribes found room for ICTs alongside existing traditions (126, 95). Here Duarte emphasizes the way in which ICT pursuance hinges on the relationships such technologies can facilitate, be they better tribal government access to federal grants, increased economic development on tribal lands, improved language literacy of tribal youth, or larger job placement for Native veterans returning from service with unused programming skill sets. The goals of ICTs—sovereignty and self-determination—remain the same, but they are performed on new platforms.

Quite unique, the book reads at times like a travel log, at others like ethnographic fieldnotes, but throughout the author articulates technical mechanisms alongside theoretical positions with ease. Across desert mountains and seasonal rainstorms, through colonial disconnection and deprivation, moving like water, Duarte weaves her words into a technoscape not unlike tribes weaving their ICTs, with defined purpose, connecting past and future through the lineage, relationship, and community dreaming.

SIERRA WATT (Pechanga Band of Luiseño) is a political science doctoral candidate at the University of Kansas.

# BETH ROSE MIDDLETON

*Unlikely Alliances: Native Nations and White Communities Join to Defend Rural Lands*
by Zoltan Grossman
University of Washington Press, 2017

ZOLTAN GROSSMAN, a geography and Native studies professor at Evergreen State College, traverses the greater western United States, documenting understudied instances of Native and rural white collaboration in the face of common environmental threats. Beyond a series of case studies, *Unlikely Alliances* offers a framework for understanding collaboration between groups that historically have had acrimonious relationships in a shared place. Drawing on theoretical perspectives from geography, critical race theory, federal Indian law, rural sociology, and Native American studies, Grossman engages questions of scale ("at what geographic scales can alliances best construct common ground?" [6]), methodology (what organizing strategies work across groups divided by race, privilege, and history?), and temporality, examining collaborations bounded by space but not necessarily by time.

Grossman begins *Unlikely Alliances* with a personal introduction explaining why—as the child of a Holocaust survivor father and a Catholic mother—finding commonality in difference is intrinsic to his identity. Indeed, he grounds the intersections of universalism and particularism as deeply personal and not mutually exclusive in either his sense of self or his lifelong commitment to work as an ally with both Native nations and rural white communities.

Highlighting shared love of land, a commitment to rural livelihoods, and place-based family ties, Grossman finds swaths of common ground between tribal members and white settlers opposing common corporate foes. He names particular political tools that each group brings to the table—such as the power of treaty rights held by Native nations, and the useful political connections held by rural white communities—and examines how these have been used effectively together. Grossman also acknowledges the messy, painful, and imperfect work of alliance building, documenting false starts and instances of entrenched conflict exacerbated by external divide-and-conquer tactics.

With over thirty years of experience working alongside Native and white rural community leaders to protect health and homelands from militarization and extraction, Grossman believes that cooperation between Native and non-Native rural organizers has "become almost commonplace" (273). He outlines three conditions central to Native/non-Native alliances—a common place, a common purpose, and a common understanding—and examines the ways in which these factors may be defined and juxtaposed in order to result in alliances that endure and accomplish their goals. He considers the development of "a more universalist nationalism" (284) grounded in Indigenous values that recognize human-land relationships as embodied, reciprocal, responsible, spiritual, and enduring.

*Unlikely Alliances* aims to serve "as a type of guide to Native and non-Native community organizers and leaders in the beginning stages of building alliances against new mines, pipelines or other projects" (xv). While the book focuses on Native-white relationships, it lays a productive foundation for additional work on cross-cultural alliances between Native nations and their other diverse neighbors (including African Americans, Chicanx or Latinx communities, Arab Americans, and Asian Americans).

*Unlikely Alliances* is particularly salient in a contemporary context of both political gridlock and increasing environmental threats. With specific attention to each rural context, Grossman acknowledges complexity and the dynamic intersecting factors that allow Native/white alliances to thrive or, conversely, to erode and dissolve. The lessons he offers from rural Montana, North Dakota, Minnesota, Nevada, and beyond support the place-based work of constructing collaboration across lines of historic conflict.

BETH ROSE MIDDLETON (Afro-Caribbean, Eastern European) is an associate professor of Native American studies at the University of California, Davis.

# MARIA SHAA TLAA WILLIAMS

*The Tao of Raven: An Alaska Native Memoir*
by Ernestine Hayes
University of Washington Press, 2017

THE TAO OF RAVEN: AN ALASKA NATIVE MEMOIR is a beautifully written and almost hypnotic narrative that is a follow-up to Hayes's previous publication, *Blonde Indian: An Alaska Native Memoir* (University of Arizona Press, 2006). Both publications chronicle her personal journey as an Indigenous woman and writer and blur the line between poetry and prose with biography. Hayes artfully weaves Indigenous creation stories and the mischievous trickster figure of Raven, creating a type of magical realism. Her writing style is musical in nature, and when reading her work aloud, the timbre and cadence of the words are like a song.

Hayes has a unique writing style that is moving and powerful and leaves the reader breathless. For example, in chapter 2, "Wolves Sing Like Old Women Keeping Ancient Songs," the author heartfully addresses her return to Alaska, with subtle references to the 1971 Alaska Native Claims Settlement Act and the impact of Christian missionaries with her own personal and family biography. The author contextualizes myth, geography, culture, and her own journey in a rich landscape of words that capture emotion, landscape, and meaning.

I read and reread many passages in *The Tao of Raven* because they are so beautiful and rich with meaning and the complexities of Indigenous identity. Both this book and her first book are masterpieces of twenty-first-century American literature and should be required reading for anyone studying literature, history, and Indigenous worldview(s). *The Tao of Raven: An Alaska Native Memoir* is a wonderful addition to anyone's reading list, and readers will be taken on a beautiful journey of experience, myth, and magic.

MARIA SHAA TLAA WILLIAMS (Tlingit) is an associate professor at the University of Alaska Anchorage in the Alaska Native studies program.

# CHRISTINE DeLUCIA

*The Place of Stone: Dighton Rock and the Erasure of America's*
  *Indigenous Past*
by Douglas Hunter
University of North Carolina Press, 2017

**THE RICHLY TEXTURED LANDSCAPES** and waterways of the Native Northeast have been powerful conduits connecting tribal communities to ancestors, histories, spiritual systems, and resources. Across this extensively marked and memorialized terrain, a petroglyph-covered stone sometimes referred to as Dighton Rock has attracted an enormous outpouring of attention over several centuries as Europeans and American colonizers attempted to interpret its significances. Douglas Hunter, a former journalist whose history dissertation formed the basis of this book, examines these multilayered histories in order to critically contextualize Euro-colonial efforts at claiming this important Indigenous locale as their own and at dissociating it from Indigenous communities, past and present. Over the course of ten roughly chronological chapters, accompanied by illustrations, he probes how Euro-colonial ministers, intellectuals, avocational historians, landowners, ethnic groups, and many others (particularly the near-obsessive Edmund Burke Delabarre) have read into this stone purported signs of early explorations and transoceanic movements by Norse, Portuguese, Phoenicians, and others. The stone's contested history demonstrates how "ever-changing versions of American antiquity and racial hierarchies spawned under colonization served to disenfranchise Native Americans from their past, and in the process from their lands, while at the same time advancing northern Europeans as the rightful claimants to those lands" (5).

Hunter clearly asserts at the outset that the stone, situated in the heart of Wampanoag homelands by Assonet and the Taunton River watershed, bears Indigenous markings. Native "provenance was apparent from the beginning of European and Anglo-American inquiries" and "was the least cumbersome and most plausible explanation" (3), yet outside observers pursued increasingly tenuous and speculative theories averring non-Indigenous origins in bids to mobilize this material feature as tangible evidence of *other,* Eurocentric histories of peopling the Northeast. This analysis is in conversation with recent studies about the logic, mechanisms, and consequences of settler colonial mythologizing and place making, such as Jean O'Brien's *Firsting and Lasting: Writing Indians out of Existence in New*

*England* (University of Minnesota Press, 2010) and Annette Kolodny's *In Search of First Contact: The Vikings of Vinland, the Peoples of the Dawnland, and the Anglo-American Anxiety of Discovery* (Duke University Press, 2012), and it offers a fine-grained account not only of the varieties but also of the converging forms of these mentalities and actions in a local context.

While the preponderance of Hunter's source material centers on Euro-colonial interpretations (and outright imaginative projections or fantasies), there are notable sections where the study takes up potential Indigenous interpretations of the feature by Mohawk travelers (chapter 4) and by Anishinaabe leader Shingwauk in dialogue with the ethnologist Henry Rowe Schoolcraft (chapter 7). These parts recognize that Euro-colonial antiquarians have never been the only parties invested in this stone; Indigenous interlocutors have also expressed interest in it, though discerning details of their readings can be challenging, given thick layers of colonialist framing. The book concludes with analysis of the twentieth-century museum at Dighton Rock State Park that has been constructed over the rock itself, creating a problematic interpretive milieu that Hunter reads as a sign of the rock's having been "transformed from an Indigenous artifact into the very statement, the very proof, of colonization" (235).

Given Hunter's commitment to critically unpacking settler colonial narratives and place-claiming processes and his attunement to the willfully overlooked or negated Indigenous significances of the stone by Euro-colonial proponents of dispossession, questions arise about the author's methodology, which evidently did not include much or any engagement or consultation with present-day Indigenous knowledge-keepers. These include the many tribal historians, cultural heritage leaders, museum and educational staff members, and others across southern New England in communities such as Aquinnah and Mashpee Wampanoag that are most directly connected to the geographies under consideration. Members of these communities have commented extensively on histories of encounter and ongoing ties to ancestral homelands. Yet "this book is not about Indigenous cultural survival" (5), the author writes in the introduction. These constrained methodological choices may have foreclosed opportunities to pursue more nuanced interactions with Indigenous forms of knowledge that could have led Hunter to interpretations different from, for example, the overly simplistic assertion that "no unfiltered Indigenous account of the meaning or purpose of the rock's markings is available" (6). Contemporary Indigenous people of southern New England have been deeply, dynamically entangled with settler colonialism for centuries, undoubtedly. But rather than seeking some pristine or pre-Columbian vantage on ancient pasts, a more insightful approach could have been to engage with these Indigenous modernities in all their multivocal complexities.

CHRISTINE DELUCIA is assistant professor of history at Mount Holyoke College and author of *Memory Lands: King Philip's War and the Place of Violence in the Northeast* (2018).

# MOLLY McGLENNEN

*Stories for a Lost Child*
by Carter Meland
Michigan State University Press, 2017

CARTER MELAND'S DEBUT NOVEL, *Stories for a Lost Child*, gracefully braids the experiences of a teenage girl, Fiona, with the writings sent to her from a person who claims to be her grandfather. Arriving in a mysterious box, the stories land in Fiona's hands eighteen years after what appears to be her Anishinaabe grandfather Robinson Heroux's disappearance into a swamp in northern Minnesota. Fiona is invited into the worlds her grandfather imagines and reveals for her, ranging from letters addressed to "the grandchild" to stories about Bigfoot, Indians in space, black holes, and addiction and poverty in Native Minneapolis. Swirling around the stories is Fiona's real-time experience of division and silence between her mother and grandmother and their relationships with Robinson. And all of this occurs one summer as Fiona is finding her way among not only her three best friends—Strep, Dane, and Chance—but also her own questions about her family's history and secrecy.

But simply synthesizing Meland's storyline does a disservice to the ambition of this novel. It is a story about stories: "You are here among these trees as well, noozis, down here with Misaabe and me," says Robinson to his imagined granddaughter. "I call you here with my words. I see you as I write. . . . These woods don't separate us from the world is what I'm trying to convey here, nor do these stories I share with you. They are a place where things come together, but not always in ways that others would recognize as harmonious" (50). Meland's novel pays attention to those strands of story that, indeed, create "a place where things come together," where meaning is made through long-tenured experience with the land and all that relates to it. Especially prescient, Fiona's grandfather writes later that "it's easier for most people to pretend things are divided rather than connected" (50). For Fiona, the stories become the conduits of truth about her past and about what it means to be descended from Anishinaabe peoples.

Meland demonstrates special attention to setting in this novel and illustrates just how important place is not only for Anishinaabeg generations ago but equally for Fiona navigating the lessons her grandfather bequeaths to her. In an exchange with her friend Chance, Fiona relays to him what she has been learning from her grandfather: "He told me that our ancestors remember we're Anishinaabe, even if we don't always remember what that means" (109). Fiona begins to tune herself to Indigenous guidance, wherever it can be found, and that fills her "with a new feeling, one she couldn't [yet] name" (128), one of light and certainty. In that moment, I can't help but think that Meland also talks directly to his reader: we are all lost without the revelation of land-based knowledge.

In line with a legacy of important Anishinaabeg writers such as Gerald Vizenor, Gordon Henry, Kimberly Blaeser, and others, Meland writes as someone who honors the medicine found in stories and believes deeply in how each of us is made of them. In fact, Meland seems to suggest that stories, as core truths, will be the way in which the planet and all her occupants will ensure a future. *Stories for a Lost Child* illustrates twenty-first-century Native peoples leaning into the warmth of Indigenous connection across generations, across time and space, and across relations. In a moving, funny, lyrical, and resonant first novel, Meland does not disappoint.

MOLLY McGLENNEN is an associate professor of English and Native American studies at Vassar College.

# LINDSAY MARSHALL

*Trickster Chases the Tale of Education*
by Sylvia Moore
McGill-Queen's University Press, 2017

**IN HIS POWERFUL INTRODUCTION** to *Noon nee-me-poo (We the Nez Perces): Culture and History of the Nez Perces*, Allen P. Slickpoo insisted on the importance of Native history written by Native scholars in conjunction with Native epistemologies. Most important, Slickpoo wrote, these books are needed in the classroom, because "it was not possible to live as a Native American for sixteen hours a day and spend the other seven or eight hours with Dick and Jane who lived in a home designed for 'middle-class' people, and not become confused and unhappy."[1] Public schools governed by Eurocentric pedagogy and organizational structures have been hostile to Indigenous knowledge, even in the rare instances when teachers have tried to incorporate community traditions into the curriculum. Because the classroom must also prepare Native students to engage in a world beyond their own communities, the conflict between the two different, often oppositional teaching traditions has historically fallen in favor of Eurocentric pedagogy, and educators have forced Indigenous knowledge and teaching practice to fit within the contradictory structure of Western education. In *Trickster Chases the Tale of Education*, Sylvia Moore challenges the foundational assumption that either tradition must give way to the other in order to incorporate them both, and she does so in an innovative format that continually forces the reader to confront her own assumptions.

Moore's work tells the story of a 2007 community-based research project involving salmon at North Queens School, a primary school adjacent to Wildcat First Nation in Caledonia, Novia Scotia. The project focused on introducing students (both from Mi'kmaw Nation and non-Indigenous) to traditional Mi'kmaw ecological knowledge by following salmon through the first stages of their life cycle. The goal of the project was "to examine the dynamics of school educators and Mi'kmaw community members working together to centre and legitimate Mi'kmaw knowledge in education" (10). As the project progressed, and especially when Moore sat down to collect and analyze her findings, she discovered that the true difficulty lay in honoring Mi'kmaw ways of knowing and learning alongside her formal training as an education researcher. Bringing Indigenous knowledge into Eurocentric education subjects it to a colonized framework, a framework that necessarily contradicts vital components of Indigenous knowledge production and sharing. Instead, Moore pushes against the notion that Indigenous knowledge should be subservient to curricular structures and presents a model in which apparent dichotomous traditions can exist in the same classroom space, honoring the importance of both perspectives without an overarching framework that reconciles their differences.

Moore is a Mi'kmaw mother and grandmother and an assistant professor of Aboriginal community-based education at the Labrador Institute of Memorial University of Newfoundland, and her decade of experience incorporating traditional knowledge and Indigenous teaching methodologies into Eurocentric classrooms is evident in this well-researched study. What is most powerful about her work, however, is her bold choice to present the study in the format of traditional storytelling. In conversation with Crow, the Trickster, Moore relates the details of the project in the form of personal narrative, even incorporating blank pages at key points in the narrative to encourage the reader to sit in silence with her as she thinks through the process. What would in many other authors' hands become a gimmick Moore wields as a persuasive tool to illustrate the efficacy and importance of her methodology. Moore's personal narrative approach offers a refreshingly introspective discussion of the research project and her process in analyzing its components, and she transparently reports the real challenges she faced in seeking the balance between the two educational traditions in a way that offers readers a productive model to follow while reminding scholars that educational research is an ongoing process, not something to conclude too hastily or tidily.

While Moore's unique structure for the book is engaging, it does not sacrifice academic rigor. The text is peppered with references to scholars and traditional knowledge-keepers whose work influences Moore's thinking, and the narrative concludes with a traditional collection of endnotes and full bibliography. While her conclusion that knowledge is fundamentally a function of relationship may seem simple, its application is rich ground for exploration in diverse school communities. In her introduction, Moore says the book is intended "for all people (Indigenous and non-Indigenous) who struggle with colonized minds" (4), a reminder that challenging colonized curriculum, while primarily for the preservation and reproduction of Native ways of knowing for Native students, is a necessary service for all students, Native and non-Native alike. Moore's unconventional work is worth taking the time to read slowly and return to again.

LINDSAY MARSHALL is a doctoral candidate in history at the University of Oklahoma.

## Note

1. Allen P. Slickpoo, *Noon nee-me-poo (We the Nez Perces): Culture and History of the Nez Perces* (Lapwai: Nez Perce Tribe of Idaho, 1973), 237.

# SHIANNA McALLISTER

*Grounded Authority: The Algonquins of Barriere Lake against the State*
by Shiri Pasternak
University of Minnesota Press, 2017

SHIRI PASTERNAK'S *Grounded Authority: The Algonquins of Barriere Lake against the State* details the coercive mechanisms that settler colonial authorities utilize to undercut the perceived threats Indigenous legal orders pose to the state. *Grounded Authority* disaggregates hierarchical conceptions of jurisdiction with an alternative way of thinking about jurisdiction through an Algonquin lens. Jurisdiction, that is, "the authority to have authority," generates a broader vocabulary that better expresses settler and Indigenous spatial encounters where sovereignty discourses fall short (7). Through an examination of the Algonquins of Barriere Lake, Pasternak describes how Canada delegated authority to Indigenous and Northern Affairs (INAC) to undermine and dismantle Algonquin jurisdiction and their customary governance system in 2010. By understanding settler-Indigenous conflict in spatial terms, Pasternak shows how distinct "legal orders meet across epistemological difference and overlap on the ground, producing the inter legal space of settler colonialism" (7). Through the language of jurisdiction, the legitimacy and legality of settler sovereignty can be critically questioned, bringing attention to the gap between Canadian assertions of sovereignty and exercise of jurisdiction on the ground.

Pasternak uses Lisa Ford's concept of "perfect settler sovereignty" to show that the Canadian state has not exercised effective jurisdiction over appropriated Indigenous lands, particularly in the Barriere Lake context (12—13).[1] In fact, the interlegal space between Canadian assertions to sovereignty and the vitality of Indigenous jurisdiction is permeated by this community's intimate and exhaustive knowledge of their lands, which is then taken up in the phrase "ontology of care." The ontology of care is a grounded legal order that "flows from relationships of respect and love for the land that are witnessed . . . through everyday practices, stories from the bush, formalized through wampum belts, and strings, and told by the fire" (27). Algonquin practices of jurisdiction are based on a principle that extends beyond the human/land dichotomy by structuring all relations on principles of respect that order the community internally within bodies, families, and the nation, as well as the external organization of authority (88). This land tenure system is based on long-term relationships of respect and care not only for the land but also for future generations (100).

Many aspects of the ontology of care are present in the 1991 Trilateral Agreement, an accord between the Algonquins of Barriere Lake, the federal government of Canada, and the Province of Quebec that acknowledges the community's right to have a say in natural resource development, as well as a share in the revenues resulting from it. However, as the years wore on, both settler governments failed to uphold this agreement despite the community's efforts to ensure they do.

Algonquin jurisdiction proved to be too great a threat to the perfection of settler sovereignty, leading to the eventual overthrow of the Algonquins of Barriere Lake's customary system of governance, which, up until that point, did not fall under the Indian Act's enforced elective system. In 2009 section 74 of the Indian Act was used as a threat to coerce the community into agreeing to a change that would alter their customary governance to fall under the jurisdiction of the Indian Act and eventually have their system replaced altogether in 2010 (200–201, 207). The deliberate mobilization of this rarely used section of the Indian Act highlights the inherent insecurity of Canadian legal orders in the face of thriving Indigenous legal orders such as the Algonquins of Barriere Lake's ontology of care.

The political struggle at Barriere Lake is similar to but also distinct from other struggles taking place in communities across Turtle Island and ultimately illuminates how settler colonial states require constant maintenance of their claim to nationhood as territorially bound entities.

Pasternak shows that despite colonial efforts, Indigenous legal authority does not disappear when settler states assert sovereignty through control over territory alone. Indeed, "Indigenous jurisdiction demonstrates enduring forms of governance that preexisted and codeveloped for centuries in relation to a plurality of imperial and colonial legalities" (15). Grounded Authority is a thorough account of the Algonquins of Barriere Lake's resilience in light of great colonial interruption that continues to this day.

Pasternak's text is appropriate for graduate-level courses and some upper-level undergraduate courses in the disciplines of Indigenous studies, political science, history, criminology, Canadian studies, and other similar fields that examine questions of Indigenous governance, jurisdiction, and sovereignty. The text is also useful for researchers studying Indigenous law, governance, settler colonial studies, and the criminalization of Indigenous communities by colonial authorities.

SHIANNA McALLISTER (Nlaka'pamux) is an MA candidate in political science with a concentration in cultural, social, and political thought at the University of Victoria.

## Note

1. Lisa Ford, *Settler Sovereignty: Jurisdiction and Indigenous People in America and Australia, 1988–1836* (Cambridge, MA: Harvard University Press, 2010).

# MICHAEL LERMA

*Native Apparitions: Critical Perspectives on Hollywood's Indians*
edited by Steve Pavlik, M. Elise Marubbio, and Tom Holm
University of Arizona Press, 2017

**NATIVE APPARITIONS** is an edited collection exhibiting three approaches to research: retrospective, individual film, and Native/industry-centered interviews (12). Essays on film legacies highlight a binary focus on "valorized noble" or "violent reactionary" Indianness. This book begins with Myrton Running Wolf's indictment of the film industry as having tremendous power and capability to force others to do what they would not otherwise do: set agendas on topics' salience and, therefore, prevent other topics from being portrayed in film and shape consciousness.[1] The title *Native Apparitions* itself is powerful: "Typically, Indian people view spirits as powers, whether negative, positive, or even neutral. Powers have to be administered . . . so at the very least they do no harm" (5, 6). Stereotypes in film are spirits with a power all their own. These scholars negate stereotypes' negative impacts.

The book begins with "Indians, American Indian Studies, and the Depiction of Indigenous Peoples in American Commercial Cinema" by Steve Pavlik, M. Elise Marubbio, and Tom Holm. This introduction calls colonizers to task in their yearning to dismiss their bloodthirsty nation-building deeds through storytelling and filmmaking. Ignoring stereotypes in film works subtly on Indigenous individuals, as well as all consumers of film.

"Reconsidering America's Errand: Wilderness and 'Indians' in Cinema" by Richard M. Wheelock argues that the fight over framing the American Indian in films and media is a continuation of the battle to frame the origin of America in a positive light. "Fighting the White Man's Wars (on the Silver Screen): A Look at the Images of Native American Servicemen in Film" by Richard Allen and Tom Holm showcases Indigenous servicemen as either betrayed scouts or superwarriors. Both of these depictions represent something "safe" for exploitation by the US military, a simplistic binary leaving colonial actors little choice but to "take the land."

"The Dys-passion of the Indian, or Tonto Goes to Town" by Chadwick Allen explores Tonto's changes across time in film and media depictions. The theme across this eighty-year history is the experiences involving settler-colonial trauma and settler colonial power. In "Look at the Heart of *The Searchers*: The Centrality of Look to John Ford's Commentary on Racism," Marubbio discusses the epiphenomenal focus on racism toward Indigenous people in spite of the more obvious sensationalization of violence toward Indigenous people and Indigenous women. The novelty of this essay is its attention to the treatment of Indigenous women in which racial and sexual tension color the storytelling.

In "Searching for Pocahontas: The Portrayal of an Indigenous Icon in Terrence Malick's *The New World*," Pavlik depicts the "real," or as historically accurate as has been portrayed, Pocahontas in *The New World.* This essay argues for the prismatic inclusion of agency exercised by Pocahontas, dismissing the "pawn" behavior previously depicted by other content.

In "The Four Horsemen of Mel Gibson's Epic *Apocalypto*: Racism, Violence, Mendacity, and Nonsense," Holm assesses *Apocalypto* as racist and inaccurate, calling Gibson to account for retelling the cliché involving Western fantasies of Indigenous savagery. This film is merely another attempt to absolve colonial actor nations of their guilt over land appropriation by way of the tired narrative that Indigenous nations brought collapse upon themselves.

In "*Avatar*: Colonization Marches On . . ." Rose Roberts questions the harmlessness and favoritism toward *Avatar* by arguing that it still fails to escape a classic film pitfall: longing for a time and place in which a "noble savage" can thrive in an ecologically sound environment overrun by imperialists. In "Through Indian Eyes: Programming Native American Cinema," Jan-Christopher Horak analyzes the multitude of stereotypes one should expect to find in classic western films and journey narratives. This work exemplifies the benefits of non-Native and Native collaboration in fighting back against stereotypes.

In "'You Have to Define Yourself as an Inuit Person, If That's What You Want to Do': An Interview with Andrew Okpeaha MacLean," Joanna Hearn, Jacqueline Land, and Andrew Okpeaha MacLean highlight Indigenous filmmakers successfully using cinematic forms in the best interest of describing and explaining Indigenous societal preferences. The new generation of Indigenous filmmakers understands the use of film but remains loyal to Indigenous cultural norms, highlighting Indigenous political marginalization and economic insecurity.

This text tirelessly brings Hollywood to account for its racism and sexism by accurately crediting American Indian studies as a discipline for pioneering the focus on accountability. The role of media in our contemporary world is becoming ever more pervasive. This work takes seriously the responsibility to question how we as Indigenous individuals are depicted. It stands up to the stereotyping monster: film.

**MICHAEL LERMA** (Purepecha) is dean of the School of Business and Social Science at Diné College and author of the books *Indigenous Sovereignty in the 21st Century* and *Guided by the Mountains*.

## Note

1. Steven Lukes, *Power: A Radical View. The Original Text with Two Major New Chapters* (New York: Palgrave Macmillan, 2005), 29.

# ROSE STREMLAU

*Indians in the Family: Adoption and the Politics of Antebellum Expansion*
by Dawn Peterson
Harvard University Press, 2017

SINCE THE EMERGENCE of the New Indian History fifty years ago, scholars have documented the dispossession of Native people through martial violence. The best new work builds on this by explaining how ideological warfare proved equally insidious. Historian Dawn Peterson ably describes how the reconceptualization of American settler colonialism as the inclusion of American Indian people in the Anglo-American sociopolitical family through adoption ultimately justified their exclusion and removal.

In an introduction, nine chapters, and an epilogue, Peterson reveals how adoption served as a metaphor for assimilation and a strategy through which whites assumed authority over American Indian land and resources, including children. Peterson begins by elucidating how American leaders engaged in "reproductive philanthropy" (29). Proponents of the civilization policy predicted that once American Indians conformed to Anglo-American gender roles, their birth rates would soar. In the second chapter, she explores the popularity of Indian adoption, transcending regional and religious divisions within Anglo-American society. Military leaders, including Andrew Jackson, and Quakers, whose pacifism precluded their participation in campaigns against Indian confederacies, advocated the adoption of Indian children into white families. For their part, American Indian leaders seized opportunities to create mediators and place their children in settings where they would learn useful skills and develop bonds with prominent American men.

In chapter 3 Peterson focuses on Silas Dinsmoor, agent to the Choctaws, to show how US officials established patriarchal households in Indian communities that included American Indian people, in this case, Choctaw James McDonald. Dinsmoor justified extending American sovereignty into Choctaw lands by correlating subjugating whole peoples with parenting their children. Peterson next turns her attention to James's mother, Molly, who she argues was representative of elite southern Indians who arranged for the education of their sons in white plantation homes as a form of diplomacy in order to train them in the "soft skills" of plantation patriarchy and to adapt to the spread of cotton agriculture. In chapter 5 Peterson characterizes Andrew Jackson's adoption of a Creek child, Lyncoya, as a rebranding of his conquest of Creeks into an act of benevolence. By describing the boy as the last of his people and bringing him into his home, Jackson created the perfect poster child representing the spread of American patriarchal control. Peterson then shifts to Thomas McKenney, a Quaker bureaucrat who held multiple positions in Indian affairs from 1816 to 1830 and who opened his home to several boys. He promoted the assimilationist ethos of the civilization policy as the political tide turned toward the views of separationist Jacksonians.

In chapter 7 Peterson turns back to the boys like James McDonald who indeed returned to their families as men adept at mediation and who sought to maintain traditional homelands while advancing the civilizing mission, including the spread of chattel slavery. Peterson next explains how Choctaw Academy, a boarding school located on an Anglo-American plantation, facilitated the centralization of the Choctaw government and reinforced the values of elites. The author concludes with a chapter explaining how adopted Native sons disappointed their host families when they returned home to become staunch and skillful opponents of removal. Those who predicted their wards would facilitate the disappearance of Native people realized they had inadvertently helped raise tribal nationalists.

Peterson skillfully draws evidence from missionary records, government documents, and personal papers, and she weaves together intellectual history and biography. Although the focus on a handful of prominent and perhaps representative historical agents makes for an enjoyable read, the discussion of the "relatively small" (5) number of adoptees should have been addressed in the text rather than buried in a footnote. Early chapters at times read like an echo chamber of a small number of voices; there was no shortage of those in the US government who denied the humanity of Indian people even during the peak of this movement encouraging the inclusion of their children in Anglo-American homes. At the same time, the emphasis on natalism and American settler colonialism is exciting and invites comparative scholarship. In addition, Peterson's analysis of Choctaw men's sexual violence toward enslaved women at Choctaw Academy is innovative and relevant to our emerging understanding of the process through which some American Indian men internalized beliefs justifying violence against women, a problem that is an epidemic in many Indian communities and perhaps the most enduring ideological violence resulting from the civilization mission's emphasis on Indian adoption of Anglo-American gender roles.

**ROSE STREMLAU** is an assistant professor of history and gender and sexuality studies at Davidson College.

# BERNADETTE JEANNE PÉREZ

*Vanishing America: Species Extinction, Racial Peril, and the Origins of Conservation*
by Miles A. Powell
Harvard University Press, 2016

HISTORIAN MILES A. POWELL examines how white manhood informed conceptions of nature in the nineteenth- and twentieth-century United States. In clear prose, Powell asks modern environmentalism to reflect on its origins in scientific racism, eugenics, immigration restriction, and human population control. According to Powell, in the late nineteenth century, white conservationists and preservationists identified the fate of the continent's wilderness with the fate of white Americans and "contributed to an enduring association between wilderness and whiteness that helps explain why many of the nation's non-white citizens continue to feel uncomfortable in parks and other sites of outdoor recreation today" (81). He urges white environmentalists to confront the movement's racist origins and work toward building a more inclusive environment.

A cultural and intellectual history of white men who had the means to shape racial and environmental policies, *Vanishing America* is structured by two key moments: the rise of a US conservation movement in the mid-nineteenth century and the emergence of post—World War II environmentalism. Powell begins with prominent mid-nineteenth-century thinkers such as Lewis Henry Morgan, Henry David Thoreau, Josiah C. Nott, and Peter Burnett, who agreed that American progress led to the extinction of "wild people" and "wild land." They disagreed over who would survive. Nott and Burnett believed that Indigenous peoples and species who resisted domestication would necessarily disappear to make way for white Americans. Morgan and Thoreau did not see vanishing people and vanishing nature as inevitable. They advocated for the preservation of Indigenous people and nature when most Americans cast settler colonial erasure as beneficial. In the late nineteenth century, a shift occurred in white racial thought. White men began to see themselves as a threatened race amid industrialization and mass migration. They worried that "rugged immigrant hordes" polluted the nation and unchecked industrial expansion destroyed the nation's evolutionary heritage. Gilded Age reformers such as George Bird Grinnell, Theodore Roosevelt, and Joseph LeConte argued that an "untamed frontier" was necessary for white male virility and worked to protect game animals from extinction and land from resource extraction. They laid the foundation for a new generation of environmental reformers, who advocated for immigration restrictions, eugenics legislation, and wild-life preservation to protect the nation from degeneracy. By the early twentieth century, "death of nature" narratives evoked nostalgia for a preindustrial past. White Americans turned vanishing Indians and dying species into spectacles and sites of national catharsis. They eulogized Ishi (the last wild Indian), Martha (the last passenger pigeon), and Booming Ben (the last heath hen) as regrettable casualties of modernity. Soothing white guilt, they "played Indian" in fraternal societies and asserted that wilderness made healthy boys and men. By midcentury, long-standing racist discourses about an imperiled and vanishing white race remained entrenched, shaping Aldo Leopold's and William Vogt's ideas of overpopulation and ecological balance.

Powell tells a fascinating history of friendships, alliances, disputes, and intellectual exchange between several generations of elite white men who jockeyed to protect an exclusionary notion of "wilderness" from frontier spaces to bounded parks. His study complements Gail Bederman's work on white manhood and Mark Spence's and Karl Jacoby's works on colonial violence and American conservation. NAIS scholars will find the text lacking in its engagement with our field and critical race scholarship. For instance, Powell's fourth chapter, "The Last of Her Tribe," examines the similarity of "lasting" narratives about Native people and animals but does not engage or cite Jean O'Brien's *Firsting and Lasting: Writing Indians out of Existence in New England.* Had he done so, he could have better connected this literary tradition to how white environmental writers and thinkers constructed Native people as out of place and time in their own lands and inserted themselves as protectors of "wild people" and "wild land." Powell mentions throughout the book that the racist undertones of American environmentalism affected how nonwhite people experienced "wilderness"—that conservationists and preservationists made people of color feel unwelcome in "America's wilds." Powell does not disentangle the experiences of Native people from those of other nonwhite people, nor does he engage the material histories of colonial and capitalist violence—of slavery, sharecropping, lynching, dispossession, relocation, segregation, and labor exploitation—that made Indigenous and nonwhite peoples (especially women) unsafe on land policed as white male provenance. More, Native and nonwhite people were not absent from national parks or land governance projects, as Mario Sifuentez, Clint Carroll, and Dianne Glave have demonstrated. Nevertheless, *Vanishing America* importantly rebukes those who treat race making and nature making as unrelated processes.

BERNADETTE JEANNE PÉREZ is the Cotsen Postdoctoral Fellow in Race and Ethnicity Studies in the Society of Fellows in the Liberal Arts at Princeton University.

# MELONIE ANCHETA

*The WSÁNEĆ and Their Neighbors: Diamond Jenness on the Coast Salish*
*of Vancouver Island, 1935*
edited by Barnett Richling
Rock's Mills Press, 2016

**I HAVE TO ADMIT** that while I was reading the preface of *The WSÁNEĆ and Their Neighbors* I was not looking forward to reading and reviewing the book. I thought this was going to be another dusty compilation of old journal notes about the weather, how many miles the author traveled each day, and critiques of the various Natives whose paths he crossed. Or, worse yet, it would be another dry, academic anthropological tour of Coast Salish country.

I am happy to report this book is everything *but* what I was fearing. Barnett Richling, Jenness's biographer, has compiled Jenness's only unpublished notes with minimal editing into a book that is immediately engaging and highly readable. Jenness's narrative is packed full of information about the lives of the WSÁNEĆ and five other Coast Salish bands. (Native groups in Canada are referred to as "bands," as opposed to "tribes" in the United States.)

With a keen ear, genuine interest in, and a high regard for Native cultures, Jenness immersed himself in the WSÁNEĆ culture and formed close relationships with a dozen Elders, giving him inside access to both the mundane and ritual lives of these Indigenous people. He recorded information from six Coast Salish First Nations bands from Vancouver Island and the Fraser River Valley, with his primary focus on the WSÁNEĆ, known today as the Saanich of lower Vancouver Island.

Diamond Jenness was one of Canada's earliest and premier anthropologists in the early part of the twentieth century. A contemporary of the "father" of "American" anthropology, Franz Boas, and other early anthropologists, including Margaret Mead, Edward Sapir, and Ruth Benedict, Jenness diverged from the rigors of academic anthropology that pertained in the infancy of that field. He typically immersed himself in the culture he was studying, participating in daily tasks and rituals, learning the language, and becoming a productive community participant. His ability to meld into these groups helped him create important connections and bonds within First Nations communities, which in turn led him to being privy to things restricted from outsiders.

Forming relationships with Coast Salish Elders, Jenness learned everything from mundane daily tasks to traditional knowledge and practices, to rituals and cosmological conceptions. He learned how the simplest to most complex tasks were accomplished, but not just the mechanics of the task itself; he was taught the importance of "being of good mind" when performing every task and for everything undertaken, there is a spirit who guides how the thing is to be done, or a spirit who guides the process. For example, Jenness relates not only the process of fishing, but how to properly make fishing equipment and tools, how to ensure a good catch, and how to treat the fish properly after catching them. He came to understand the reasons for the complex relationships formed among community members, their antecedents, and the intricate and intimate relationship people had with the natural world, as well as their cosmos.

Laid out in twelve chapters, a section of Coast Salish myths, and five appendices, this book is neatly organized. Richling's preface gives us background on Jenness and his work and sets the stage for the book. Part 1 is a compendium of everything from economics through social structure, ritual activities, daily tasks, warfare, medicine, and more. Part 2 is a collection of Coast Salish mythological tales. The five appendices include Coast Salish vocabularies, how to play a popular children's game, place-names, and orthography.

Jenness does not impose on either his subjects or his readers his interpretations, analysis, speculations, and suppositions. He reports. Jenness simply, concisely, and thoroughly reports what he is learning in an engaging and interesting manner; thus, *The WSÁNEĆ and Their Neighbors* feels as intimate as if we are sitting at the kitchen table with Jenness over coffee.

MELONIE ANCHETA is the authority on color use and the pigments and paint technology of Northwest Coast Native Americans. She is the founder, owner, and head researcher at Native Paint Revealed (www.nativepaint revealed.com).

# ARICA L. COLEMAN

Anglo-Native Virginia: Trade, Conversion, and Indian Slavery
   in the Old Dominion, 1646–1722
by Kristalyn Marie Shefveland
University of Georgia Press, 2016

KRISTALYN MARIE SHEFVELAND has written a succinct history of Anglo-Native relations in Virginia, focusing on the tributary system, trading routes, Indian
slave trade, and, to a lesser extent, conversion in the Coastal Plain and Pied-
mont regions during the midcolonial period. While the Virginia colony and
the Powhatan Indians are the central focus of the book, the story includes
"foreign" tribes such as the powerful Iroquois League of New York and the
Occaneechi, Catawba, and Tuscarora Indians of the Carolinas, which demonstrate the complexity of Anglo-Native relations with tributary and nontrib-
utary Indians within a broad geopolitical scope.

   With the signing of the treaty of 1646 after the English defeat of the
Pamunkey Indians in the 1644 uprising, led by Opechancanough, a new chapter in Anglo-Native relations began with the rise of the Indian tributary system, bookended by the Albany Treaty of 1722. This period saw an increase in
trade of furs, skins, and Indian slaves, which tributary Indians bartered with
the English for guns, powder, and shot. Competition was fierce as colonists
such as Abraham Wood, William Byrd, and Alexander Spotswood struggled
to maintain alliances with tributary Indians while keeping foreign or enemy
Indians at bay so as to establish and maintain a monopoly on Virginia trading routes.

   Bacon's rebellion in 1676 aimed to end the tributary system as Nathaniel
Bacon sought to break the Occaneechi stronghold over the trading route,
which would increase his access to the Indian slave market. Once the rebellion was put down by Governor William Berkeley, the tributary system was
restored with the 1677 Treaty of Middle Plantation. Trade resumed and the
violence increased as human captivity, once based on social control before
contact, was transformed into a market economy that demanded constant
slave raids for profit.

   By the early eighteenth century, a "new paradigm" in Anglo-Native bar-
tering emerged as colonists began requesting Indian children as leverage
during tributary negotiations. Due to the increased fear of slave raids, Indians acquiesced to such demands, as the colonists promised to protect the

children from enslavement. Unsurprisingly, the colonists could not provide adequate protection for their Indian allies or their children.

The Treaty at Albany of 1722 was reached with the cooperation of Governor Alexander Spotswood of Virginia and the governors of Maryland, Pennsylvania, and New York with the Iroquoian League (which now included the southern Tuscarora) agreeing that death or enslavement overseas would be the penalty for "any southern Indian who ventured north of the Potomac or passed west of the [Blue Ridge] mountains" and any of the Iroquois League "who went south or east of the boundaries." The treaty was upheld until 1738.

Shefveland's book provides a general history that will be useful to undergraduates and others with little knowledge of the subject. Her discussion of Indian slavery and the Indian slave trade enriches her study, yet it also highlights its limitations. First, without the discussion of Indian slavery, much of the work she presents on tributary Indians, particularly as it relates to the Powhatan, has been adequately covered, as demonstrated by her abundant use of secondary sources. The work would have benefited from a more thoroughgoing exploration of the Iroquois and Sioux tribes in the Virginia region.

Second, the Anglo-Native paradigm has run its course and should be expanded to include other social phenomena. Case in point, Virginia recognized three classes of slaves: Negro, Indian, and mulatto. Yet Shefveland makes only a passing mention of African slavery and fails to explore its confluence with Indian slavery. Also, she collapses the Negro and mulatto categories into the single category "African," which as my work and that of Jack D. Forbes demonstrate is problematic. Not only did the Indian and African slave trades overlap during this period, but racial categories did not have the same meanings they do today. Hence, Negro was not synonymous with African. With a good portion of the book previously published, expanding its breadth and depth would have added value to this study. Recommended.

ARICA L. COLEMAN is a scholar of U.S. history and comparative ethnic studies. She is also a *Time Magazine* contributor.

# DANIEL USNER

*Great Crossings: Indians, Settlers, and Slaves in the Age of Jackson*
by Christina Snyder
Oxford University Press, 2016

CHRISTINA SNYDER concludes this book with a timely lesson from its subject, the Choctaw Academy at Great Crossings, Kentucky. American Indians, African Americans, and European Americans who resided and worked there during that school's quarter-century existence "remind us that progress cannot be taken for granted." Invoking an Indigenous model of time, Snyder warns against Americans' all-too-characteristic amnesia over "unpleasant historical truths" like those inherited from the Jacksonian era: "intolerance, exclusion, and racial injustice." With the promise of liberty still eluding many Americans, "circling back to old paths" just might provide "the opportunity to cultivate change." *Great Crossings* is a remarkable study of how a road "paved by collaboration and alliance" in the aftermath of the American Revolution became "bloodied and then divided" in the Age of Jackson (314–17).

The prodigious archival research and creative analytical narrative that went into this history of Choctaw Academy would alone be quite an accomplishment, but the particular way that Snyder explains both the rise and fall of this forgotten institution ensures that *Great Crossings* will become a landmark book in Indigenous studies. By closely examining various individuals who came together at a boarding school started by the Choctaw Nation and run by Richard Mentor Johnson, Snyder fully captures parallel and intersecting dimensions of their lives. During the 1820s Peter Pitchlyn and other Choctaw leaders recognized non-Native education as a new instrument for serving their people, but they objected to the proselytizing that accompanied schools established by religious organizations. Johnson meanwhile transitioned from his reputation as a frontier soldier and War of 1812 hero to become a slave-owning planter and politician. This unlikely convergence of pathways resulted in Choctaw Academy being founded about a dozen miles northwest of Lexington, Kentucky.

Choctaw Academy at Great Crossings was a community that embodied a promising vision of the future but that succumbed all too quickly to the dragging effects of its own time. With lucid analysis and luminous prose, Snyder explains how profound contradictions in antebellum American society shaped life and learning at this multiracial community in the upper South. In Johnson's relationship with his slave Julia Chinn and with their two daughters, we learn about an enslaved plantation wife heavily involved in running the academy and intimately influential in shaping her white partner-owner's vision as benevolent patriarch and reformist politician. Intertwined with the story of Johnson's family are contradictions also abounding inside the school, where by the mid-1830s nearly two hundred students from different Native nations resided at one time. While the US War Department saw schooling as a means of pacification and assimilation, American Indian supporters of the academy saw it as an additional strategy in their ongoing struggle to retain land and sovereignty. And while anxious whites tried to thicken racial boundaries amid accelerating socioeconomic change, both Indians and African Americans drew on middle-class identity and privilege to challenge mounting racism. Although both Indian gentlemen and black ladies defied in a similar way the judgments made by powerful men like Johnson, each group nonetheless had its own reason for standing apart from each other. Clashes inside Great Crossings, as Snyder closely demonstrates, "reveal what is often hidden in histories of antebellum America—a social world shared by whites, blacks, and Indians, one shaped partly by the intimacy created by slavery" (114).

At the heart of Snyder's inquiry is her attention to how Indigenous students and their families confronted government policy that was shifting ideologically toward racialization and removal. In defense of their political identity and personal integrity against this deepening threat, pupils initiated ways to challenge how they were treated and what they were taught at Choctaw Academy. To explore this encounter, Snyder vividly captures the school's daily routine, curriculum, residential condition, and social life. The flight of Anishinaabe teacher John Jones and Miami pupil George Hunt with two enslaved nieces of Julia was a significant moment in the school's history, dramatically displaying "undercurrents of resistance that would eventually surface to destroy Choctaw Academy" (195). Occurring soon after Johnson became the Democratic Party's vice presidential candidate for the 1836 election, this episode received widespread coverage from journalists whose characterization of the fugitives reflected a hardening of racial politics. The brutal whipping of Parthena Chinn that followed her capture and then Johnson's sale of her and her children to a slave trader provide poignant evidence of how "notoriously harsh" slavery on the cotton frontier was becoming (214).

Protest against deteriorating conditions and mishandling of tribal funds at Great Crossings had escalated significantly by the end of the 1830s, with a petition sent directly to the secretary of war by Dr. Adam Nail (Choctaw), a former student teaching at the academy. The Choctaw General Council soon thereafter appointed Peter Pitchlyn as superintendent of Choctaw schools, and his investigation of academy records found plenty of evidence of Johnson's and his associates' mismanagement and embezzlement of funds paid by Indian nations. Mounting opposition to Johnson's behavior and the closing of his school by 1848, as Snyder aptly explains, was part of "a not-so-quiet revolution . . . underway in Indian country" (235). Wanting to redeem their children and reclaim control, the Choctaw nation started its own school system in Indian Territory and, in this and other ways, exercised its share of power in the United States. In a comparable expression of autonomy after the Civil War, former slaves would leave Kentucky to become homesteaders in Kansas.

*Great Crossings* warrants attention from a wide multidisciplinary readership. From the short-lived experiment at Choctaw Academy, Snyder offers new insight into race, class, slavery, education, and other aspects of antebellum American society. She even shares a foreshadowing glimpse into what would become the United States' Indian boarding-school system later in the century. This book, moreover, contributes plenty to our understanding of how integral and intricate Indigenous experiences have been throughout American history.

DANIEL USNER is a professor of history at Vanderbilt University.

# DEANNE GRANT

*Peace Weavers: Uniting the Salish Coast through Cross-Cultural Marriages*
by Candace Wellman
Washington State University Press, 2017

CANDACE WELLMAN'S *Peace Weavers: Uniting the Salish Coast through Cross-Cultural Marriages* exposes a disregarded history of intermarriages in the Pacific Northwest Coast Salish Territory during the mid-1800s. Wellman uses the metaphor of weaving to describe how four Native women who married white settlers acted as "peace weavers," blending ties across people and cultures. She uses four primary methods for this book: public and private archival collections, research by professional historians, the work of independent historians and scholars, and perfectionist family historians and genealogists. The result is a multilayered approach to exposing these women's histories with great attempts to gather information from various sources.

*Peace Weavers* consists of an introduction to Coast Salish territory during this time period, with four chapters (one for each woman) focusing on their lives during that time and a conclusion. Historians of Native America, as well as those interested in the history of early intermarriage between white Americans and Native Americans, will find this book especially interesting. By focusing on the lives of four Coast Salish women, Wellman provides intimate knowledge of their lives, detailing various hardships and specifics of life at this time. Wellman analyzes layers to their lives, which include stories of numerous births and deaths, separations, community politics, securing land rights, and, of course, marriage. Each chapter centers on one of four Native women: Caroline Kavanaugh (Samish and Swinomish), Mary Phillips (S'Klallam), Clara Tennant (Lhaq'temish/Lummi), and Nellie Carr (Sto:lo). Every marriage is uniquely described, with detailed stories from archival research and family history filling in information on their lives.

Wellman exposes the power dynamics involved in legitimating marriages, including prohibiting intermarriage based on religion. She describes how the Catholic Church banned Spanish marriage to non-Catholics, leaving people living in the Northwest Coast Salish territory with the only option of tribal custom marriage. Rather than analyze the reasons why intermarriage was discouraged, Wellman provides background to the meaning making of tribal custom marriages. The tribal custom marriages relied heavily upon cultural gifting systems, with the wedding being the setting to exchange gifts between families. Native beliefs of family obligations were significant to the marriage ceremony, meaning the gifts a husband provided represented the wife's value to the community and her family. When a Native woman married, the family understood this as the loss of a valuable contributor in the way of gathering plants, cultivating crops, and making cedar mats and baskets, for which restitution must be paid.

The most valuable contributions of the book are those rooted in Indigenous epistemologies, including the representations of Native women as beneficial to family and community and the meaning making of tribal custom marriages. Wellman addresses a specific cultural clash within the social understandings of marriage, given that Native people and Americans understood marriage differently at this time. Despite compelling cultural implications for marriage, there are examples of custom marriages being treated as not "real" or on par with civil or religious authorities that provided marital paperwork. "Legitimate" marriages dominated and coincided with charges of "fornication" for couples outside of marriage and heavy fines to control and discourage intermarriage.

Wellman notes that her work is meant to bring to light "untold" stories of women's lives, given the lack of attention given to Native women's histories in the United States and active attempts to erase Native peoples from US history. Wellman specifically addresses attempts to keep hidden Native presence as she exposes how at the time many newspapers would exclude the names of Native wives in family obituaries. Despite being married for many years to early settlers, Native wives were largely made invisible as long-term wives, mothers of children, and formidable and well-known members of the local community.

Regardless, the women had valuable knowledge of how to live off the land all while maintaining hereditary resource claims, as was part of Caroline's story. Wellman clearly shows the agency Native women possessed in their abilities to remarry and actively portrays the women as knowledgeable, strong, and independent. The women are described not only as culturally diverse and resource rich but as able to endure despite challenging life circumstances, including stillborn children, deaths of many community members from disease, and even imprisonment for Mary and two of her young children.

DEANNE GRANT (Pawnee) is an ethnic studies doctoral candidate at the University of Colorado Boulder.

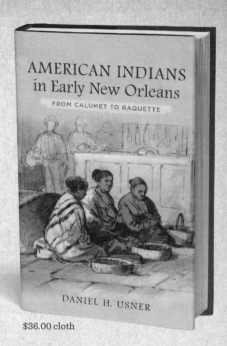
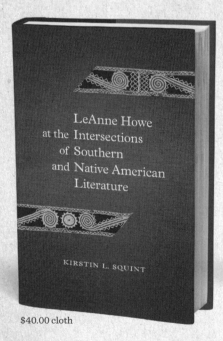
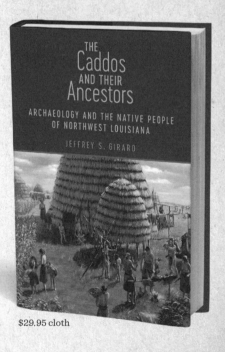

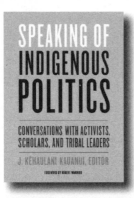

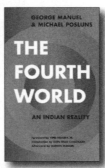

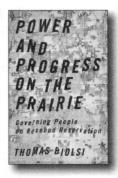